Forgotten Four:
Notre Dame's Greatest Backfield and the 1953 Undefeated Season

The Forgotten Four:
Notre Dame's Greatest Backfield and the 1953 Season

By
DONALD J. HUBBARD
MARK O. HUBBARD

CORBY BOOKS
Notre Dame, Indiana

Forgotten Four
Notre Dame's Greatest Backfield
And The 1953 Undefeated Season

10 9 8 7 6 5 4 3 2

Manufactured in the United States of America

Published by
CORBY BOOKS
A Division of Corby Publishing
P.O. 93
Notre Dame, IN 46556
(574) 784-3482

wwbsite: corbypublishing.com

To Virginia P. Thorne,
who so loved the Irish and passed on her love to us.
And to the Lads of '53.

ACKNOWLEDGMENTS

We would like to extend special thanks to the staffs of the Boston Public Library, particularly Elise Orringer and Susan Applegate at Interlibrary Loans and the entire Microfiche Department.

Thanks also go out to the staffs at Notre Dame Archives and the Sports Information Department.

Jack McCormick (NDLaw '84) proved an able and enthusiastic researcher, finding many "lost" players and alumni.

No more gracious or wonderful subjects for a biography could be had than Ralph Guglielmi, Joe Heap, John Lattner and Neil Worden, who devoted hours of their time to bringing this project to its fruition.

All of the players, coaches, managers, alumni and all others who permitted us to interview them are due our thanks. Particular thanks go out to Bob Taylor, Wayne Edmonds, Jack Lee, Tom McHugh, Dave Metz, Ray Bubick and Bob Rigali who sent us their scrapbooks and other personal items for review.

Any time we hit a curve in the road, Jack Lee and Joe Doyle placed us back in the right direction.

Thank you to all of the patient interview subjects, who responded to our letters and constant phone calls: Bob Arrix, Jim Bigelow, the late Patsy Bisceglia, Jim Bolger, Terry Brennan, Joe Bush, Leo Callaghan, Tom Carey, John Da-

FORGOTTEN FOUR | viii

rago, Jack Dumas, Dick Fitzgerald, Dick Frasor, Armando Galardo, Dan Hammer, JoAnn Heap, Dick Hendricks, Fr. Theodore Hesburgh, George Hubbard, Dr. Nicholas Johns, Bob Joseph, Jack Kegaly, Charlie Keller, Paul Kelley, John Lujack, Fred Mann, Gene Martell, Bob Martin, Paul Matz, Jim Mense, Jim Milota, Rockne Morrissey, Pat Nakfoor, George Nicula, Art Nowack, John O'Hara, Sam Palumbo, Tony Pasquesi, Russ Quilhot, Bob Ready, Bob Ritchie, the late Paul Robst, Don Schaefer, W. Thomas Short, Dick Szymanski, Bob Toneff, Frank Varrichione and George Wilson.

Final thanks go out to our families, for Donald to Lori, Billy and Caroline and for Mark to Bridget and Matt.

TABLE OF CONTENTS

FIRST QUARTER

SECOND QUARTER

THIRD QUARTER

FOURTH QUARTER

FOREWORD
By Joe Doyle

As an underclassman in the glory years of Notre Dame football in the 1940s, comparisons were the mainstay of our sports discussions.

The Irish were winning game after game on the field, and our after-hours discussions were loaded with questions. Was the sometimes 1946 backfield of John Lujack, Jim Mello, Terry Brennan and Emil Sitko, for example, better than the Four Horsemen of 1924? The rules were different, the nay-sayers pointed out. Some of our present day players didn't play defense and Coach Frank Leahy didn't always use the same backs.

We wondered if George Gipp was the greatest-ever player. Or whether the Ohio State game of 1935 was the best game of the century. Almost every discussion would get very argumentative. We were lacking in any authoritative voice.

Later when I became closer aligned with the Notre Dame team as a writer (and then sports editor and columnist), I discovered that Irish fans were just as argumentative, and just as lacking in authoritative opinions.

Harry Stuhldreher, the quarterback of the Four Horsemen of 1924, surely was such a voice. Harry had coached for years at Wisconsin and I not only saw many of his games, but I had close relationships with some of his players on his best Badger team of 1942. Thus, we had some things in common and I was always welcome in his company.

One afternoon in 1953, Harry was in the office of athletic director and Mr. Notre Dame, Ed "Moose" Krause, when the Moose mentioned to me (although I surely knew) that Harry was a member of that great backfield of 1924.

"Well," said Harry, "That is true but the best backfield in Notre Dame history is playing right now for us. Sure, we were good, and so were Rock's great teams of 1929-30, but right now, these kids are better.

"(Ralph) Guglielmi, (Joe) Heap, (Johnny) Lattner and (Neil) Worden may not climb on horses and get all that acclaim, but they are better than we were. And 1929-30, too."

He went into some comparisons. Guglielmi was better than he was. Worden is tougher than (Elmer) Layden, and Lattner is well ahead of (Jim) Crowley and Don Miller. Heap is faster than any of us were, he said, and a great receiver, too.

Moose brought up Rock's last teams when he was a freshman. "They didn't play as a unit for two seasons, as we did, and Frank Carideo was the one constant," countered Harry. "Marchie Schwartz was good, but he wasn't here in 1929. (Joe) Savoldi was good, too, but he didn't finish."

The 1953 foursome had played together in 1952. And as Harry pointed out, they can play defense just as well or maybe better than the boys of 1924.

When I summarized Harry's thoughts in my *According*

to Doyle column, several knowledgeable Irish fans wondered if I would be beseeched by irate fans who questioned the ratings. I was not; in fact, most correspondents liked Harry's thoughts.

Although I had not seen either of Rockne's great teams, I had always thought the guys of 1952 and '53 were better. In my first year as sports editor, Leahy fought back from the dismal worst year (4-4-1) of 1950 and fielded a team that battled back to a 7-2-1 record, despite a 35-0 thrashing at Michigan State. But freshman Guglielmi arrived just in time to win that "big" one over Southern Cal in the Coliseum.

Little did I realize that after many years, my fondness for that backfield and that team would be chronicled in the *Forgotten Four*.

Forgotten Four? No way will they be forgotten. They were the nucleus of Frank Leahy's greatest comeback era. And when it was, the man we called The Master named his greatest college-age team.

He could not, and would not, forget the great teams of the 1940s, the four national titles won—1943, 1946, 1947 and 1949. Those teams were older, more experienced and much deeper in talent. Lattner, Guglielmi, Heap and Worden were college-age athletes and in Notre Dame lore will never be forgotten.

Only Lattner of that great backfield played defense in 1952. But he was the loneliest man on the field when the ball changed hands, offensive players would head for the bench, leaving only Lattner on the field. And when that tough defense of 1952 made the opponents surrender the ball, all 10 would leave and Lattner would be joined by 10 from the offense. What a sight, time after time, and what a season, again 7-2-1, but including victories over conference champions Texas, Southern California, Oklahoma and co-Big Ten champ Purdue. The tie, incidentally, was against Ivy Leagues' best, Penn.

That 1952 team with its 7-2-1 record finished third in the national championship rankings, setting the stage, of course, for the undefeated season of 1953. And for the great Johnny Lattner to win the Heisman trophy.

Much as I admired that 1953 backfield, I was equally enamored by the great line of 1953, a group that eventually sent six players to careers of nine years or more in the National Football League. Not even the great Seven Blocks of Granite (of Fordham fame) could match that.

Dan Shannon and unheralded captain Don Penza were the ends, but the real strength was in the middle, tackles Art Hunter and Frank Varrichione, center Jim Schrader and guards Menil Mavraides and sophomore Ray Lemek. Reserves for that line were such 1952 regulars as Dick Szymanski, Jackie Lee, Sam Palumbo and Wayne Edmonds.

Hunter, Varrichione, Lemek, Schrader, Szymanski, and reserve Ed Cook went on to long NFL careers. Guglielmi played eight years as a pro, but the other backs were limited to one or two years.

Forgotten Four? Indeed, I will never forget that entire team: Lattner won the most honors, the Heisman, of course, but fullback Worden gained more yards, more than 2000. Heap was the leading receiver for three years, and boy, could Guglielmi fling that ball, 3117 yards in all.

The Hall of Fame named Lattner rather quickly and

then finally Guglielmi. Worden didn't rate because he never was a first team All-American, just the heart and soul of those remarkable Leahy teams.

That's why they never will be forgotten.

South Bend, Indiana

PREFACE

Between the Notre Dame Fighting Irish football team's National Championships in 1949 and 1964, there is little history which celebrates the excellence of the players and (some of the) coaches and far too little about the teams and the players at all. There is some mention of Paul Hornung and his Heisman and Frank Leahy and his tortured last years as head coach and Terry Brennan's firing before Christmas, but too little recognition of the wonderful characters who graced the team and the administration as the University faced the modern world.

To ignore this era in Irish history is to miss out on the vital changes in the University from an almost monastic institution to one of the leading intellectual centers in the world. The type of Irish football player generally changed too, not a seasoned veteran of combat in the Second World War, but someone perhaps more willing to challenge the status quo, both on and off the field.

In his Heisman Trophy acceptance speech in New York in December, 1953, that year's winner, Notre Dame's John Lattner emphatically stated that "Without a good team behind him there is no such thing as a so-called star." The modest Lattner had much to be thankful for in terms of the character and ability of the teammates that worked with him and his coaches that year to produce an undefeated season for the Fighting Irish. In a break during the Heisman ceremonies, Lattner had his picture taken with the members of Notre Dame's most renowned backfield, the "Four Horsemen" of Crowley, Stuhldreher, Layden and Miller. The 1953 Notre Dame backfield was not the most renowned, but it was the best.

In the early fifties, the Irish lined up their best backfield ever with Ralph Guglielmi at quarterback, Neil Worden at fullback and John Lattner and Joe Heap at halfback. This backfield constituted the only backfield in history to have all of its players drafted in the first round of the NFL draft. But the excellence did not end there, as six of its linemen enjoyed careers in the NFL of at least 9 years in length. Many other players experienced professional careers and almost to a man left Notre Dame to become successful businessmen and family men, true credits to their families, both at home and at Notre Dame Avenue.

In 1953, these young men came together, assembled by head coach Frank Leahy and went undefeated against the finest competition by far in the country. The title of this book is *The Forgotten Four*, after the four backs who blazed paths so glorious that their feats need to be remembered and never forgotten. To the Forgotten Four and their remarkable coaches and teammates, we remember you and we honor you. And what's more, we are glad that you were on our side.

PROLOGUE
FEAST AND FAMINE

On December 3, 1949, the feast day of St. Francis Xavier, the football program at the University of Notre Dame stood at the apex of intercollegiate sports. Led by head coach Frank Leahy, the squad had just completed another undefeated season, en route to selection in the AP poll as National Champions for the fourth time since 1943. The seniors on the team had not lost a single game in the past four years, as they spent much of the year pondering whether to play in the NFL, or perhaps make even more money in the business world. Their 6′5″, 250 pound star lineman Leon Hart stood poised to receive both the Maxwell Trophy and the Heisman Trophy, awarded each year to the nation's finest football player, the third time in the past seven years that a Notre Dame man had won the Heisman.

Soon, once the professional football draft took place, Hart would be chosen as the first round pick of the Detroit Lions, and all told, twelve of his teammates merited selection by various teams that year.

Frank Leahy was worried, concerned not only that his "lads" might not win their fourth championship in five years, but that they might suffer dramatic reverses in the succeeding campaign. Few took him seriously, Leahy always badmouthed his team's chances against inferior opponents, only to roll over them on Saturdays. Some opponents like Army, which had won the National Championship in1945, had ended their series with the Fighting Irish, an admission that as World War II closed, it no longer realistically stood a chance of competing with their traditional foe.

Most scoffed at Leahy's alarm, listing the many All-Americans who remained on the team for the 1950 season:

Bob Williams, the star quarterback, an All-American in '49 who had finished fifth in the Heisman voting. Williams was one year away from being chosen by the Chicago Bears as a first-round draft choice and in 1988 was inducted into the College Football Hall of Fame;

Jerry Groom, captain in waiting for 1950, a consensus All-American selection awaited him his senior year for service as the star center and linebacker, after which he played for the Chicago Cardinals (as their first-round draft selection, sixth choice overall), and entered into the College Hall of Fame in 1994;

Bob Toneff, a massive defensive lineman, who later starred with the Washington Redskins and San Francisco 49ers, elected to four Pro Bowls during his pro career; Chet Ostrowski, a star defensive end who later played five years for the Redskins; Jim Mutscheller, a big and tough wide receiver who starred for eight years with the Colts, catching Johnny Unitas' passes and earning All-Pro recognition along the way.

Yes, Notre Dame still had weapons in its arsenal, yet its returning players were lighter and many, like Groom, had to play both on offense and defense to shore up holes in its roster. The 1950 season presented challenges unique to a Frank Leahy coached team, as the school had cut down on the number of scholarships it granted and many state schools emerged to challenge the traditional supremacy of the Irish.

Each year since the 1920s, the Notre Dame football team staged an Old Timers' Game in which former players suited up as an opposing team and played a game in the spring against next fall's varsity team. Only twice in the nearly three decades since the inception of this exhibition series had the former ND players ever defeated the varsity, and those games stood out more as anomalies than anything else, the typical "if these teams played ten times, the varsity would win" type of statistical quirks.

In early May, some of the Old Timers began to make noises about winning in ways much louder and more menacing than in years past. Having co-captained the 1949 champions, Leon Hart spoke for many of his senior classmates when he said, "We fellows who are being graduated this year have never played in a losing Notre Dame game and we don't intend for the first loss to come Saturday."

Not only were all of the graduating seniors eligible for the game, but all alumni players, many of them on professional teams, participated too if they wished. To fill out the "Old-Timers" roster, fourth and fifth string undergraduates also helped provide depth for the Old Timers, even though they had, in many instances, never played a down in a real intercollegiate contest yet.

From all over the stars joined seniors such as Hart and Jim Martin, Emil "Six Yard" Sitko, Bob Dove, Corwin

Clatt, Steve Oracko, Bob Lally, Ed Hudak, Larry Coutre and Gus Cifelli all expected to suit up against the varsity, while quarterback Frank Tripucka set up arrangements to arrive for the game by train.

Paul Neville, a Notre Dame grad and the sports editor of the *South Bend Tribune* observed at the outset of the 1950 spring practice that "When Frank Leahy is perturbed about the progress of a Notre Dame football practice session he clasps his hands behind the back and stalks a few feet away from the team he is observing." In that spring, Leahy found himself clasping his hands in back quite often as he scrutinized his future club with too few players and relative lack of stars.

On Saturday, May 13, 1950, the Old Timers systematically destroyed the varsity in the annual Old Timers' Game before 25,000 spectators. The Old Timers absolutely chewed up the Irish offensive line, once they got past Bob Toneff and Paul Burns, and Bob Williams threw from his heels all afternoon and rarely completed a pass to two very talented ends, Jim Mutscheller and Chet Ostrowski.

The Old Timers won 25-7, an outcome that could have been worse, except Tripucka never suited up because he did not arrive at the stadium due to a train strike, so varsity second-stringer John Mazur directed the Old Timers. Dejected, after the game Frank Leahy said, "There were a lot of good football players on the field, but all were graduates. We had better get used to scores like this."

Frank Leahy saw a bleak mid-spring and an even more apocalyptic future fall, but he also sent out his coaches to recruit the next generation of stars, often closing the deal himself when meeting in his office an awe-struck young man and telling him or one of his parents how terrific the prospect would look in a green uniform and gold helmet.

And as was his custom, Frank Leahy engaged in hyperbole when gloomy, never much for gushing with praise when enthusiastic. The varsity still had some good players, and one of the "Old Timers" was actually someone named Neil Worden, who left high school early to train with the Irish in the spring rather than enjoy the last half of senior year in his home town of Milwaukee, Wisconsin. Jesus famously designated St. Peter as the rock upon which He decided to build his Church and likewise, Frank Leahy meant to rebuild his team around one of the truest of Notre Dame men, Neil Worden. Frankly, Frank Leahy had the stronger foundation upon which to build.

And in the fall, other freshmen would come to join Neil Worden. While Leon Hart and his fellow seniors led their mates to that one last title in '49, high schoolers like Johnny Lattner, Art Hunter, Jim Schrader, Tom McHugh and Don Penza filtered in for visits and perhaps good seats at a ballgame and answered the call to be a Notre Dame man. They knew the lyrics to the Fight Song; they choked up when they first saw the Golden Dome atop the Administration Building; and they did not see impending doom, but rather a rich tradition of sportsmanship and achievement found at its finest in South Bend, Indiana.

While Frank Leahy fretted, young men dreamed of gold.

The Bull

FRED MILLER did almost everything well. He played left tackle for Notre Dame's inspirational head coach Knute Rockne, captaining the squad in 1928 and earning All-American honors and eventual induction into the College Football Hall of Fame. When Rockne delivered his famous "Win one for the Gipper" speech during the half-time of a game against Army, it inspired Fred Miller and his teammates to victory that day. After graduation, he worked in a number of his family's business enterprises in and around Milwaukee, Wisconsin, becoming vice-president of Miller Brewing in 1936, and ascending to the presidency of the company in 1948.

Under his stewardship, Miller Brewing rapidly expanded, and, in a few years, Fred had transformed the business from a prominent local brewery to one of the most prosperous national beer brewers in the United States. Miller beer did not make Milwaukee famous. Fred Miller did.

He also maintained close ties with his alma mater and its head football coach, Frank Leahy, a former teammate of his. For a man so distinguished as an athlete and a businessman, Fred Miller surprisingly conveyed a soft spoken demeanor, not an introvert by any means but a pleasant man quietly content with his accomplishments. As successful as he had become as his family's brewery developed into one of the largest in the nation, Fred's first passion remained football.

1

He not only recruited promising athletes, but actually commuted from Milwaukee to South Bend as often as possible to coach the linemen, often personally landing his plane on the football practice field. In many sidelines photographs of that era, the man who somehow keeps popping up in the background, unknown to most people today, is Fred Miller.

As a Milwaukee native, high school senior Neil Worden knew some of the accomplished background of Fred Miller, a man with whom he had an appointment to meet in the fall of 1949. He had heard that Miller had played an instrumental role in procuring a teammate of his, Jim Paterski, for the Irish the previous year. One evening, Neil's *babcia* (grandmother) handed him the telephone at their home and he began to speak to the estimable Mr. Miller, who arranged an appointment to stop by with one of the Irish coaches, Bernie Crimmins.

The clean-pressed and dapper Fred Miller probably spent little time in Worden's neighborhood, then a working-class Polish area on the city's South side, although many of his employees called that section home. For those Southside Poles who did not work for Miller, most gravitated to the giant sprawling Allen-Bradley plant, home of the world's largest "four sided clocks," four gigantic timepieces facing in each direction of the compass. At night the clocks lit up and were called "the Polish moons." The giant eyes of T.J. Eckleburg, metaphorically looming over Fitzgerald's *The Great Gatsby,* had nothing on the clocks at Allen-Bradley.

No matter where one moved, one could not escape the passage of time kept at each edge of the compass by the Allen-Bradley clocks, and for young Neil Worden, they seemed inexorably to tick away the moments until he joined his neighbors with a brown lunch bag to work at the factory. Against the advancing hands of the giant clocks, Neil Worden only had the Drive, the omnipresent internal will of the young man to excel in all things.

Others may let him down and perhaps he did not have many privileges growing up, but the Drive never abandoned him, and by extension he never wanted to let anyone else down either. If he had to get his grades up a bit to satisfy the admissions requirements for a school like Notre Dame, he got his grades up a lot. If he had to master one physical discipline to become a better all-around athlete, he deferred to the Drive. After awhile it no longer became a drive to excel so much as it had become second nature. He personified the Drive.

Unlike most of the Irish recruits, Worden had not experienced a parochial school pedigree, having attended Rutherford B. Hayes grammar school and Pulaski High School, where he not only starred as a running back in football, but also participated in track, basketball and gymnastics. An obscure president meant little to Neil or his neighbors, but Pulaski did—in Polish neighborhoods across the nation such as Middlefield, Connecticut or South Bend, Indiana— Casimir Pulaski, a revolutionary war hero from Poland meant so much more.

In Europe, Pulaski fought in vain only to see his native Poland divided and absorbed by the great powers of Central Europe. In Paris, Benjamin Franklin recruited him for the American cause and Pulaski gratefully accepted the offer, joining George Washington and helping to organize American troops, ultimately becoming the "Father of the American Cavalry." This dashing figure died in the Battle of Savannah, after taking over the command from the wounded commanding officer. Perhaps Pulaski did not inspire Neil Worden much more than Rutherford B. Hayes, but like the famed Polish cavalryman, no one ever doubted Worden's courage. He simply had it.

Millions of boys in the 1940s watched Notre Dame high-light reels in their local theatres or read about their heroes, and perhaps the more ambitious, began to daydream about one day donning the green jerseys of the Irish. One might imagine taking over for the swift handsome back Creighton Miller or taking a pass from Angelo Bertelli, the "Spring-field Rifle," or perhaps joining George Connor in spearing an enemy who had the misfortune of crossing into the flats with the ball.

Young Neil Worden entertained little of these romantic notions as he focused on one man, the team's head coach, Frank Leahy. Worden did not want to attend and play ball for Notre Dame to win one for the Gipper, he simply wanted to play for the individual whom he perceived was the finest coach in the nation and become part of the preeminent foot-ball program. The traditions and the Fight Song and the All-Americans meant little to Worden; sustained excellence meant almost everything.

So if he had to improve his grades he did so, but he also passed up competitive swimming so he could take gymnas-tics to increase his body's balance, a valuable tool to possess when linemen keep hitting with vicious intent. He ran the hurdles to jump higher, finishing first in Milwaukee his se-nior year. In 1949, he earned All-City and All-State recog-nition in football, and if he fulfilled his considerable athletic promise, he exceeded his potential in other areas, all with an eye toward gaining the attention of the Great Leahy.

When Fred Miller came to Neil's grandmother's home, the estimable visitor may have presented a somewhat stately image, one balanced off by the more earthy personality of Assistant Coach Crimmins, a street-wise kid out of Louisville whose brother reputedly ran the largest bookmaking operation in that Kentucky city, and yet Miller projected refinement without snobbery. Due to his profound love for Notre Dame and his cognizance of some thin recruiting classes the past couple of years, Miller needed Neil Worden more than the young man needed him. Neil Worden was going to get a football scholarship from a top-flight program; Miller and Crimmins needed to seal the deal for their school on this exceptional fullback.

Besides the Irish, such powerhouses as Wisconsin, Minnesota, Indiana, Michigan, Army, Navy and Iowa all sought his services on their squads. Against the lure of these schools, many of them co-educational, Worden received a ticket in the fall of 1949, to see one of Notre Dame's home victories by its undefeated National Championship team, led by Heisman Trophy winner Leon Hart, quarterback Bob Williams and World War II hero Jungle Jim Martin. Everything they seemed to do worked.

Mainly because of his respect for Coach Frank Leahy and his remarkable success at Notre Dame, Worden accepted the offer. What he did not appreciate at the time, few in the general public did, is despite the '49 team having just won another national championship, the future held little promise for the ensuing years. It was not so much that the 1950 team did not have talent, as much as it did not have as much depth and physical size, trademarks of the great clubs of the '40s. The school needed to rebuild its depleted ranks quickly, and since freshmen were prohibited from playing, Coach Leahy and his men had to hope that the 1950 edition had just enough to cover the underlying weaknesses of the program as they enticed new stars to sign up.

In the process they procured for the University one of its toughest players in its history, a man that in his thoughts and in his words, in what he did and in what he failed to do, performed it with honesty and right through the middle of the field, into the teeth of the opposing defense. If other people let him down, Neil Worden became that much more determined to excel at all phases of his life.

Perhaps Miller and Crimmins played on this sentiment a bit, because they made it clear that they wanted him right away, in lieu of his enjoying the second half of his senior year, ripping him away from his grandmother and his friends and from a relatively carefree spring, during which he needed no more credits for his diploma. Eschewing sweethearts and proms and nights out with his buddies, he went to work.

Each year, two or three young men graduate from their high school in December of their senior year and start classes at Notre Dame after the Christmas break. Neil was due to graduate just before Christmas, and as his football season had just ended, Miller and Crimmins arrived at a good time to offer their potential recruit a full scholarship starting in January, 1950.

Neil Worden fell in a mutually agreeable place because he enrolled in the University just after it had rolled off another huge season and before any potential embarrassment occurred in 1950, with an undermanned squad seeking to replicate the feats of the great teams of the '40s.

While Frank Leahy and his staff papered over the flaws

of the Fighting Irish, the University of Notre Dame and American society in general stood poised on the verge of seismic change. The end of the Second World War brought prosperity, which in turn permitted young people to leave their close-knit communities, whether it be an ethnic enclave in a major city or a small rural community, and alleviated the need in many cases for three generations of a family to reside together.

The Church, which united so many Notre Dame students in the 1940s, had not maintained pace with the changes in American society and with its adherents moving from one parish to another, or none at all, another unifying force weakened.

Neither Neil Worden nor many others in his generation perceived these sociological shifts. If anything, by packing up his bags and embarking on a one way trip to college, he was entering a much more traditional environment than he or most other American lay Catholics knew, even at that time.

As all Notre Dame students returned in January, 1950 to begin their second semester, Neil Worden took the deceptively long train trip from Milwaukee to South Bend. After his arrival on campus, he detrained and moved into Walsh Hall, a dormitory catering almost exclusively to seniors with whom he had little in common, bunking with another new student, a veteran who had just been admitted to the school.

Worden fell into an odd slot on campus. He started studies before his class had graduated from high school. He lived in a senior class dorm as a new student and practiced with the varsity players in the winter and the spring of 1950, even though come the following fall the NCAA refused to allow him to play with the varsity during their games. The practices in early 1950 also did not resemble other varsity practices, as Coach Bill Earley did not run young Neil in scrimmages as an offensive back, but mainly restricted him to running, conditioning and running through ropes. Occasionally, he played a bit on defense, but otherwise did not fit in much of anywhere, at which time he returned to his dorm room, surrounded by seniors, many of whom had established their friendships with each other four years earlier. They were nice to him by and large, but not friends.

Neil may have grown more discouraged had he known that, in general, only a small host of the freshmen who started out with the team ended up with it four years later. For instance, of the more than fifty young men in the class of freshmen who went out for the team in the fall of 1949, only eight were "available for varsity duty" three years later.

Of this group who preceded Worden to South Bend by only four months, in a survey by Leahy a few years later "[n]ine members are playing for other schools; another eight are still in school at Notre Dame but are no longer interested in trying out for the varsity; five flunked out or are otherwise ineligible. Another five received injuries that have prevented further competition. Five are in service."

He never got on that well with backs coach Billy Earley, but Earley certainly appreciated the talent he worked with, and pressed Worden as hard as possible. The backfield coach never seemed to get over how someone so relatively small as Worden packed so much of a punch. Once during a weigh-in, Worden tipped the scales at a skinny 176 pounds, causing Earley to write down the weight as 192, commenting, "No fullback at Notre Dame only weighs 176!" Instantly, Neil Worden gained 16 pounds by an edict of his coach.

Loneliness did not deter him from his goals. When asked to carry the ball to test the upperclassmen's defense, he often sprang free for a long run or a touchdown. Leahy noticed. One day in the spring of 1950, while Worden walked back to Walsh Hall after practice, a car began to follow him and then park right in his path. His head coach, not a huge believer in praising his players very much, pulled down his window and flatly told him, "Oooh lad, one day you are going to break a lot of records at Notre Dame!" At which point Leahy drove off, having made the young man's day.

He did not know anyone and missed his friends back home, but he did have the examples of success. There was Bob Williams, the All-American quarterback who had charted the school's fourth National Championship in seven years, a man whom the young Worden considered "a prince." Although they no longer played with the Irish and soon awaited long careers in the NFL, Leon Hart and Jungle Jim Martin still strolled campus, much larger than their classmates and a young man from Pulaski High in Milwaukee.

In the years ahead, the Notre Dame sports information department over-reported the height and weight of their fullback Worden, and this detracts from a pure appreciation of what he brought to any team he played for. By the standards of early 1950s football, Worden paled with contemporary fullbacks in physical proportions, and yet he always excelled for the simple reason that he approached every hand-off of the ball to him as if he meant to run through a brick wall and expected to see the other side for his efforts. His weight deceived, as he also possessed a 19" neck, a valuable tool for burrowing his way through small holes in the opposing defenses.

He once ran—or more accurately served as a human battering ram—for seven running plays in succession. His appreciative teammates nicknamed him "Bull." Serious on the field, Bull loved to laugh with his friends and tell stories and engage in whatever hi-jinks presented themselves to him and his cohorts. He never just smiled with his lips alone: his eyes twinkled, his cheeks turned crimson, his eye brows arched and even as a young man his forehead wrinkled. His smile developed like a wonderfully choreographed symphony.

And he learned how to play to a crowd, both in the stadium and in speaking in public. Years after he retired, in a gathering of his '53 Irish teammates, Neil Worden strode up to the dais to speak, with a magazine in his hand. Once behind the podium, with a grand flourish Neil opened the magazine and put on his glasses and in a stentorian tone, related to the crowd that he had recently read a most inaccurate and disgraceful article in *Notre Dame Magazine*, the official alumni publication.

Bull Worden always spoke his mind, and the roomful of grown men, many of whom had not only survived Leahy's scrimmages but had served in Korea and Vietnam and had raised families afterward, all stood erect and at attention in their seats. As if to say, "If Neil thinks this is important, then we had better listen."

Having drawn the crowd into the supposed outrage, Neil then delivered the punch line, that the article had praised team kicker and occasional running back Bobby Joseph as one of the greatest all-around athletes at Notre Dame, at which time his old teammates realized that Neil had pulled a fast one on them and let go a sustained roar of laughter. Even Bobby Joseph, the master of ceremonies at the function, had to laugh. The point resonated though, that while Neil Worden could make his friends laugh, he always had their deep respect.

Since he came from a big city and had not attended Catholic schools growing up, Worden lived it up in comparison to most of his teammates, who had to slowly learn how to have a good time and bend the rules of the University, although he knew how to stop short of detection and "campusing," the Fighting Irish version of being grounded. Perhaps because the administration did not believe he would ever rise three times a week and attend chapel services, someone appointed him the monitor of these wake-up calls so that he had to awaken early three times a week to present the sign-up sheets to his classmates.

As much as the restrictions bothered him, Worden accepted them because he had come to the conclusion that he needed some pretty tight rules to guide him, that the way of living back home clashed with ability to achieve his long-term goals. He did not like them, quite often rebelled against them, but in the end knew he needed structure and limits. Thanks to Fred Miller's recommendation, he had plenty of this at Notre Dame.

Fred Miller did almost everything well, but he did not rival Charles Lindbergh or Charles Yeager as a pilot. Terry Brennan, star running back for the Fighting Irish in the 1940s once gladly hopped a ride with Miller back to his home in Milwaukee, only to discover that his host lacked essential skills in the sky. Embarking from South Bend, Indiana, Miller was warned about a storm standing between him and Milwaukee, but he did not heed the warning and loaded up the plane and took off.

Before long he hit the storm and had to turn back, a difficult task since he did not know how to fly from instruments, only from sight. The Midway Airfield in Chicago refused to clear his landing as the weather prohibited it and the flight quickly went off track after Lake Michigan, and with gas running out, Miller ditched the plane in a Northern Indiana cornfield, successfully saving his life and those of all his passengers.

Miller's faulty flying became so notorious that in the early 1950s, former Irish All-American and after dinner speaker extraordinaire Ziggy Czarobski once related the following story at a testimonial:

"I was stationed on an island that was so top-secret that only two planes flew over it in 14 months. One was a Jap Zero looking for Japan and another was Fred Miller looking for South Bend."

So Fred Miller recognized his limitations and hired the Laird brothers, a top team of aviators to fly him around. But even doing the responsible thing is sometimes not enough. Like his mentor Knute Rockne, Fred Miller died in a plane crash in Milwaukee on December 17, 1954, alongside his young son, a student at Notre Dame. A rescuer approached a badly burned Fred Miller and asked if he needed help, causing Miller to exclaim, "My God, don't bother about me. There are three others in the plane."

Grace under pressure, that was Fred Miller. The University of Notre Dame in January of 1950 expected nothing less from Neil Worden or anyone else enrolled there.

The Old Man

ESTABLISHED LEGEND has it that Blues singer Robert Johnson sold his soul to Satan and came back as the finest guitarist ever. An equally cherished story has come down through the ages that legendary Notre Dame Coach Knute Rockne once shared a hospital room with one of his players, prized pupil Frank Leahy to whom he conveyed his accumulated wisdom and schemes.

Some of the story is true. Frank Leahy did stay at the hospital with his old coach and football talk probably did enter into their conversation frequently. The tale provides a nice link between these towering coaches, yet insufficiently explains the younger man's later success. Leahy achieved greatness in his own fashion, and while his mentor helped him on his path, Leahy succeeded where so many of Rockne's other protégés met with mixed results because of his own brilliance and single-minded dedication to his vocation.

Hailing from Winner, South Dakota, a boom town that never really boomed, Leahy arrived at Notre Dame almost by accident and earned a place on Rockne's line. He played in 1928 and 1929, but he never starred and injuries marred what career he may have had by the next year, and yet even in this he proved fortunate as he got to keep Rockne company in the hospital and essentially accept anointment as his one-day successor.

Rockne of course died in a plane accident on March 31,

1931 in Kansas, with Leahy much too young to have anyone consider him as a possible replacement as head coach at his alma mater. But events had already taken him east to start his coaching career.

Tommy Mills of Georgetown University, then hailing a powerful football program, hired Frank Leahy for his first job as an assistant coach in 1931. Leahy lasted one year in Washington, D.C., shifting to Michigan State University under its head coach (and former Four Horseman of Notre Dame) Sleepy Jim Crowley. When Crowley accepted the head coaching position in 1933 with Fordham University, Leahy followed the Horseman there.

At Fordham, Leahy coached the vaunted "Seven Blocks of Granite" line, which included Johnny Druze and future Packer legend, Vince Lombardi. His successes as an assistant led him to his first hiring as a head football coach, with Boston College, starting in 1939. In his first year he coached the team to a 9-1 regular season record, clouded only by that one regular season loss and a loss to Clemson in the Cotton Bowl by a field goal. The next year, his team went 10-0 and defeated Tennessee in the Sugar Bowl, thus earning him a promotion in 1941 to the head coaching position at Notre Dame.

His first three Irish teams recorded a record totaling 24-3-3, and in 1943, he earned his first National Championship at the helm of the Irish.

Although he had just won a National Championship, he shifted his offense from the standard box in the backfield utilized by Rockne to a T-formation with the quarterback under center, a fullback directly behind the quarterback and two halfbacks to either side of the fullback. The change was initially resisted by Domers (that nickname given to students matriculating under the Golden Dome) as an act almost as heretical as Luther posting his Ninety-Five Theses on the doors of Wittenberg's Castle Church in 1517. But Leahy correctly saw that the future of college football lay in the T, with a quarterback orchestrating the offense and serving more as a passer and less as a runner himself. It suited his slow moving but accurate passing quarterback, Angelo Bertelli, the "Springfield Rifle," to a tee. The T-formation caught on and Leahy kept winning.

World War II interrupted his quest temporarily as he served in the Navy, turning over his reins to Ed McKeever one year and Hugh Devore the next. After Leahy returned from the war in time for the 1946 season, he led his lads to four straight undefeated seasons, earning national titles in '46, '47 and '49.

Leahy achieved his success due to mastery of the x's and o's of both his team and the opposition, skill at optimizing his athletes' performances and stellar recruiting. Just look at his quarterbacks: lose Heisman trophy winner Angelo Bertelli and replace him with Boley Dancewicz (first player chosen in the 1946 draft by the Boston Yanks) and John Lujack, another Heisman recipient. When Lujack goes pro, no problem, plug in Frank Tripucka and then follow him with All-American Bob Williams. And do not forget George Ratterman, a back-up in this era who enjoyed a long career as a pro primarily with the Cleveland Browns.

In the early 1950s this incredible depth had dried up, victim in part of a university-imposed decline in scholarships, but not wholly. Fewer scholarships meant that Leahy and his staff needed to exert more care in their assembly of a freshman class. The relatively weak senior class in the fall of 1950, indicated that the coaches did not enlist their best group in the winter of 1946 and spring of 1947.

By 1949, the head coach had learned to recruit players under different circumstances—or at least bend university rules beyond recognition, because the new decade heralded the advent of some very fine football careers for the young men who committed to Notre Dame.

Still, Frank Leahy served as much a symbol of the 1940s as Betty Grable had, or as Elvis soon would become in the 1950s, and he in many ways became imprisoned by an earlier era that made sense to him. Leahy was a very traditional Catholic and politically conservative man, and while he coached with a keen eye to innovation, with advancing age he perceived the existence of fewer touchstones for him to rely on.

Notre Dame had subsisted on Catholic ethnics, who saw their own aspirations embodied by this wonderful university which won national championships. The same Irish, Italians, Germans, Poles, Slavs and Cajuns who had formed the backbone of the undefeated teams would continue to do so as the '50s dawned, but by the end of the decade African-American athletes began their ascent and indeed dominance in the skill positions. Leahy was no bigot; he coached African-American back Lou Montgomery at Boston College ten years earlier and under his stewardship, Notre Dame desegregated. Again, conservatism bound him, and had he desegregated the Irish faster and more vigorously, he may have won more championships in the '50s than the four he captured in the '40s.

Other recruiting challenges developed or worsened, starting with Notre Dame's steadfast status as an all-boys school even as other universities became coeducational, providing more of an appealing social atmosphere to a young athlete. Leahy had a few other ideas why the squads at his schools had thinned, chiefly citing the heightened entrance requirements for student-athletes and the advanced expectations for them once they started their courses.

A dispersal of talent had occurred, causing Leahy to concede that, "There's even more talent. . .there are more schools paying attention to football. Twenty years ago [he gave this interview in 1952], there was probably only a handful of outstanding teams. Today, there are dozens of schools crowding each other for national recognition."

He also believed that state universities had begun to tug at a player's loyalties, and more importantly, money had become a factor. Over time, Notre Dame would gain massive financial profits from its athletic teams, but this windfall had not yet shown up in the University's coffers to any appreciable extent. Although he did not state it, some players and fans had detected what they felt constituted a deemphasization of the football program.

His lads had changed too. The post-war teams had returned older war veterans who knew how to obey authority, execute orders and in many cases, had endured combat. The teams of the early '50s contained very few veterans in comparison, and indeed, most incoming freshmen were encouraged to sign up for either the Air Force or Navy ROTC programs, not to avoid the draft per se, but certainly to defer one's service to country until after graduation. Many players in the '50s believed that Leahy and some of his coaches deliberately tried to toughen them up, sometimes with potentially disastrous results.

Social attitudes were ripe for change also. The conservative church of Latin Masses and women with hats on during Mass did not disappear in the 1950s, but even religious leaders like Angelo Cardinal Roncalli, the future Pope John XXIII, foresaw that the traditional church no longer met the needs or expectations of many believers and by 1962, Vatican II convened to address modernism in the church. No one on the early 1950's teams wore long hair or smoked pot and few grumbled much about church, but the restlessness remained.

With the dawning of the 1950s, Leahy increasingly had to battle the administration of the University itself, as his intense desire to win and to take whatever steps necessary to secure victory clashed with many of the priests who ran Notre Dame, and who had a responsibility to the student body as a whole. During the early 1950s, sports scandals erupted in intercollegiate basketball and football programs and the Holy Cross Fathers fretted that one day a cataclysmic controversy might engulf the University, with a genesis in the football program. Leahy bent rules but always figured that he had pushed the envelope, not broken it. Opinions differed, both inside and outside of Notre Dame on that issue.

He also shifted from being an extremely hard worker to a workaholic, spending several nights away from his home to study film or go over assignments for the next practice or game. His health began to suffer. In his early forties in 1950, the job had aged him well beyond his years, causing his players to refer to him as the Old Man.

Leahy fought to preserve the past, even though in many ways he personified restlessness as he sought perfection, always trying to stay slightly in front of opposing coaches and never being satisfied despite the success he and his players obtained. His biographer, Wells Twombly, best captured the enigmatic nature of his subject; yet because Twombly allowed himself to become close to Leahy, he missed the often hypocritical nature of his subject.

For instance, in his dedication of the biography, *Shake Down the Thunder*, Twombly honors Leahy as such:

> Dedicated to the memory of Frank Leahy,
> Who genuinely believed in all the
> old frontier verities, now dying.
> Who chased the American Dream with
> a single-minded passion.
> Who may have been America's last
> knight-errant.

In portraying Leahy as a chivalrous and romantic figure, Twombly lost sight of the occasions when his subject erred. It is a curious biography, published in 1974, after Leahy died from leukemia, but very much a work conscious of its subject's final days, and in a final irony, a tome published not long before Twombly himself died. In many ways, it is a book written in black crepe, not so much a celebration of a great man as a requiem for a Quixotic figure.

Even as the bio leads up to the 1953 campaign, it focuses on the considerable controversy that whipsawed around Leahy that year, but ultimately misses the mark in failing to account for the dedication of the man and appreciation for the victories that he and his lads ultimately won. The season was a mini-opera, perhaps unnecessarily so, but it ended on a high note. Had Twombly captured the pitch a bit better, adjusted his tuning, he might have preserved Leahy completely.

Frank Leahy had the rare ability to change sport and seemingly to read the mind of the opposition coaches, but he had difficulty otherwise in adjusting to the times. He and his wife Floss had a large family, eight children, but even she knew that his lads on the football team all too often monopolized his thoughts, and his lads were changing. They largely had not fought in wars, not yet anyway, and some rolled their eyes at curious restrictions imposed on them by their school and football team.

With perhaps one major exception. The men who played varsity football for Notre Dame all possessed a burning ambition to win and as changes manifested themselves around the young men as the '50s dawned, this remained constant and for Frank Leahy, for now, this was enough.

John Lattner Walks Down Notre Dame Avenue

POOR NEIL WORDEN stood alone as the first recruit of the Class of '54 during the long and lonely winter of 1950, in a Senior Hall with a roommate he scarcely knew; but with the coming of June, reinforcements arrived in the form of his fellow classmates and future teammates.

Officially, freshmen enrolled on the second Tuesday in September in 1950; but for many football prospects, any time after high school graduation they might be encouraged to come to campus early and spend the summer there orienting themselves to university life. A bit of that did exist—one could live on campus and eat at the dining hall—but primarily the early residences constituted no more than a means for Frank Leahy to start indoctrinating a young man into the life expected of a Fighting Irish football player and to commence conditioning each athlete as soon as practicable, or trying out an athlete to determine if he possessed the skill and dedication required of a Notre Dame man.

This invitation led Joe Morrissey to fill up his Buick one early summer morning to drive from Cincinnati, Ohio, to South Bend to drop off three recruits, his own son Rockne and friends Bill Hall and Jim Bolger. The elder Morrissey had played football for the great Knute Rockne in the late 1920s and had babysat for some of his head coach's children on the side. Of course, that explained the derivation of his own son's name, with young Rockne trying out for a spot on the Irish backfield.

Rock Morrissey's friend from Purcell High in Cincy, Bill Hall, had not only been awarded a scholarship in football from the defending national championship team at ND, but also had received the offer of a basketball scholarship from Adolph Rupp, the coach of the defending national championship Kentucky club. Hall, nicknamed Igor for his 6'5", 210-pound frame, intended to try out for end.

Jim Bolger, another friend from Purcell joined the group, and once up in South Bend, promptly received an offer from coach Bernie Crimmins. Unfortunately, Frank Leahy either was not in town or did not meet with young Bolger, as the head coach possessed very keen powers of persuasion and might have enticed the recruit to join up.

Instead, Jim Bolger ultimately only entertained offers from three major league baseball teams, the Cleveland Indians, Chicago Cubs and Cincinnati, ultimately deciding on signing with the hometown Reds. Bolger got in a couple of major league baseball games soon after he returned from Notre Dame and earned some distinction as the youngest player in the majors the next two years. He finished off his career with the Cubs, but the story does not end there. Years later, Jim's son, a star football player at Cincinnati's Elder High, joined the Fighting Irish football team, playing three varsity campaigns for Ara Parseghian.

While the Irish missed out on talented athlete Jim Bolger, they succeeded in obtaining Rock Morrissey and Bill Hall. So Morrissey and Hall started conditioning drills to work themselves into the extremely high level of fitness expected of an Irish footballer. Bit by bit others joined them over the summer, enticed by the possibility of making a favorable impression on the coaches while other incoming freshmen sat around the beach, impressing no one but maybe a few girls. Some had scholarships, some only had try-outs.

The school opened up some dorm space for the incoming students; it did not cost much to board someone during the summer, no heat or air conditioning required, plus the football team did bring in some money. For eight weeks, about two dozen young men, fresh from their graduation parties, worked out by sprinting and performing calisthenics and running though ropes (Leahy had his lads run through a long row of ropes in lieu of a column of car tires, because the former exercises made the players raise their legs higher).

The new men endured a purgatory of blocking drills, one of the coaches' favorites involving running into a series of defenders, each ten yards in back of the other, until the gauntlet had been run. Players smashed into each other in close one-on-one blocking drills and then the proper scrimmages began, with full contact in the middle of the summer. Once the drills ended, the men often napped or tended to a course or two in the school by attending classes and laboratories and writing papers and studying for tests.

About one third of the young men who started early with the football program in June (between their senior year in high school and the official start of their freshman year in college), ended up with the varsity four years later. Some quit during the summer and enrolled elsewhere and others fell off along the way, while those who stayed made the team the central reality in their lives the next four years.

The elder Morrissey did not leave campus right away. A

number of people he had known while he played football still worked for the University, so he became reacquainted with them a bit before he sensed that Rock and his friend no longer needed him around, at which time he took his car and drove it back home.

The best was yet to come. After the Cincinnati contingent dropped off its precious cargo and other parents goodbyed their sons to the trusting hands of Our Lady and Frank Leahy, the next wave of early arrivals occurred in mid-August when a number of prospects arrived, including Fred Mangialardi, an end from St. Phillip's High School in Chicago, and Paul Robst, a lineman from St. George's in Evanston, just north of Chicago.

Tackles coach Bob McBride had invited young Mangialardi for a visit and wisely also extended an invite to his mother. Mrs. Mangialardi fell in love with the spacious and idyllic campus and her son recognized a similar epiphany after having an audience with the great Frank Leahy. In all his other visits, with Big Ten schools, Mangialardi did not work out, but Coach McBride had him blocking him over and over to test his mettle. Mangialardi passed and earned his scholarship.

Paul Robst had come from a similar Chicago Catholic High School background as Mangialardi. He had a distinct memory of trying to tackle Fenwick's star back John Lattner in a game, only to get hit in the chest by Lattner's fast churning knees. But Robst possessed the necessary size and athleticism and he too obtained a full boat at Notre Dame and came to work out in mid-August with a congregation quickly approaching two score.

The early enrollments meant only one thing, more in-struction for the freshmen. With heightened supervision, the proper conditioning of athletes occurred before Labor Day, freeing up time thereafter so the young men could con-centrate more on learning blocking schemes and techniques, running offenses and defenses and providing the varsity with reasonable facsimiles of college football players. The last task proved most crucial, since the older boys practiced against the frosh in preparation for their games against other programs.

It also gave the coaches insight into projecting who most likely would survive to play varsity football at the school in the future, with the full knowledge that over half of the prospects had no chance of ever winning a letter (called a monogram) in football, at least not at the University of Notre Dame.

Later on, once the players got older, it became a true survival of the resilient, but at the early stages of develop-ment, the players received encouragement, a pat on the back or on the old leather helmet (at best a faded gold color with an iron cross stripe running along the middle and sides), as each prospect tried his hardest to impress the coaching staff. Athletic talent at this stage needed evaluation, then once the best had come forward, at least preliminarily, the weeding out began. By then, motivation by the coaches most often took a more negative turn, even for the chosen ones, and sev-eral young men had already established themselves.

The best was yet to come.

In the second week of September in 1950, a carload of Notre Dame men and their luggage drove from Chicago to South Bend, Indiana, for the start of school, a group that included the driver Joe Rigali (a senior at ND), his brother Bob and John Lattner, the prized freshman running back for the Fighting Irish football backfield. The trip today, normally less than a two-hour drive for a fast car and a good radar detector, took closer to four hours then, as the current Toll Road had not yet been constructed.

Picked up from his West Chicago home at 6:00 p.m. that evening, by the time Lattner and his friends approached the outskirts of South Bend, Indiana, night had fallen and a thick and vaporous fog had enshrouded them. Between the bustle of Chicago and surrounding industrial hubs such as Hammond and Gary, Indiana, there stood little but farm-land before South Bend, the home of the Studebaker Motor Company and Bendix, a mostly Polish-American town, with an influx of African-American families coming up from the South to escape Jim Crow laws for good paying work at the plants.

After a drive largely spent whisking past rows of corn-fields, the car arrived just outside of the University of Notre Dame, parked in a spot, perhaps a legal space, perhaps not. In any event, there they stopped and unloaded their gear and the small party hiked up the long stretch of Notre Dame Avenue towards campus. Lattner had engaged in the good natured conversation on the car ride over but part of his gre-gariousness masked an almost instant homesickness and a feeling of uncertainty that despite his high school exploits, perhaps he did not possess the skill and athleticism to thrive at his new campus.

He missed his folks, Bill and Mae already, along with his brother and sister. He had also by this time been dat-ing for two years the girl he meant to someday marry, Peg

McAllister, whom he started dating on his sixteenth birthday. He went to Fenwick High (a Catholic powerhouse football team in the highly competitive Chicago Catholic League) and she attended Trinity Catholic in Chicago, and he left her behind and also his friends, many of whom remained in Chicago. The break hurt more than he feared.

Joe Rigali already attended the school and was about to start his final year there, so he entertained little of the same concerns. He knew his way around and how to avoid trouble. His brother Bob, a star back and teammate of Lattner's at Fenwick High School, had come here to exploit the legacy of his father Joseph, who had played football a generation earlier for Knute Rockne. Rebuffing recruiters from such schools as Wisconsin, Alabama and Illinois, Bob had come to make some memories of his own. He also excelled at basketball despite his lack of height, having captained the Fenwick cagers the year before.

His teammate at Fenwick in the backfield, John Lattner, did not have the same pedigree, but had come to the attention of the ND coaches by dint of his 18 yard per carry average in his senior year. Besides Notre Dame, seventy other suitors had contacted Lattner to entice him to join their team and attend their school for free on an athletic scholarship. He doubted his own ability at times in part because some of the recruiters at other schools had intimated to him that he was not Notre Dame material, but that their program might accommodate his "limitations" more.

And some programs sought to do more than fit his needs, they catered to luxurious dreams, such as the folks at Indiana University who "suppl[ied] him with a white summer tux and a stunning brunette date for a dance." Some schools' alumni opened their hearts and more to him. All told, he visited six heartland schools other than Notre Dame, those being Michigan, Illinois, Purdue, Kentucky, Kansas and Indiana. ND had relatively little to offer, but his mother and the priests at Fenwick High pushed him toward South Bend, so he followed their advice.

Fretful Frank Leahy did not cease worrying about Lattner attending Notre Dame even with a commitment to do so, a legitimate concern in that other college representatives did not terminate their contacts with the young man. Rumors spread that after Leahy landed his prize recruit, he procured Lattner a summer job at a nuclear power plant in Joliet, Illinois, a facility so secured and guarded, that other teams' coaches failed in all of their attempts to obtain clearance and contact him there.

So while Lattner spent his summer cloistered in a nuclear power plant, he continued to struggle with self-doubt, not based on any objective evidence but springing more from modesty, a sincere feeling that he had nothing on his fellow man. Lattner's self-effacing nature was not an act or a manifestation of a phony image, he simply accepted the gifts given to him and never became impressed with himself.

Plus, he did not grow up on an estate adjoining his country club but rather grew up in West Chicago, where he often had to fight his way back home, receiving many a bloody nose and returning the favor on more than one occasion. He also had a famous misadventure on St. Patrick's Day during sixth grade, when he jumped into his father's '36 Ford with two friends and started it up. The situation deteriorated rapidly as young John wheeled the vehicle wildly onto some trolley tracks, where he froze and his friends jumped out and ran as fast as possible back to their homes.

Making a bad situation worse, John then manipulated his truck off the tracks and kept on driving until he had crossed the street, jumped the curb and kept on going until he had cruised through the front of a nearby butcher's shop with cold meat flying everywhere.

It was a tough time, and often he had to ward off his peers by getting into fistfights until one person or the other had had enough. So for every person slapping his back during his youth, he had others either throwing a punch at him or reminding him he was not the Second Coming.

With this in his background, it took that hike up Notre Dame Avenue for the first time to alleviate his fears, accompanied by his friends as the fog parted a bit and he perceived the outlines of the top of the University's Administration Building, capped by its Dome, all lit up and golden and beautiful, a beacon for his doubts. A lump formed in his throat and inspiration overcame him. For the first time since leaving home he began to feel that he might be alright, that he had made the right choice for a college.

It is a good thing he stayed. Possessed of almost a boundless grace and athleticism—he even looked perfect while punting—Lattner had a far greater gift even at that age. Probably equal parts the product of nature and nurture, he was one of the nicest sports stars of that or any other generation. While some of the Irish players in the 1940s believed their press releases, Lattner quietly set an example for all of his friends and teammates: athletic talent is a gift from God, humility is a reflection of God and an acknowledgment that gift can be taken away. Grace and class cannot. Even more so than the dome on top of the Administration Building, Lattner set the gold standard at Notre Dame in the early 1950s.

Orientation

LATTNER CARRIED his gear into his dorm room at Zahm Hall, one of the four dormitories on the campus restricted solely to freshmen, the other three being Breen-Phillips, Farley and St. Edwards. He had arrived a couple of days before most of his incoming classmates, so he had time to kill, hanging out with Bob Rigali and awaiting his new roommate, an aspiring baseball player. Rigali staked out his own space at Breen-Phillips, awaiting the formal commencement of the Freshman Orientation events.

Soon other football prospects began arriving on campus, Joe Bush, whose brothers Jack and Mike played football for Notre Dame and whose father played in the early NFL, with the long-defunct Louisville Colonels. Joe roomed his first year with his brother Jack, easing his transition onto campus, while simultaneously placing him in an upper class hall, Badin. It helped too, that a high school classmate from Iowa, quarterback Bob Martin, joined him in college and on the team.

Fair-haired Don Penza, an end from a large family in Kenosha, Wisconsin, and Art Hunter, a massive lineman from Akron, Ohio, joined Menil "Minnie" Mavraides from Jack Kerouac's hometown of Lowell, Massachusetts. Minnie may not have possessed the magic tongue of Kerouac, who had preceded him as a star at Lowell High School by a handful of years, but he did have a golden toe with which he kicked winning field goals.

Center Jim Schrader, soon to become Neil Worden's best friend, joined Fran Paterra, a back from McKeesport, Pennsylvania. Joe Katchik, a 6'9" end from Plymouth, Pennsylvania, checked in as the tallest member of the class, while Tom McHugh from Central Catholic High School in Toledo, Ohio, proved to be one of the more precocious souls.

Not the most mischievous, however, not as long as Bobby Joseph, a superb all-around athlete from Martins Ferry, Ohio, matriculated at Our Lady's University. A Syrian-American, Joseph promised to become the 1950's version of former All-American Ziggy Czarobski, a comic foil for Frank Leahy and his even tougher assistant coaches.

Over thirty freshmen formed the ranks of this football class, some of whom went on to win monograms at Notre Dame while others either dropped out or incurred career ending injuries during their undergraduate term.

The brief respite that Lattner and Rigali had enjoyed soon ended as not only did prospective new teammates start arriving, but hundreds of their classmates funneled into the quadrangle by train and automobile, to see their new rooms and halls and meet their assigned roommate. For all incoming students, the Administration had established an ambitious orientation program.

On that first official welcoming day, new students had to register for their courses in the Drill Hall between 8:00 a.m. and 5:00 p.m., which sounds reasonable enough except they also had to take placement tests on that day during the same period. The school weekly, the *Scholastic* quipped, "[y]ou can always spot the Freshman during the registration periods in the Drill Hall. They're the ones who fill in their census cards legibly, smile when their I.D. photos are being taken, and don't ask for class schedule changes."

It did not end there. For two hours that day, starting at 12:30 sharp in the afternoon each freshman (and if he chose, his family) ate a luncheon with the hall rectors and prefects. For those who had never seen the campus before, tours ran throughout the morning and afternoon for an hour apiece on the hour. Most of the freshmen football players that day also suited up for practice.

At 7:00 each evening, each student then had to run over to the chapel in his hall and listen to his rector speak, no doubt impressing on each young man the honor bestowed upon them to attend Our Lady's school and the responsibilities that came with that distinction. At 8:00 p.m., the freshmen then had to run over to Washington Hall to watch a screening of *Knute Rockne, All-American.*

Of course, this film chronicled the life of the University's first truly great coach, and it starred Pat O'Brien as Rockne and one-day U.S. President Ronald Reagan as superstar George Gipp. Reagan played Gipp as a watered-down wise guy, little resembling the true ballplayer who pretty much broke every rule on campus, at one point enduring expulsion.

In the sanitized version, Gipp gets sick and then quickly becomes deathly ill, with Coach Rockne summoned to his bed as sort of a quasi-religious last rite before the Gipper meets the Great Referee in the Sky. Whatever he truly said to his coach on his death bed (or whether his coach was even present) is open to debate, but the film version clearly laid out its preferred version, hewing to what the "Rock" told his players once at half-time to rally them to victory:

> Now I'm going to tell you something I've kept to myself for years. None of you ever knew George Gipp. He was long before your time, but you all know what a tradition he is at Notre Dame. And the last thing he said to me, "Rock," he said, "sometime when the team is up against it and the breaks are beating the boys, tell them to go out there with all they've got and win just one for the Gipper. I don't know where I'll be then, Rock," he said, "but I'll know about it and I'll be happy."

Maybe Gipp said it or maybe not, but the film ends with Knute Rockne's death on the Plains of Kansas, and for generations thereafter, Notre Dame students and alumni have cried during the movie, vowing to not let down the coach and to win one for the Gipper.

By the time John Lattner left Washington Hall on the 11th, he had choked up and had dedicated himself to emulating the sanitized Gipp and sailing into anyone who dared badmouth Notre Dame, as he ambled back to his new home. Subtly, Notre Dame had begun to fill some of the voids in his life caused by his move from home. So inspired, he said his prayers and jumped into his dorm bed for the night, determined to not let down the University.

Lattner and his classmates had four Colleges in the University from which to choose their major: Science, Commerce (Business), Arts and Letters, and Engineering. Technically the football players had the same choices, but in subtle ways they generally got steered away from Science and Engineering due to the laboratories that too often cut into afternoon practices. Probably the majority gravitated to Commerce, although some like Neil Worden went into Arts and Letters.

At the time the University still had a physical education major in the school of arts and letters, and Neil and a few other ballplayers pursued this degree. In some colleges the major may have been a joke with hulks playing bombardment all day long, but Notre Dame did the opposite, loading up the major with science courses so that it more resembled a pre-med course.

A few intrepid souls pursued pre-med and engineering, but the coaches did not look kindly upon it as fellows came to practice late or on some days not at all, and at least one back who later became a doctor thought that Coach Earley in particular penalized him for dedicating himself to medicine and not enough to the Split T-formation.

It mattered little the first year, because most students, regardless of their major or department, essentially took liberal arts courses. Students learned to write well and to pursue theology and philosophy, heavily weighted to the accumulated works of St. Thomas Aquinas.

After a hectic first day, the pace slowed down from an orientation standpoint, with the only formal function involving one's meeting the school administrators, again at Washington Hall, in the evening after supper. A highlight film of the 1949 Notre Dame National Championship team also was shown.

The lull ended on September 13 with the start of the Freshmen Missions, an event kicked off that day with a 6:30 a.m. service in each dorm, a routine repeated for the next two days. Each evening during the Mission, the students were supposed to trudge over to the Basilica of the Sacred Heart at 6:30 to hear talks that President Cavanaugh had prepared on the topics of "Living in the State of Grace," "A Life of Study," and "Devotion to the Blessed Virgin."

On the second day of the Mission, after attending the morning Mass, classes began at 8:00 a.m. sharp. The day after the Mission ended, the freshmen finally had a bit of a break when they received invitations to attend the varsity football scrimmage at 2:00 in the afternoon. To this point, the freshmen had received an indoctrination heavily weighted with love of God and devotion to the Fighting Irish football team and had slept so little, that many no longer retained the ability to distinguish between the two.

Expecting each plebe to know the songs of the college, the *Scholastic* printed the lyrics of the Fight Song (which probably more people in America knew than the National Anthem), the Hike Song and When Irish Backs Go Marching By. No longer outsiders, Lattner, Rigali, Morrissey, McHugh, Paterra and Worden were Irish running backs and the lyrics had direct bearing on how they must comport themselves in their new roles:

> And when the Irish backs go marching by
> The cheering thousands shout their battle cry:
> For Notre Dame men are marching into the game,
> Fighting the fight for you, Notre Dame
> And when the Irish line goes smashing through
> They'll sweep the foemen's ranks away;
> When Notre Dame men fight for Gold and Blue,
> Then Notre Dame men will win the day.

Two brothers, Michael Shea and John Shea, who had obtained degrees from Notre Dame in the early part of the twentieth century, composed the Fight Song, which has two parts, the first of which virtually no one outside of South Bend recognizes today. Michael Shea became a priest and in the spirit of ecumenism, performed the song for the first time in a Congregational Church in Holyoke, Massachusetts. The song debuted at Notre Dame the next year in the Administration Building and the second verse quickly grabbed hold of a nation:

Cheer, cheer for old Notre Dame,
Wake up the echoes cheering her name,
Send a volley cheer on high,
Shake down the thunder from the sky.
What though the odds be great or small,
Old Notre Dame will win over all,
While her loyal sons are marching onward to victory.

And yet the song that most profoundly impacted the undergraduates was always *Notre Dame Our Mother*. Written to commemorate Knute Rockne's funeral, then president Father Charles O'Donnell wrote the lyrics and an alumnus, Joseph Casasanta added the tune. It became a tradition in the late twentieth century for the team to gather in by the student section at the end of a home game and sing it out, accompanied by the Marching Band:

Notre Dame, our Mother
Tender, strong and true
Proudly in the heavens,
Gleams thy gold and blue.
Glory's mantle cloaks thee
Golden is thy fame,
And our hearts forever,
Praise thee, Notre Dame.
And our hearts forever,
Love thee, Notre Dame.

Notre Dame of course, as a name roughly translated from French to English, means Our Mother and is a reference to the Blessed Virgin Mary, Mother of Jesus Christ. And yet in listening to the song itself, it is unclear if the lyrics concern Mary, the school named Notre Dame or the third possibility of "all of the above." Young Catholics learn at an early age the concept of the Holy Trinity, the three distinct and indivisible beings of God: God the Father, the Son and the Holy Spirit.

In *Notre Dame Our Mother,* it appears as if Mary has two distinct and indivisible beings, one as the Mother of God and the other as the personification of Notre Dame itself. Of course, the University has never proffered that preposterous theory and yet, folks like Frank Leahy might be excused if from time to time they blurred the distinction. Football players who missed an assignment or fumbled a ball often heard from the Coach about how they had committed a grave sin against "Our Lady" and they too, probably needed some leeway in determining who or what exactly he referred to.

Just precious days ago many of these same strapping youths had sat by their radios and tried to memorize the lyrics of the Weavers number one hit, *Good Night Irene,* an adaptation of Leadbelly's borrowing of an old folk tune:

> Stop rambling, stop your gambling,
> Stop staying out late at night
> Go home to your wife and family
> Stay there by your fireside bright

Good advice for an incoming Domer, but soon the Weavers would be blackballed, a casualty of what became known as McCarthyism, and at ND, conformity dictated an observance of the traditional.

And Notre Dame had its traditions, although at this period they remained surprisingly few, such as no undergraduate

could walk up the front steps to the Administration Building (on top of which perched the famous Golden Dome), but
had to resort to walking in through a lower entrance. Also,
no smoking in the quadrangle, a strange rule since at such
a strict school smoking probably could have been prohibited
but in truth, the weekly campus paper ran advertisements for
Chesterfield and other brands. The young men also had to
wear ties at dinner, but in a rare instance of rebellion, many
wore tee shirts to dinner with a tie.

Yet the indoctrination did not end with the end of orientation and the commencement of classes. The student
newspaper, for the first time ever, had published a welcoming issue to new students, with the expectations of the Notre
Dame man clearly articulated in the editorial page:

> A Notre Dame man "is not a Notre Dame man for just the
> four years he attends courses. He is a Notre Dame man for
> life...If he goes astray he's not the only one to receive criti-
> cism-he puts Our Lady under attack also...Your boyhood
> is over and done with. Now you have to learn how to be a
> man...you have to learn to be a Catholic man."

A heavy load to lay on the lap of any young man, particularly
if the individual who needed to learn to be a Catholic man
fit into the category that approximately 8% of non-Catholics
in the student body did, including the highly touted Greek
Orthodox guard from Lowell, Massachusetts, Minnie Mavraides. Then again, that year the students were urged to
pray for the conversion of the Soviet Union, then an atheistic
and communist state, so how hard would it be to bring the
other 8% of the students over to the Church?

For those who did not understand the rules of the University already, the *Scholastic* reiterated them again. With the
exception of one night each week, each new student had to be

in his dorm room at 10:00 p.m. with lights out by 11:00 p.m. One switch extinguished the lights on each floor. On only one day a student may stay out until 12:30 a.m.

Getting up early made sense since three times a week from Monday through Saturday, each student in the school had to sign in with a monitor (a chore given to football players) before 7:00 a.m. in front of the hall chapel. At that time the *Scholastic* opined that a student "should" then attend the service that subsequently began, yet the phrase "should" conveyed a sense that an option was involved. If a student did not sign in and attend the service, he often was "campused," which meant he lost his privilege to stay out that one precious night past midnight, thus enduring virtual house arrest. Someone might also be campused for other infractions such as gambling; girls or beer in the room, with closed doors, almost always culminated in expulsion.

Charitably, the administration mandated that no Saturday classes extend beyond the noon hour, which meant by logical extension that only on Sundays, the day of rest, did the classrooms close down. Many peculiar regulations and bits of advice differed little from a Physical Education Department guide prepared in 1902, which advised the young men to eschew wearing "close-fitting, hard rimmed hats," and which warned against eating "fresh breads, goose, green corn and dandelion."

For John Lattner and his fellow recruits, they not only had to follow the rules of the University, practice and play hard in football and serve in ROTC (Reserve Officer Training Corp), they also had to maintain a 77 average to retain eligibility. Non-football undergrads had to achieve only a 70 average to pass. Confusingly, at the end of four years, if an individual posted an average between 70 and 77 percent, the University permitted him to graduate but not obtain a degree.

Plus there were no girls on campus!

Against these formidable obstacles, Domers balanced the ledger with some indisputable facts. While the post-war GI Bill paid for veterans to attend college in sizable numbers, many people did not have the ability or means to enroll in higher learning like the poor suffering lads in South Bend. And most football players had scholarships.

Additionally, while the administration enforced its strict rules, the newcomers had access to the University's private 18 hole golf course, clay and concrete tennis courts, handball and squash courts, swimming and diving (both at the Rockne Memorial building and the lakes on campus), basketball courts, boxing rings, wrestling arenas and tumbling rooms for gymnastics buffs. Intramural basketball, football, baseball, softball and bowling leagues flourished, although the keglers had to travel to downtown South Bend on Sunday afternoons to find bowling lanes. When the boys returned to their rooms, the maid service had tidied up after them, a luxury very few of them enjoyed back home.

Touring actors, singers and lecturers stopped by often to augment the arts, while the aspiring artists in the undergrad ranks had the option to try out for the Freshman Band, Senior Band, Orchestra, Glee Club or renowned Marching Band, while actors auditioned for the University Theater. Politicians vied for Student Council seats, although freshmen did not have seats on that organization. Scribes scribbled for the *Scholastic*, *The Dome*, the *Juggler* (literary, almost all of its writers and editors wore glasses), *Technical Review* (engineering) or the *Law Review* at the Law School, the oldest Catholic law school in America.

The University tried to keep the students out of downtown South Bend, a task made easier by the commonly held observation that "what is there to do in South Bend? Not much, is the answer, unless you are resourceful." Enterprising freshmen soon discovered bars far off campus that catered to an underage crowd, serving beer, never hard stuff.

But all of the lakes and tennis courts and bands could not match the warm weather or plentitudes of young women co-eds other schools had to offer. Many of the football players sacrificed the opportunity to encounter more attractive things in life because they felt they had the opportunity to play for the greatest coach and the most heralded program in the country, and if they starred enough and had their faces printed on the covers of national magazines, the women would follow. Or so they told themselves.

Yet, the scholarship football athletes measured only a tiny fraction of the entire student body; no, something else drew young men to a frosty climate with strict rules and an all male campus.

Notre Dame had God on its side. At least that's what Frank Leahy thought. Perhaps in a more sober moment he only believed that he had Mary the Mother of Jesus in his corner, but in a pinch he could ask Mary to intercede on behalf of him and his lads. In the end it mattered little what Leahy thought, as the school, long before it had a football squad had been founded by Fathers of the Holy Cross. The priests planted a university on barren land and survived a fire in 1879, which almost spelled an end to the venture, because they believed.

They believed and they made it easy for others to believe that Notre Dame had its foundation on consecrated ground, a sacred place founded on a childlike trust that God's will would be honored, that Catholics across America might feel a part of something bigger, something greater, a foot in heaven and a sliver of the American dream. Older priests and young men prayed together and learned together and when those young men became men, they had the opportunity to accomplish great goals, to honor God and their own talents.

A little bit out of the way, behind the Basilica of the Sacred Heart, stands the Grotto, a quiet little cave modeled after the Lourdes shrine in France. Here, football players and their classmates and teachers and families knelt down in the dignity of their own reflection and worshipped God in the most elemental form of prayer, an admission that no one, no matter how great on earth, possesses ultimate answers of the universe, yet has the equal and inalienable right to continue to try to seek them out.

If you knew that you have God on your side, you can accomplish most anything. Notre Dame men, in general, believed they had God on their side and that they had chosen the right place to go to school.

Like many private colleges and universities in the early 1950s, Notre Dame maintained its single sex status, a policy not in effect in the state schools which increasingly began to dominate the standings in the National Collegiate Top 20 rankings. Across a highway, though, stood another single sex institution named St. Mary's College catering to women only.

Ideally, every man at Notre Dame would decide upon considerable personal reflection and encouragement from the floor rectors to join the priesthood. Realistically, relatively few men chose that path in each class, so the next best alternative lay in ensuring that the nice young men of Zahm and the other frosh halls met nice young Catholic girls to create in the future large and happy Catholic families. In advancement of this objective, each year toward the third week in September, the two institutions staged a joint picnic at South Bend's Potowatomi Park.

Lattner and Rigali missed the event as they had girlfriends back home but many of their classmates bought up the tickets to this event with dispatch before the 400 tickets allotted to the school ran out. Photographs of the event show young women being warily watched by groups of men with their hands in their pockets, in a tentative bow to the mating ritual. Most of the men remained bashful, and either kept standing or playing volleyball, but a few of the more adventurous ones asked young ladies to stroll with them to explore the local zoo. The editors of the *Scholastic* felt for their young charges, commenting that, "the best advice is to go on over and fend for yourself."

Briefly, St. Mary's had teas, where their students danced with the Notre Dame boys. Not long after arriving in South Bend, Neil Worden attended one of the teas, not to dance, but in the hopes of scoring some good refreshments. Tiring of watching his peers dance, he asked a young woman where to find the punch and cookies, and received back a most unfriendly face, like he had just used her tooth brush. It turns out there was not even tea at the teas, so Worden quickly departed, hungry, but wiser for the experience.

Like many of the pupils on campus, and virtually all of the football players, Lattner had signed up for ROTC, with

Johnny, Joe Bush, Ray Bubick and several others choosing the Air Force, while Fred Mangialardi and a few others opted for the Navy. In that era, particularly since the Korean War had begun, the selective service draft remained in force, and at times a ballplayer might find himself at an armed services base, not a gridiron as had happened to a recent Irish ballplayer, Frank Epstein.

Notre Dame wanted to keep its young football players on campus and away from wars and training camps, while they endured an equally demanding regimen under the guidance of such men as line coach Bob McBride and Prefect of Discipline, Father Charles I. McCarragher.

Black Mac and Toneff

MOST DOMERS at mid-century referred to the Prefect of Discipline, Father Charles I. McCarragher, as "Black Mac." Born in Mt. Vernon, New York, on June 5, 1909, Fr. McCarragher early in his career exhibited considerable promise as an academician, with a concentration in criminology and sociology, but that was not his "calling," as his temperament better suited him to keep the young men under his charge in line.

In fairness, the position of the Prefect of Discipline in a strict Catholic university of hormonally charged young men had to have taxed the soul of any person foolish enough to accept the appointment. Too harsh and the students hated you, too soft and the alumni and parents might come down on you.

Given these allowances, Fr. McCarragher relished his job and all too often acted harshly when a situation merited a measure of Christian charity. Every young man from that era has their favorite Black Mac story; for instance, before his appointment as the Prefect of Discipline in 1952, McCarragher served as the rector of the freshman Zahm Hall, and one student noted that Black Mac occasionally ran down the floors of the dorm just before midnight with one sneaker and one shoe on.

McCarragher did not engage in this ritual as some sort of quirk, but rather he sought to catch students with lights on

47

in their room after the 11:00 p.m. enforced darkness period. The sneaker muffled the sound completely so it sounded as if he walked slowly (with only the shoe making noise on the off-beat) when in fact he flew down the hall. So by the time a frosh heard the shoe drop the first time, it was already too late. In effect for every two strides taken, the nocturnal student only heard one.

Another student, while one day playing football with his hall mates along one of the borders of the University's eighteen hole golf course, sent an errant tossed ball or shanked kick over the fence and onto the golf course. Unbeknownst to him, protocol required that he go walk about a half mile out of his way to the entrance to the golf course to retrieve the ball and then exit the same meandering way. Naturally he jumped the fence and grabbed the ball and hopped back over, only to get caught by one of the rectors and taken to Black Mac McCarragher.

Scared out of his wits, the young man sat in front of McCarragher, who told him, "I don't think you are the type of person that Notre Dame is looking for." All this for jumping over a fence to get a football. He did not receive a suspension but had to endure this humiliation for a minor offense at best. Others did not get off so luckily.

One evening, four students with a BB gun made the grave mistake of shooting it into an adjoining hall. Notoriously inaccurate, this BB went through a window of another student's room. The priests set up a dragnet right away and nabbed the shooter and his friends, not a difficult task, and they all had their day with Black Mac, who kicked them all out.

Some wayward young men only survived visits with Mc-

Carragher due to divine intervention, or at the least a power-ful bishop back home. Each Notre Dame student had three class cuts a semester, after which the student flunked out of the course. In a logic class, one student faced a dilemma of either not attending an important family event back in Ohio or cutting his fourth class and receiving an automatic "F." Since the professor was blind, the intrepid student had asked a friend in the class to answer his name during roll call, a plan which would have worked had the second student at-tended the class and answered the roll, which he did not.

After returning back to campus from his family celebra-tion, the student learned that his friend had let him down and when he spoke to the professor, he was told that since he had exceeded the allowable number of cuts, he had thus re-ceived a zero in the class and could never hold student office ever at the University.

The rector at the student's hall, Fr. Charles Sheedy, pleaded for him and almost three weeks and eight more class cuts later, the student had his meeting with Black Mac Mc-Carragher. McCarragher informed him that he would be allowed back in the class, but first asked the student to list his total number of class cuts, which now totaled about a dozen, prompting Black Mac to turn a redder shade of crim-son, wadded up the form and hollered, "Get your [expletive deleted] butt back to class!"

On another occasion, one of the football players attempted to sneak out after hours, choosing as his escape route the park-ing lot then situated by the engineering building and the law school, an area often patrolled by Fr. Mac and another priest, Fr. McAulliffe. The ballplayer soon recognized the errors of his way when he spotted Fr. McAulliffe in his path, so the young man pulled down his head to try to escape detection and ran right by the padre, giving him a shoulder in the process.

The next day, the young man said his goodbyes to his friends and left the campus with his bags packed, never to return.

Fr. McCarragher largely did not discriminate among the student body, never turning his eyes away from any indiscretions and flouting of the rules by the football players while disciplining the remaining student body with vigor and severity. Black Mac pounced on everyone who violated the policies of Our Lady's University, and while Frank Leahy might bend a rule here, there and everywhere, Mac had little tolerance for tolerance.

In part, McCarragher reflected the strictness of the Catholic Church of his era, where the Baltimore Catechism answered questions of the faithful with certainty and where right was right and wrong was sin. Venial sins were like misdemeanors and there might be a bit of leeway there, but mortal sins like theft and murder and missing Mass were punishable by eternal damnation unless one sought forgiveness, received forgiveness from a God more merciful than Black Mac, and resolved to change his or her ways.

Also, as a very visible Catholic institution, Notre Dame needed its students to act like gentlemen and reflect well upon the University, so for that additional reason, Black Mac had a mandate to enforce rigorous adherence to the rules and regulations of the campus.

Unfortunately, during this era, not enough people questioned the need for such strictness, or what this often cruel behavior did to the faithful and ultimately to the loyalty to the Church by its members. Vatican II was still over a decade away, and until then, Black Mac and others had their rules to follow and their punishments to dole out to the wicked, so the students largely obeyed and bowed their heads and prayed a lot and some begged for change. And change eventually came, but not in the early 1950s and not at Our Lady's University.

The typical Notre Dame student feared Black Mac and some of his more zealous disciples, but they did not have to face the tough Irish football coaches each day. For aspiring linemen in particular, they might survive Coach Leahy's biting remarks, or a coach running them through the paces after practice or Fr. McCarragher's strict regulation, but then they had to encounter the sternest test yet, the sheer power of tackle Bob Toneff.

Born on June 23, 1930 in Detroit, Toneff grew up in Barberton, Ohio (outside of Akron) and graduated from Barberton High. Unlike many of the Irish recruits of the day, neither he nor his parents particularly possessed any aspirations for him to attend Notre Dame, and Bob assumed that his path led to Ohio State, where his brother already played football.

A local furniture store owner and ND bird-dog scout named Tom Wygant had other ideas. Wygant finagled a meeting for Toneff with Frank Leahy, and like many recruits of this era, this recruit sat mesmerized as the great coach laid out his case to persuade him to come to South Bend. Knowing that Toneff was unlikely to be influenced with tales of Rockne and the Four Horsemen, Leahy stressed the strong academics at the University and the potential of obtaining a great job in the future. Leahy sold the school and conveyed to the young man a sense that the head coach might be a bit of an easy touch.

As Toneff later admitted, "Oh, what a bad read that was!"

And yet if Leahy's body language lied, Bob Toneff had another reason for looking at schools other than Ohio State. While one impulse drew him there because of the prior presence of his brother, an opposing consideration drove him away. He wanted to establish his own reputation, independent of his brother and he felt he could only achieve this objective by leaving home. While other schools such as Georgia and Kentucky beckoned, his time with Leahy divined his path to Notre Dame.

When Toneff enrolled in the fall of 1948, returning World II veterans dominated the Fighting Irish squad. Jungle Jim Martin had returned from the war with stories of secret missions and long swims through enemy waters in the South Pacific. Revisionists have since suggested that some of Martin's exploits might have fallen victim to embellishment in the retelling, yet simply analyzing the undeniable facts of his service established him as a genuine American war hero.

Gruff end Leon Hart, while not a veteran, was a huge athletic man, a fierce blocker on offense who also sprang loose for receptions, while disrupting opponent's offensive lines on defense. En route to a 1949 Heisman Award and later, All-Pro recognition with the Detroit Lions, Hart virtually created the tight end position.

Additionally, the Irish stocked the backfield with star quarterbacks Frank Tripucka and Bob Williams, featuring running backs Frank Spaniel, Emil "Six Yard" Sitko, Terry Brennan, John Panelli and Larry Coutre.

Later a running back for the Green Bay Packers, Coutre

had notoriously poor vision. In a game against North Carolina, the Irish faced a fourth down situation, so quarterback
Bob Williams heaved the ball thirty yards to Coutre for the
first down, causing Coach Leahy to lament, "Couldn't you
throw it to someone who could see?"

Freshmen in 1948 did not play varsity, yet Toneff started
at right defensive tackle the next year, at which time he encountered Coach Bob McBride for the first time. Off the
football field, it is difficult to find a more gentlemanly soul
than Bob Toneff. Throughout his life Toneff naturally exuded his elemental self: a kind, good-natured, articulate, hu-
morous, perceptive, modest, warm-hearted friend and family
man.

The hard-laughing, knee-slapping side of Bob Toneff
certainly did not escape the attention of Bob McBride, up
from Mt. Carmel as he began his line coaching duties at ND
in 1949. At first, McBride might have perceived these traits
and mistakenly concluded that Toneff might carry them
onto the practice and playing field, a costly error on the line
coach's part. McBride invited Toneff to his after-practice
blocking sessions, and rather than toughing the player up,
Toneff tenderized the coach. On each occasion that Mc-
Bride threw an elbow into Toneff's eye, Toneff biblically returned it with more force and bad intention. When McBride
pushed too hard, Toneff threw a punch at him. McBride
could teach the young lineman technique, he never could
make him any tougher than he already was. McBride had a
burgeoning superstar protégé on his hands.

Having started on the 1949 National Championship team,
Toneff thrived at tackle on the weaker all-around Irish squads
in '50 and '51. In his last year with the Irish, Toneff earned
All-American honors and was drafted in the second round

by the San Francisco '49ers. After serving with the armed forces in Germany, he enjoyed a twelve-year career in the NFL, evenly split between the '49ers and the Redskins, toting home four Pro Bowl selections during his remarkable career.

It has substantially become clichéd and hackneyed to suggest that a sports player "never received the recognition he deserved," and in Bob Toneff's instance, it is inaccurate, as his All-American accolades, his participation in the Senior and East-West Shrine Bowls and his multiple Pro Bowls attest.

Still, he has not been accorded anywhere near the repeated mention of other Irish greats of the late 1940s, and several reasons suggest why. Although he started as a sophomore on a championship club, his junior and senior years coincided with a steep decline in the program, a development that drew attention to players from more successful teams.

There is more. Despite his talent and accomplishments, Bob Toneff never spoke in the first or third person about his work. Modestly, Bob always chose to marvel at the accomplishments of his teammates or respected foes and keenly broke down the elements of their game that made them great, eschewing self-aggrandizement. In a somewhat related vein, while many of his teammates later settled in an area of the Midwest close to South Bend, Bob settled around San Francisco, far from the Fighting Irish crowd, so he did not appear regularly at alumni events or games, although he did catch games.

Incoming freshmen in the falls of '50 and '51 did not see the magnanimous side of Bob Toneff so much because their

age differences and separate dormitory arrangements discouraged any socialization they may have experienced with
him on the campus grounds. What they saw was a man who
outweighed them and who carried unrelenting nastiness onto
the field. This was the Bob Toneff they knew at the time.

Akron's Art Hunter, a graduate of St. Vincent High
School in that city, had played against Toneff's team in schoolboy football, but by college gave up about 25-30 pounds to
his former adversary. Toneff later lined up against Hunter
in the NFL and always considered him "tough, big and a
good blocker." Similarly, he felt that Jim Schrader "knew
what the hell he was doing."

A tackle named Dick Hilinski did not fare half as well
as some of his peers. Toneff ran into him on a number of occasions, knocking him out at least twice. One day, after
practice, some time in 1951, lineman Jack Lee and fullback
Del Gander looked out of a dorm window at Alumni Hall
in horror to see poor Hilinski keel over onto the quadrangle
grass.

Hilinski had experienced a typically harrowing day posting up against Toneff in blocking drills, and it took several minutes for Lee and Gander to revive him. Thereafter,
Hilinski left the Notre Dame campus to transfer to Ohio
State, where he later earned All-Big Ten honors and played
on their 1954 National Championship team. But his days at
ND had ended and Bob Toneff perhaps in some small way
hastened the departure. Tragically, Hilinski died in a car
accident in the fall of 1955, when his car went off the road.

But if his teammates suffered after blocking him in drills
and scrimmages, Toneff also sustained abuse dollopped

upon him by Leahy and the coaching staff, all of whom descended upon him in 1951, as some type of disappointment. For Toneff, the negativity had its desired effect as he struggled all year to exceed the expectations of the staff, a seemingly impossible task given their constant chiding, but someone noticed as Bob Toneff earned his All-American selection in 1951.

He did much more, as any teammate who experienced sustained contact with him can attest. He taught his younger teammates how to block with ferocity and yet maintain cheerfulness, a playful nature off the field. He imparted proper technique and how to battle it out with an opponent, lessons he learned from the star linemen he encountered in the '40s like Martin, Hart, Walt Grothaus and Bill Wightkin. He bore the brunt of his coaches' taunts not because he did not excel, but because at the end of the last decade they had a platoon of Bob Toneffs at their disposal and now they had only one available.

The fact that they had one Bob Toneff though, helps to explain how Notre Dame football rose from the ashes in the early '50s, as he contributed mightily to rebuilding his team and the young men that survived going against him in many cases went on to enjoy long careers in the NFL. But first they learned how to excel in the trenches at Our Lady's University.

The Irish Prepare for the Fall

NOTRE DAME once had an equipment manager named Jack McAlllister, a bit of a curmudgeon on the outside but a quiet guy who called everyone a "pissant" on the inside. A short wiry man with snow white hair, Jack had cleaned uniforms and guarded gear for over a quarter century by the fall of '50, harkening back to the days of the great Rockne and the Four Horsemen. He watched over the precious assets of uniforms, cleats, pads and helmets tenaciously, recouping the torn jerseys and beat up shoes each year for safe-keeping and delivery to the freshman football players for the next year. Joe Rigali, Bob's brother, helped keep track of the equipment as a campus job.

After the initiation period for freshmen had ended, the scholarship athletes lined up on September 17, 1950 to be issued their gear for the ensuing campaign. As Johnny Lattner approached McAllister, he understood the equipment manager only wanted to hear the player's name and high school, so when his turn arrived, he barked out, "Lattner, Fenwick High!"

McAllister scanned the list, did not see anyone or anything with that name and informed him that he was not entitled to any equipment as he did not have a scholarship and did not belong on the team. Politely, Lattner protested that indeed he had taken a scholarship at Our Lady's School and that…"Hey you pissant!" barked McAllister, "go and see your coach and take it up with him!" So Johnny Lattner, late the recipient of over seventy scholarship offers from colleges and universities, slinked out of the queue, leaving a very terrified teammate behind him to encounter the Equipment Nazi.

Chastened for something he had not done, Lattner loped up to the varsity backs coach Bill Earley, and to freshman coach Benny Sheridan, and explained the predicament: "that old man doesn't want to give me my uniform." The coaches rolled their eyes and explained to McAllister that he needed to issue gear to the young recruit, so he complied and gave Lattner a pair of old oblong cleats a size or two off his normal foot dimensions, together with a smelly old leather helmet, pads that looked like relics of another century and hand-me-downs of a jersey and pants. Johnny Lattner had hit the big time.

The treatment was not unusual. Years earlier one of freshman tackle Joe Bush's brothers had stood in line for his equipment and McAllister denied him his request because he was "too small to play." Like Lattner, Joe's brother had to go back to his coaches to straighten out McAllister, but no one really changed him much. He protected Leahy and he knew where all the bodies were figuratively buried and he was much better in the tent pissing out than vice versa. Players came and went, Jack McAllister remained.

With the flurry of fall sign-ups, freshman orientation activities and practices, Neil Worden could be excused from taking a bit of rest on the top bunk of his dorm, this fall no longer ensconced with seniors he did not know nor was likely to become acquainted with. This time he roomed with someone his own age and a person who shared his zest for adventure, Bobby Joseph, from Martins Ferry, Ohio.

Someone in student housing or on the coaching staff must have immediately intuited that Worden and Joseph were characters, so rather than room them with unsuspecting and impressionable virginal football recruits, wisely the two joyous young men bunked with each other. They could not corrupt each other, it was too late for that, but they could have a great time together, which they most always did.

During a rest on the top bunk of their beds, Worden was awakened one afternoon by Joseph and introduced to another freshman football player, end Joe Katchik. Wearily, Worden opened his lids and took sight for the first time of the tallest man he had ever seen, and at 6'9" in height, almost a foot taller than he and Joseph. Worden at first figured that Katchik was standing on a stool or on the edge of the mattress on the bottom bunk, but no, it was all Katchik. The long end enjoyed pushing the envelope a bit, and the trio became fast friends, living life with what passed for the fast lane in 1950's Notre Dame.

Across campus, massive tackle Ray Bubick did not travel far from his boyhood home in South Bend to Notre Dame's Cartier Field. A product of Riley High School, Bubick came to ND upon the recommendation of the future Mayor of South Bend, Babe Voorde, and someone must have scouted one or more of his schoolboy varsity contests because he received a full football scholarship without ever having met Frank Leahy or worked out against line coaches Bob McBride or Joe McArdle. To complete the run of luck, the 6'4" strong man got his own room at Breen-Phillips his freshman year. There are of course two types of luck, and at his first scrimmage, he encountered the other kind when the coaches paired him up against Bob Toneff in a blocking drill and Toneff promptly broke Bubick's nose.

Like most of his classmates, Bubick had signed up for the Air Force ROTC on campus so in addition to his studies and football practices, he attended two classes and marched separately for two additional hours each week. About the only airplane Ray and his friends saw that year was that flown in by Fred Miller from the Miller Brewing Company.

Otherwise, his ROTC classes consisted mainly of learning about the rules and regulations of the Air Force and its history and tradition. Since the USAF came into existence only after the Second World War, it had but a brief history to study. The students nevertheless had to review the congressional legislation that promulgated the separate air wing. The courses got a bit more interesting with time, and between junior and senior years the ROTC required the young airmen to go on base for six weeks; but for now, the courses did not meander much into anything remotely interesting or even technically challenging.

As a new wing of the armed services instituting an ROTC program from scratch, the Air Force had uniforms supposedly for everyone, but it had not fitted out its regular uniforms for some of the massive football linemen. So for tackles such as Bubick, the Corp only provided pink pants and an olive drab dress coat at the beginning. In nice weather the young men drilled by Cartier Field; and in inclement conditions, they marched in the old Field House. The investment the Air Force made in its recruits panned out in many instances, as Bubick and others later made the Air Force their career.

Representing a minority of freshman football players, Fred Mangialardi signed up for the Navy ROTC. Mangialardi absolutely loved the Navy and made his closest friends, of which he had many, more in the NROTC than on the football team. Unlike the Air Force, the Navy men did not do a lot of marching, but spent much of the first year studying the history of the United States Navy and its traditions. It doled out more work than the Air Force, but Mangialardi for one enjoyed it so much that it did not seem too bad.

While nearly all football recruits also belonged to a branch of the ROTC, their real work did not take place in military history classes or drill halls and fields, but rather on the Cartier Field practice facility.

Not all were created equal. A later team head coach estimated that a third of recruits in general excelled, another third performed adequately with the remainder players who did not live up to their potential or who sustained crippling injuries. Joining "can't miss" prospects like John Lattner and Neil Worden on the freshman team in the 1950s were other young men with their own aspirations.

It took no time for his teammates and friends to christen large lineman Carl Trail "Mark Trail," after the popular comic strip character, who survives to this day, espousing the reduction of "carelessness and abusive activity such as littering, vandalism and theft, and wildlife poaching." It also took little time for John Darago to earn the nickname "Fog" because of his thick glasses, which fogged up during practice, making his eyes impenetrable at times. He came over from St. Vincent's High School with Art Hunter, his inseparable friend there, although in South Bend they lived in different halls and drifted apart a bit over time. The young center played basketball in the Ohio state finals and had the stern task of blocking Bob Toneff both as an opponent in high school and on the practice field at ND.

Ed Sarna, the first prize recruit for the Irish from South River, New Jersey (with Joe Theisman the second), as a very young man sat in Yankee Stadium and heard Babe Ruth deliver his farewell speech. A physical education major, he listed "hunting, fishing and trapping" as his hobbies, and had hopes of breaking into the team's backfield. A funny and engaging man, he later developed into a pretty fair boxer in the college's annual charity bouts.

Halfback Jim Lapash and fullback Jim McClure impressed the coaches early but then disappeared, remembered if at all only vaguely by their freshman teammates. They may have transferred out, but again no one is certain.

Larry Ash came from mountain country in Colorado and had played against Joe Bush in a high school All-American team in Nashville. Bush's high school friend from Iowa, quarterback Bob Martin, stayed after practice with the eager and likable Ash, working on their tackling technique. The clean-cut popular young man aspired to become a Navy pilot, and died tragically shortly after graduating from Notre Dame, when his plane augered in outside of Pittsburgh.

Art Nowack, a lineman and sometimes linebacker from Rochester, New York, had attended Aquinas Prep before he enrolled as a freshman at the University of Portland, a school which promptly dropped football entirely after that fall of 1949. Irish back Jack Landry invited Art to visit Notre Dame and Coach Bernie Crimmins and a meeting was set up, but the closer Art got to South Bend, the more nervous he became, so he kept on traveling past without stopping by as appointed. After Portland's program became defunct,Landry extended him another invitation but demanded that he keep his appointment this time—which he did, earning a scholarship to join the freshman team for 1950.

Nowack joined another lineman named Al Petranick, a young Czech guard from Johnson City, New York, trying out for the interior line. A physics and mechanics buff, he signed up for the College of Engineering, but found enough spare time to effect a bit of a Renaissance man aspect, enjoying dancing and Sinclair Lewis' "Arrowsmith." Another new player, Tom "O.B." O'Brien, hailed from the Connecticut countryside and walked around seemingly everywhere with a pair of devices that he used to strengthen his wrists. When he did not flex his wrists with these tools, he hung them out of his pants pockets. One of his frosh teammates recalled him over a half century later as very clumsy.

Having spawned such receiving stars as Leon Hart and Jim Mutscheller, by acclimation the end position reputedly stocked the finest incoming athletes by far. This group included Joe Katchik, Art Hunter, Minnie Mavraides, Fred Mangialardi and the young man from Kenosha named Don Penza. Recruited by Fred Miller, Penza hailed from a very large family, with the youngest member a little brother named Frank Leahy Penza. Perhaps the potentially most talented end, Entee Shine, one of Notre Dame's first African-American players had come over from Central High in South Bend. Known more for his prowess on the basketball court, he had the potential to become the greatest end in Notre Dame's history.

In addition to scholarship athletes, another couple dozen or so freshman tried out for the team, some in the summer before freshmen year with mixed results as some of these players never enrolled at the University. Some other young men stepped onto campus after Labor Day and almost immediately jumped into pads and began hitting each other and trying to block and tackle varsity men in practice. A pre-med student named John O'Hara had played some competitive high school football in Colorado, so early during his time at ND he walked into the Athletic Director's office and asked for information about joining the team. Out walked the AD himself, kindly Moose Krause, and asked O'Hara his height and weight and told him there might be a space on the team for him. So Moose gave him the information about the time and location of practices and, like that, O'Hara had joined the freshman team.

Sometimes alumni encouraged a talented athlete to suit up, an approach that worked with Thomas Short, an end from Moberly, Missouri, who heeded the advice of Red Hagan, a fullback from the '32 and '33 teams. Many other fellows needed little encouragement from anyone else, having always wished to play for Notre Dame, so if a potential recruit had enough size or speed to dream, he often got an old jersey and some other standard issue equipment.

Particularly in the case of non-scholarship walk-ons, a young man might check in with the team after considering whether to do so, but for the scholarship men and those who had tried out during the summer, in addition to the multitudinous other activities required of a freshman on their first day of class, the first year footballers also practiced for the first time. They did not start working right away with Frank Leahy, who "cast[ed] more than one envious glance at a handful of the freshmen grid hopefuls who were limbering up under Coach Bennie (sic) Sheridan's scrutiny." The current senior class had some excellent players, just not enough of them, and Leahy needed his freshmen now, but the rules prohibited it so he could only watch and work with the three thin classes of players at his disposal.

Five coaches guided the Irish acolytes that fall, with Sheridan the head coach. Benny played left-halfback for the Irish in the late 1930s, leading the Irish in scoring in 1938 with 24 points and in punt return average in '38 and '39 under coach Layden. He played in the 1940 Senior Bowl and with a Fort Riley team during the Second World War, but by 1950 he knew his role, to teach and weed out freshman players.

Dick Riley, Phil Cantwell, Bob Lally and Babe Voorde assisted Sheridan. Riley had coached at Kings College in Wilkes-Barre, Pennsylvania, but he came out west in part to work in sales for the Schwarz Paper Company in South Bend. Typically the Irish culled the ranks of the irretrievably injured scholarship ballplayers to serve as assistant coaches for the frosh, a good description of the background of Cantwell, an oft-injured end while a player for the Irish. Bob Lally starred at guard on the '49 team and had started law school at ND, helping out with the coaching chores in his spare time, while local politician Babe Voorde "had done a lot of scouting for the Irish," as the *South Bend Tribune* described his background.

The freshmen, though ineligible to play varsity and considered a team, never actually played any games against any other colleges. Oftentimes, they merely served as sacrificial lambs to the varsity in their blocking drills and scrimmages, having no chance to seriously give the much larger and far more experienced upperclassmen any true challenge. When Leahy did not pit these young men against the varsity, Sheridan and his assistants worked on their conditioning with constant calisthenics and some fundamental instructions on how to run, block and kick on a collegiate level.

Otherwise, they had to adopt the persona of the varsity's next opposing players, and more importantly learn the opposing team's plays and replicate the execution of them on short notice for the edification of the varsity. On September 16, less than a week after the freshmen came to campus, they suited up with fourth stringers and acted out North Carolina plays, which the *South Bend Tribune*'s Paul Neville adjudged more of a workout than a scrimmage.

Probably on this occasion, newcomer Paul Robst, playing the defensive line, ran into a big pileup and in the midst of bodies flailing all over, junior tackle Bob Toneff's shoe bashed into his face. The force of Toneff's kick drove one of Robst's teeth to penetrate right through the outside skin below his lip, requiring several stitches. The *Chicago Tribune* believed that the neophytes played well, not having given up a point on defense until the second quarter, "Altho [the varsity had been] given the ball most of the time in an effort to improve its attack..."

The frosh came "within a couple feet" of scoring a touchdown and on a second occasion penetrated the varsity's ten yard line, eventually succumbing to the varsity 32-0. But not before badly dinking up some of the veteran players, most notably back Billy Barrett, tackles Bill Flynn and Jim

Mahoney, guard Tom Seaman, linebacker Dave Flood "and a few others." A truly pyrrhic victory for the varsity.

Concurrent with the loss of healthy varsity players, probably the first freshman football recruit to drop out of the program was Entee Shine, who left the team to devote his energies to playing basketball at the University. If Leahy hoped that Shine might mature into the first African-American monogram (varsity letter) winner in football at ND, those hopes irretrievably vanished. Shine had started at left end in a recent scrimmage, so he had a role on the team, he simply did not want to fill it.

The coaches perceived exceptional athletic ability in Shine, a view held by many of his teammates. Several decades later, one of them recalled the two weeks Entee Shine suited up and believed he had the potential to be a special end. Shine did play some basketball for the Irish before transferring to another school, but the Los Angeles Rams thought enough of his potential to later draft him with a 27th round pick.

At about the same time, another prospect, Joe Morgan, left the campus and transferred out to Ohio State. Morgan had envisioned a career both in football and track at Notre Dame and got neither, perhaps concluding that the tough scrimmages might curtail both ambitions.

Finally, one freshman received a condom in the mail from his girlfriend back home and before the envelope hit the floor, he was out the door for good, never to return. Meanwhile, his erstwhile teammates continued to master the I-formation of the North Carolina Tar Heels to prepare the varsity for their first game of the season.

On September 23, 1950, the freshmen had their next opportunity to play the varsity, this time in a full scrimmage, and their only one in the stadium that year. Frank Leahy did not see the game, as he traveled south to see and scout the University of North Carolina. Interestingly, the evening before the scrimmage, the local paper ran the starting line-ups of both the ND varsity and frosh squads.

The starting line-up of the varsity is only mildly note-worthy, as they obviously were going to start such stars as Bob Williams, Bob Toneff, Chet Ostrowski and Jim Mutscheller. More intriguing is the evaluation that the coaches made of approximately thirty players and their talents in less than two weeks since they first enrolled at Notre Dame in the drill hall.

John Lattner as a starting halfback was a no-brainer, but Benny Sheridan also started Bob Martin at quarterback, Jim Lapash at fullback and Fran Paterra at the other halfback slot. On the line, the coaches led with Minnie Mavraides at left end, Joe Katchik at right end, Ray Bubick and Joe Bush at tackles, Frank Kettles and Al Petranick at guards and Bernie Fieler at center. Only four of these young men suited up at the University of Notre Dame as ballplayers three years later as seniors, illustrating the limits of talent evaluation, particu-larly at such an early stage in a young player's development.

Of course the freshmen got killed, losing 40-0. While All-American Bob Williams completed short passes at will, the freshman defensive line showed promise (and the un-derlying weakness of the varsity offensive line) as Joe Doyle of the *South Bend Tribune* saw it, Williams "found himself rushed to the point where he was hitting only about a third of the time." On a less positive note for the new players, Doyle also noted, "The complete lack of an offense by the frosh was even more astonishing." The freshmen never marched beyond the 30 yard line of the varsity.

By Monday, Leahy had returned with his scouting evaluation of North Carolina, and the freshmen entered the practice field decked out in jerseys with the numbers of the North Carolina starters affixed, as Leahy ran his offense against the freshmen. The novices soon learned to subordinate their egos to the greater good of the team, and one of their earliest auditions involved play-acting as Tar Heels so that their elders might prepare however imperfectly against them.

Two days later, Leahy ran a dummy scrimmage with his starters and second-teamers. Unlike a full blown scrimmage, which replicated game conditions, in a dummy scrimmage the players did not tackle each other nor did they run into blocking dummies. Meanwhile, the third and fourth team varsity men scrimmaged against the freshmen on Cartier Field.

The coaches planned for the attrition of the newest team members, they wanted their eventual varsity roster members to fit a certain mold. Most importantly for the short term, they needed cannon fodder to throw against the current varsity to prepare them for their first game, and the Irish did defeat North Carolina—barely—to preserve their 39-game unbeaten streak. Playing before the home crowd, Bob Williams passed for two touchdowns to end Jim Mutscheller, the last time with less than three minutes left in the game for a 14-7 decision.

Frank Leahy knew what the narrow victory meant. As recently as the year before, the Irish would have rolled over an opponent like the Tar Heels, but now had just enough to eke out a victory. His team faced a much stronger team in Purdue the next week and Leahy openly worried about defeat for his team, announcing, "We're going to go to work on fundamentals."

What this meant is a week of torture for his players, and in the trickle down theory of who was going to receive the most painful punishment, it fell to the freshmen to absorb the hits of the varsity and the frustration of the coaches. In non-theoretical terms, Leahy altered his usual practice of giving the first teamers a day off from practice on Monday in favor of a scrimmage and a focus on blocking and pass defense.

The next Saturday, his concern proved well-founded, as Dale Samuels, one of many fine quarterbacks from Purdue, systematically picked apart the Irish defense while the offense failed to answer each opposing score.

Although Notre Dame had defeated Purdue in Ross-Ade Stadium the previous season, the Irish lost at home in 1950 to the Boilermakers by a 28-14 margin. Reportedly, thereafter, the Irish's sports information director, Charlie Callahan, walked around dazed, almost in a paralytic state. The club had not lost a game since December 1, 1945 against Great Lakes, a team filled with older servicemen and college all-stars in the first year Hugh Devore coached at ND (the second occasion was in 1963, the year before Ara Parseghian came to coach). Indeed, Frank Leahy had not lost a game as the Irish coach since November 27, 1943, again against Great Lakes, but at least that year the team had won a National Championship, its first under him.

The loss stunned many, even outside of the campus where some publications boldly anointed ND National Champions in their pre-season publications. The defeat definitely unnerved Frank Leahy, a perfectionist if there ever was one, but he had foretold the result after seeing his lads practice. He knew that the losses would continue to mount. Meanwhile, in Lafayette, Indiana, a spontaneous celebration, several days in length, erupted on the Purdue campus.

Classy Irish team captain, Jerry Groom, who previously had never known a defeat as a football player under Leahy, walked into the Purdue dressing room and later onto their team buses to make certain he congratulated each and every Boilermaker player. Then he joined his teammates to shower and dress and walk to the dining hall as the team that broke their own winning streak.

That night, the Notre Dame players collectively walked into the dining hall together, most not very hungry. Expecting nothing, they received a long and raucous chorus of cheers from the student body, "believed to be the most tumultuous reception ever given a team by the student body."

As one ray of hope, the *Scholastic* printed a team photograph of the freshmen, the Hamburger Squad, with a platoon of prospects intently gazing at the photographer. The accompanying article lauded the efforts and prospects of several of the members, and had the prohibition against using freshmen not been in effect in '50, Leahy almost certainly would have raided the roster for about a dozen of the young men.

By this time, many of the freshmen, both ballplayers and civilians, had hit a wall academically, struggling to bridge the difference between high school and quite rigorous college courses. In the middle of October, weekly talks commenced for those interested (after evening prayers) to hone their skills at such tasks as test taking, paper writing, military service and draft deferment, and budgeting one's time; a tour of the library was conducted for those who treated the edifice as a foreign entity.

The famed multi-floor Hesburgh Library, with its looming Touchdown Jesus with His arms lifted gloriously toward the heavens and high over an end zone to the stadium, did not exist yet. The University housed most of its volumes in a library tucked away near the Old Log Chapel in the ancient area of the campus. Most buildings looked about the same back then, with the exception of the rust-colored Dining Hall and the gold-domed Administration Building, with tan uniformity the norm for most of the structures.

Meanwhile the campus braced for a large Rosary devotion to take place at the stadium, while General Johnson planned to visit the Air Force ROTC. Knights of Columbus members dropped off pledge cards in each dorm room requesting a commitment from each student to say the rosary daily, no small task. At the rosary rally, about 40,000 attended, or just below the expected yield for a home football game. It was an age of faith, both in the Church and Notre Dame football.

Having lost to Purdue, the varsity girded for its first team flight ever, to visit New Orleans as the guests of Tulane University for an October 14th game. The idea had percolated in Executive Vice-President Fr. Theodore Hesburgh's mind for over a year, after having endured with the team the ordeal of the long train ride out to the West Coast to play Washington, an odyssey that took the better part of a week to accomplish. With the dawn of the new decade, Notre Dame men would travel in style.

The Fall Sets In

DESPITE HAVING LOST only for the first time in over four years, the Irish fell from first all the way down to tenth place in the AP poll in one week, after Purdue. It received some slightly good news when Chet Ostrowski, thought to have sustained a concussion in the game, merely had a broken nose. Sensing the profound disappointment, Frank Leahy told his players to "forget it," as he prepared them for their next game with the Tulane Green Wave.

To prepare for Tulane, the team ran some passing drills and a defensive line scrimmage to prepare for their opponents, who outweighed them considerably along the line. Scouting for Tulane, one-time Notre Dame player Andy Pilney reported back to New Orleans that the Irish lacked the depth of years past. The report leaked, and Leahy probably was divided between declaring Pilney a traitor or determining if he had any eligibility left and inviting him to fill in at his alma mater.

Generally, Leahy would have liked to run a full contact scrimmage, but with mounting injuries such as speedy sophomore linebacker Dave Flood with a shoulder separation, in mid-week he only scheduled a dummy scrimmage between the varsity and the freshmen. On Friday, en route to New

Orleans, the team took its first ever flight and upon landing, left for their lodgings at the St. Charles Hotel.

Over 73,000 fans bought tickets for the game in the Sugar Bowl, and for the locals, satisfaction came early as the Green Wave scored a touchdown five plays after taking the opening kickoff. The partisans went wild, but unbeknownst to them, Tulane had just made their last offensive score of the day.

A central viciousness underscored the game, the last scheduled between the two teams for the foreseeable future, with "Halfback Bill Barrett and Guard Paul Burns ...taken to Touro hospital for observation of head injuries." The Irish ground game stagnated, with 34 yards total to the Green Wave's 224.

To win, quarterback Bob Williams had to take over the game, which he did, evening the score with a 54-yard touchdown bomb to his back (and local New Orleans Jesuit High legend) John Petitbon to tie the game. The Green Wave employed an eight man front and they constantly threw Williams down for losses and "badly bruised" his shoulder and though Williams stayed in the game, a second back, Jack Landry, left the game having received a bouncing blow to the head that left him dazed and unable to play. With Bill Gay also dinked up, the Irish had lost their three best running backs.

And still Bob Williams dug in, throwing for 225 yards, an impressive total for the era, and he also averaged 40 yards for the seven punts he made for his team. When fullback Del Gander scored the team's second touchdown early in the second quarter, the two offenses stopped scoring. A second-half sack of Williams gave Tulane the last points scored that afternoon, as ND survived for a 13-9 victory.

Having seen Williams endure so much punishment from Tulane's defensive line, Leahy installed a two quarterback formation with back-up John Mazur on the field with Williams, as the rolls of the injured lengthened. Already thin, some of the Irish back-ups ended up playing nearly the whole game, remaining on the field for offensive and defensive series. But Notre Dame endured and won.

The narrow win over Tulane put ND back in the win column, but *Chicago Tribune* columnist and Irish alum Arch Ward pointed out flaws in the offense. While lavishly praising All-American quarterback Bob Williams, Ward lamented, "There is no Emil Sitko, John Panelli or other line-buster to provide the threat up the middle that great teams must have." It was almost a template for Rick Pitino's comment, several decades later as a Celtic coach in tough times, that "Larry, Kevin and Robert are not coming through that door."

Ward had it partly correct. After producing numerous quality backs for years, the ranks withered, the starters were not All-Americans and they lacked depth at the positions. But other pressing problems remained with no solution that fall. The defense too, lacked depth and quality and many of the best players had to play both offense and defense, while their opponents sent fresh players against them.

And Ward needed to sit down at some freshman practices to see John Lattner, Neil Worden and Tom McHugh, who were ineligible to assist the varsity in '50, but who had more talent than most backs their age. Better times would come.

Or would they?

On the Monday after the game, the starters rested, while the freshmen scrimmaged, against the reserves no less. A thankless task for the rookies, but one made worse by the fact they were not even priming the varsity for their next game. It could hardly be any other way, with Barrett hurt and lineman Paul Burns suffering from a likely left upper broken jaw.

Lamented Leahy, "In all my years of coaching football... I have never seen a team as badly battered as our club is right now." On Wednesday's workout, he did not even have his players wear their pads, as he conducted the whole practice with his lads wearing their tee-shirts. Team trainer Hugh Burns reported twenty varsity players had undergone treatment after they left the Tulane game, either during it or upon their return to South Bend. It did, however, lessen the infliction of pain upon the poor freshmen, who barely touched the varsity the week after Tulane due to the condition of so many of the varsity starters.

Approaching their October 21 game against Indiana, the coaching staff had another pressing concern to divert their attention: the club had scheduled a "B" game against the junior varsity of the University of Illinois, and between the depleted varsity ranks and the off-limit freshmen, ND barely had enough players to match up against the Illini. At times that year, the Irish suited up a player like Dave Flood for the B game and then sent him soon thereafter into the varsity game as well. Necessity being the mother of invention the team scrounged together enough players to tie Illinois on the Friday before the varsity game. If only the varsity had been so lucky the next day against Indiana.

Indiana had not defeated the Irish in 45 years, and in 1949, Bob Williams, Jim Martin, Six Yard Sitko and Leon Hart decimated the Hoosiers by a score of 49-6. In 1950, IU turned the tables.

Bodies kept falling all over the field. Just as Bob Williams began completing passes to Jim Mutscheller, the redoubtable quarterback was flattened trying to pass in the third quarter and was helped off the field. Junior QB John Mazur, a future head coach of the New England Patriots, came in but did not turn matters around. Tackle Jim Dunlay was carried off the field and even seemingly indestructible Bob Toneff limped off at one point.

Fullback Del Gander scraped away yardage for the Irish all afternoon, and scored their only touchdown, but even a late return by Williams failed to fully ignite the Irish, who bowed to their down state rival by a final score of 20-7. In what was becoming almost a customary development, another campus in Indiana thereafter went wild in celebration, this time in Bloomington.

While Hoosiers partied and Irish varsity football players checked into the infirmary and again felt the sting of failure, the freshmen back at South Bend chomped at the bit, football players who did not play football games. The constant battering of the freshman hamburger squad at the hands of the much larger and better trained varsity had its toll on much more than the marginal players. John Lattner for one, despite his exalted status as a national blue chip recruit, had had more than enough of the constant punishing by the varsity and the incessant demands by the coaches.

On one play, he ran past stout junior teammate Bob Toneff, causing Frank Leahy to praise the back and admonish the defender, "Oooh, freshman, didn't you realize this is Mr. Toneff and you ran right over him." Leahy called the same play and Lattner took the ball and ran it into the same hole, only this time, embarrassed and in his proper position, massive Bob Toneff drilled sacrificial lamb Lattner deep into the turf at Cartier Field. He never had a chance.

And then during another one of the scrimmages against the varsity, perhaps partly out of anger, Lattner tackled a varsity back with such intensity, he almost buried the poor upperclassman. Frank Leahy noticed. In his half-brogue, the Old Man complimented Lattner, "Ooh, keep up the good work, son. There's no telling how far you can go at Notre Dame if you do. You can go as far as you like with hard work." Some players needed constant stroking, Lattner did not, he just wanted to know that the coach appreciated his efforts and the acknowledgment helped him continue on through the punishing practices with no games against other schools.

Having lost to Indiana, the student body arose to engage in a week-long pep rally with signs and placards springing up all over campus supporting the beleaguered coaches and players, and were subjected to an intense emotional build-up that had them tingling...by kickoff time. President Cavanaugh tempered the enthusiasm a bit by predicting a 2-3 touchdown margin loss for the Irish against Michigan State, although he did promise that, "We are not reconciling ourselves to a period of losses."

The freshmen mostly acted as cheerleaders during the week, because with so many lame varsity members, Leahy scarcely could risk more injuries (or more serious ones) to his starters.

Meanwhile the student body continued to stoke school spirit, staging a massive torch light procession on the evening of Friday, October 27, the night before the Michigan State game. The parade started at Farley Hall at 7:00 p.m.

and wended its way with hundreds of students holding 400 signs and posters, led by a band. The congregation ended up behind the tennis courts where a giant bonfire lit up the area, culminating in a pep rally led by Father Hesburgh, Frank Leahy and team captain Jerry Groom.

The players, students, faculty and alumni left energized, ready to root their team past Michigan State the following afternoon.

"Notre Dame Should
Be Ashamed!"

LIKE ALL FRESHMEN-INELIGIBLE ballplayers in 1950, Johnny Lattner would have loved to sit on the bench or watch a game in the stands, but he sold programs outside of the stadium during home games and then often wandered back to his dorm. Just before the home game against Michigan State in late October began, Red Noonan, the local bird-dog scout who had first brought Lattner to the attention of Notre Dame, saw him ending his program duties and offered him a free ticket into the game.

Although fortified with only a windbreaker, Johnny jumped at the chance and in a few minutes had a seat next to Noonan right behind the dug-out on the home team side of the field. Freezing, Lattner still felt exhilarated, enjoying his fortune of seeing the fellows he practiced against each week in an exciting nip and tuck game against a strong Spartan club. Until Noonan asked Lattner how his father's recent operation back in Chicago went.

The news shocked Lattner, he had never heard that his father was ill, never mind had recently come out of an operation. Since Noonan had asked him the question and John had no answers concerning the condition of Bill Lattner, he sat through the entire game wondering and worrying about his father. To make matters worse, Notre Dame lost to another Midwestern rival that it had destroyed the year before. Michigan State won 36-33 and the Irish record sunk to two wins, three losses.

After the game ended, Lattner thanked Noonan for the ticket and then shot over to his dorm to telephone his mother, who indeed told him that his father had gone to the hospital and had survived the operation, which temporarily relieved him. What the young Irish back did not know then, and would not discover for another two months, was that his father had cancer.

The world kept turning. On November 1, 1950, the lads at Notre Dame awoke to the news that Puerto Rican separatists had attacked the Blair House, President Truman's residence during the White House rehabilitation and nearly succeeded in assassinating him. Also, Pope Pius XII proclaimed as dogma that after the Blessed Virgin Mary died, she was assumed into heaven in body and soul, therefore providing the men at Notre Dame a bit more theology to master.

Leahy probably paid some notice to these events, but he focused on the probability that he had to fly to Cleveland to play the Naval Academy without the services of back John Petitbon who suffered a neck injury during the MSU game. He promoted Frank Johnston from his B squad, and worked on defense all week long to stifle the reputedly explosive Middies' offense.

At least this Saturday Leahy caught a break as back Jack Landry bailed out his team with a terrific performance running the ball. Team captain Jerry Groom played all 60 minutes of the 19-10 win against Navy. Reflecting some of the angst directed against Bob Toneff by Leahy, the *South Bend Tribune*'s Paul Neville noted that Toneff "began moving across the line of scrimmage against Navy and operated for the first time this season as though he was interested in All-American honors."

The plaudits for the Irish kept coming, with Jim Mutscheller receiving high praise from Coach Druze as "probably the best pass receiver I've seen in some time… And that covers a lot of good boys, Bob Dove, Jack Zilly, and even Leon Hart." Paul Neville passed on to his readers the tidbit that John Lattner "was doing pretty well with the freshman team."

In preparing for the next game against the University of Pittsburgh, Notre Dame's last home game of the year, most of the work occurred indoors at the Field House with the onset of inclement weather. It mattered little to the Irish as they soundly defeated Pitt 18-7. Quarterback Bob Williams began to break some hallowed records, including one set by Angelo Bertelli.

Billy Barrett took off his cast and started practicing with the team again, but accompanying this hopeful sign came news of an influenza outbreak which sent several ND varsity men to the infirmary. Despite this bad news, the Irish still figured to defeat the Iowa Hawkeyes, a squad that had recently suffered a most unholy drubbing, losing to Ohio State by 83-21.

Of course, little came easy to the Irish that year and at the end of the first quarter, they trailed Iowa by two touchdowns. Inspired drives by led by Bob Williams and junior quarterback John Mazur brought the team back to a 14-14 tie, which is where matters rested. Meanwhile, out in Los

Angeles, columnist Francis X. Flaherty reported that Frank Leahy planned to announce his retirement as the ND coach to take a job leading the Rams, a decision prompted by "de-emphasis [of] Notre Dame football and bigger money as Leahy's reasons for quitting."

Leahy promptly issued a denial, and began to plot schemes against the last opponent of the season, Southern Cal, in two weeks. Paul Neville quipped that Flaherty got the story wrong, that Leahy instead had decided to coach the rejuvenated local Woodrow Wilson High School team.

Leahy desperately wanted a season-ending win against Southern Cal at the Coliseum on December 3, but he did not get it, losing 9-7. The team outplayed the Trojans, outpacing them in first downs earned by 13-1, but USC got a safety and then on a kickoff their runner returned it 94 yards for a touchdown. Petitbon nearly negated that score after intercepting a Trojan pass and running it back almost all of the way to the end zone, but he was hit just short of the goal line, and had to be carried off the field, by Bob Toneff among others.

Gay and Barrett fell to injuries and in the fourth quarter the indomitable Bob Williams was carried off the field unconscious after gaining five yards on a run while teammate Murray Johnson went to the hospital with him in the same ambulance, the latter player sustaining an ankle injury requiring x-rays. At one point, Captain Jerry Groom even collapsed. Fortunately, Leahy did not have to witness the horror in person, as he lay in his bed back home recovering from the flu.

The team flew back home and instead of the throngs of fans awaiting them, as had occurred at the conclusion of the glorious previous season, only Chet Grant and former player Larry Danbom met the boys at the airport. When the buses came to the campus circle, a slightly larger crowd showed up, probably under fifty students, as the players marched off to their dorm or the Grotto or somewhere else which helped them to forget. Paul Neville of the *South Bend Tribune* editorialized the situation, "Notre Dame should be ashamed."

The Cavalry Arrives!

FRANK LEAHY went right to work after the dispiriting season-ending loss at Southern California, or more to the point, his lads did. Most of the freshmen had played multiple sports in high school, so typically after football season ended, basketball began and then in the spring, track or baseball.

Occasionally, a Notre Dame football player embarked on another sport for the winter or spring, but it came with the knowledge that the football season never truly ended at the University. Because two of his older brothers had played for Leahy previously, Joe Bush knew that he would have to continue to work out once the regular season ended. So as the young football players began to seriously engage in studies for their first semester examinations, they also began to work out as varsity football players for the first time.

Generally, the pace of the workouts changed, not so much getting easier, but less emphasis was placed on scrimmaging or dummy scrimmaging and certainly no one studied other teams' plays and play-acted them out with the varsity. Leahy believed in conditioned athletes, so calisthenics and drill work prevailed. The Old Man had known that 1950 might prove rough and it pretty much ended as hideously as advertised, but now the promising athletes that he had recruited the year before became available to him and he could set to rebuilding his team.

On December 12, the Irish announced the election of Jim Mutscheller as their captain for the next campaign and on the next evening, staged their annual banquet, an event that in advance Paul Neville likened to a wake.

Notre Dame's President, Father Cavanaugh, saved the evening by announcing a pay raise for Leahy and then delivering a thoughtful and very moving address. After discussing the past year, Cavanaugh emphasized the following:

"Rumors are rampant, since our 1950 squad lost a few games, that Notre Dame is in the process of de-emphasizing football. This is absolutely untrue. Bear in mind now that Notre Dame never did over-emphasize football. Football and other forms of athletics have been, and will continue to be, an important part in the training of the whole man at Notre Dame....I reiterate: We shall always want Notre Dame men to play to win so long as there is a Notre Dame."

"Do you think Notre Dame will be weak next fall? It seems to me that there is a new kind of determination written in the faces of the coaches and the boys who are with us this evening. I have a feeling that a wonderful Notre Dame team is forming in their hearts and minds and that this coming spring practice, and the fall that follows, may be long remembered. Our coaches and our boys believe in Notre Dame; they know we believe in them, that we will go all the way down the line for them, that we pray for them, not only to win football games, but to play to win and win fairly, in the whole game of life. To the weak of heart, I say, keep your eye on the Notre Dame team of '51."

Of course, Fr. Cavanaugh brought down the house. He had reaffirmed the critical importance of the football program to the school, as part of a rubric of expecting the Notre Dame man to strive to win at all things. Had de-emphasis of the football program either overtly or tacitly occurred (primarily through slashing scholarships), which Fr. Cavanaugh denied, he nevertheless assured the players, coaches, alumni and fans that as a matter of policy, the administration meant to fully support the program in the future.

From here on, the administration left no doubt that with Notre Dame football, the retreat had ended and Leahy's lads would fight another day with the full backing of the administrators. First though, his lads had to pass their courses and average out with 77 or higher in their courses. The pink warning slips that had fallen in the middle of the semester served as constant reminders to all students that failure awaited the non-vigilant. Leahy had little use for poorly conditioned athletes but he literally had no use for one that had flunked out.

Having finished their last first semester classes, John Lattner and Frank Kettles ventured to an out of the way section of downtown South Bend, off of Michigan Avenue, to drink a few beers in celebration of their good fortune. On the way out they bought a pack of cigarettes for Father Charles McCarragher. The next day, they breathlessly delivered the pack, which apparently smelled of beer, as a present to Black Mac. If the good father smelled anything, he kept it to himself and wished the young footballers a happy and safe Christmas break, and closed the door to his office.

Unlike the previous January when Neil Worden blazed a lonely trail for his incoming class, a number of new players joined the squad in the second semester. Having seen quite enough of losing in the fall of 1950, Frank Leahy brought as many as two dozen new players onto campus in the winter of 1951.

From the existing student population, one of these recruits, George Hubbard, had not played football in high school and did not try out for the frosh squad in the fall, but since he had good speed, he passed himself off as a defensive halfback and drew the standard issue of equipment. Another, Armando Galardo from Cleveland, proved a keeper for Leahy.

From New Orleans, Leahy scored a massive coup in landing running back Joe Heap and his friend Butzi Zimmerman, a deal that had been contemplated and cultivated for some time. A couple of years earlier a Notre Dame bird dog scout named Harold Sporl had recommended John Petitbon from Jesuit High School in New Orleans to Frank Leahy, and Petitbon had had to date a very good career for the Irish. So when Sporl sent word up to South Bend about these talented players, Frank Leahy came down to see for himself.

Butzi Zimmerman had starred at quarterback at Holy Cross High School, and his potential recruitment answered an immediate need with the impending graduation of All-American Bob Williams. In his backfield starred Joe Heap, who incidentally had reigned as Louisiana State Champion in the 100-yard dash, 200-yard dash, low hurdles, broad jump and triple jump.

Like Lattner up in Chicago, everyone wanted Joe Heap to play on their football teams, with the then powerful service academies pushing hard, along with Alabama and LSU emerging as the strongest suitors. Joe's devout Catholic dad, Edwin Heap, had different ideas for his son, and he strongly suggested he consider attending Notre Dame.

Mr. Heap very very strongly suggested to his son that he

attend the University.

So Joe took a visit up to South Bend and stayed at a dorm, hosted by none other than fellow New Orleans native John Petitbon. Petitbon took him for a tour and showed him around, but rather than complete the trip with the usual movie and burger, the guide brought Joe to a bar and bought him a number of beers, enough to seal the deal. Joe Heap was coming to Notre Dame.

Inauspiciously, the star back entered Notre Dame in January as a student for the first time. A bus took him to the front circle and alighting from it, young Heap stepped on a slice of ice and fell on his butt. Goodbye bayous, welcome to the winters in South Bend.

His first practice did not go much better. With the fierce weather, the backs practiced in the Navy Drill Hall with its concrete floors and six minutes into practice, Joe fell again, this time cracking his hand. Even when matters improved, he merely shifted into the arduous regime of a freshman back at Notre Dame, with Coach Bill Earley expecting much from him and the hitting beginning with his often much larger and older teammates as soon as the spring thaw set in and scrimmages started outdoors.

Probably his enduring optimism and good-nature buttressed him during the difficult winter days. Later in life, like most Delta Louisianans, Heap had to evacuate during the wake of Hurricane Katrina, but his younger years certainly provided him with competition and opportunities to excel, and by extension, occasions to test his mettle.

Although he carried the deep, rich New Orleans accent butchered in movies like *The Big Easy*, he did not have a drop of Cajun blood in his veins. Instead, his father was English, while his mother was Irish and German. Segregation decimated a whole generation of African-American athletes as it had in the past, but in a state whose football recruits were dominated by sons of the confederacy or Cajuns, Heap stood alone.

His recruitment by Notre Dame itself was an anomaly, as the University had largely been hemmed in to the Midwest, New England and the Atlantic states above the Mason-Dixon line. At times, a Texan like George Strohmeyer might filter through, but almost all of the Irish's limited recruiting in the South was restricted to the French parishes in and surrounding New Orleans. Joe Heap played in a Catholic enclave, so he had at least some chance of scrutiny by Irish scouts and coaches.

One of ten children of Edwin and Florence Heap (eight boys, two girls) Joseph Lawrence Heap was born on October 26, 1931 in New Orleans, spending most of his childhood and adolescence in the Gentilly neighborhood. Joe's father had attended the seminary, and although he decided not to become a priest, he raised his brood strictly in the Catholic faith. His Dad had a very good job with the Illinois Central Railroad as an assistant general freight manager, making enough money to buy a summer home in the country, where Joe and his family loved to hunt and fish.

On Saturdays, the family flocked around the radio to listen to Notre Dame football broadcasts, but always with the proviso that Joe and all of his brothers and sisters went to confession every Saturday, whether he had done something wrong since the previous week or not. If the game went a bit late, Joe and company had to leave home to confess, and hope the lines of other penitents were not that long, in the hope of returning home to catch the end of a game.

Along with faith, sports dominated Heap's early life, peculiar for an era without Soccer Moms and Little Leagues and travel teams and the AAU for grammar school children. First at St. James the Major and then at Holy Cross High School, young Joe competed against other parish squads in track, basketball and softball. Today, this network would be recognized as part of the CYO, or Catholic Youth Organization, but it is not certain if any of Heap's activities were channeled through that national group or remained local.

Mistakenly and fairly repeatedly listed as a native of Albita Springs in Louisiana, or at the least having been born there, Heap's family actually did not move there until Joe had reached his junior year in high school. To accommodate this relocation but to retain his place at Holy Cross, Joe became a boarder, and thus stayed in New Orleans. Until of course, Notre Dame came beckoning.

Reeling from a couple undermanned sub-par recruiting classes in the late '40s, Frank Leahy accelerated his efforts to land another bumper class to augment the players he brought in for the fall of 1950. With the 1950 season unfolding into a disaster, Coach decided to personally persuade Joe Heap and his friend Butzi Zimmerman (and more particularly their fathers) to sign up for four years under full scholarship at Our Lady's University.

They all met at Antoines in New Orleans, most likely during the weekend that ND flew down to Tulane for their narrow and quite physical 13-9 victory there. Leahy put on his best show, spending equal time on the values of athletics, academics and spirituality that his school embodied. Leahy particularly persuaded Joe's father that ND provided the most proper Catholic atmosphere for his son and after the party finished eating and Leahy picked up the check, Joe's father tipped his hand and indicated that he really wanted

Joe to attend the University of Notre Dame. Joe needed little persuading at this point; he always wanted to go there. With his family's strong backing, Joe decided to depart from Holy Cross High after the fall of '50 to join Notre Dame for their spring 1951 practices.

When the students returned to campus from Christmas break, they had mid-term examinations to sit for. After exams, around February 3 of 1951, the team commenced its spring practice, and while some old faces like Bob Williams no longer had to show up as they prepared for graduation and their careers outside of Notre Dame, the freshmen all moved up to practice with the varsity and even more new personages graced the team.

Strong lineman Bob Taylor rolled into town from Pekin High in Illinois, having earned all of his high school credits, an academic career that included one year playing for Bob McBride at Mt. Carmel High in Chicago, before his family moved from the city. In the late 1940s-early 1950s, Aquinas Prep in Rochester, New York, had become a virtual minor league camp for aspiring Notre Dame players. Sophomore Tom Seaman had prepped there, and now in the spring of '51, two more of its players, roommates Frank Varrichione and Jack Lee, left to join the Irish.

The transition did have its difficulties. Mike Holovak had recruited both players for his Boston College team, a seemingly natural fit with Lee a native of Medford, Massachusetts, and Varrichione hailing from a few towns west of Boston in Natick. They had agreed to play for the Eagles, but when Frank Leahy offered these two fine linemen scholarships at Notre Dame, they quickly switched their allegiances and bought tickets for the next train to South

Bend, a slight Holovak never forgot.

Lee had grown up in an environment quite different from his fellow Medford native Elizabeth Short, the famed "Black Dahlia," whose brutal murder in Los Angeles a few years before had shocked the public. Lee lived an idyllic existence as his father Eddie Lee ran the old Boston Garden, and young Jack's adolescence and young adulthood was joyfully filled with Bruins and Celtics and the aroma of Red Auerbach's cigars. Idyllic enough that he had never heard of the Black Dahlia.

On the train ride in from Rochester to South Bend in the beginning of 1951, Lee and Varrichione bumped into a fellow after the Cleveland station who looked like a football player, so they struck up a conversation with Sam Palumbo, coincidentally another mid-year recruit to Notre Dame. From East Cleveland, the good-natured but hardnosed and talented Palumbo played the line like they did, and after he concluded his career for the Irish, he suited up for his hometown Browns, and then later the Packers and the Bills.

That was not all. In the previous year, McArdle had attempted to recruit two star linemen from the excellent Lowell High School team in Massachusetts, but had only succeeded in bringing Minnie Mavraides to South Bend. Another lineman, tackle and true gentleman Bob Ready stayed behind, enticed by an offer from the Dartmouth Club of Lowell to play for a post-graduate year at Cheshire Academy in Connecticut, as a prelude to acceptance at Dartmouth and service on their football team.

Somehow signals had gotten crossed, and now the potential of playing for Dartmouth had seemingly disappeared for Ready, so Coach Joe McArdle caught wind of this development and returned to his home town of Lowell to complete his Christmas wish list. This time, Ready and his family proved more receptive to the Irish offer and not to leave a thing to chance, McArdle eyeballed Ready all the way from Lowell to South Bend to begin winter training, offering to Ready at one point, "Bob, I never could figure out why a nice Irish boy like you ever wanted to play for those blue-blood Yankee bastards up in Dartmouth!" Once together with Mavraides, the Massachusetts men took train trips home together, starting with pitcher of beer drinking contests in a pub across from the station. Often, they gave unsuspecting trainmen and conductors "hot foots."

After enrolling, Taylor, Varrichione, Lee, Palumbo and Ready became full team members by working out after the January mid-term examinations. While their coaches did not believe in coddling their charges, they did not immediately subject them to outdoor practices in the austere Northern Indiana winters. The offensive drills required precision in all facets, an objective not easily obtainable in drifts of snow and ice puddles.

Feisty equipment manager Jack McAllister issued young Jack Lee a tee shirt, a pair of socks and a jock strap. Upon trying out the jock strap, Lee learned that it had been stretched so badly out of shape over time that when he tried it on, it fell to his knees. When he tried to return it, McAllister would have none of it, suggesting, "You pissant, you ought to get bigger!"

As linemen, the three new men from Massachusetts and all of their other new friends on the line went to Bob McBride's lair, the University handball courts for some instruction on blocking technique. One of the more popular exercises was the lunge drills for offensive linemen, who back then could not use their hands nearly as much as today. Instead, they crooked their elbows and met their fists along their sternum, a form exhibited in many publicity shots and football cards of the era.

Without the ability to use hands much, it was imperative that linemen got off to a powerful and quick jump against the defensive linemen, a task greatly eased by mastering lunge drills, where a blocker lunged at his opponent with maximum force. The quicker out of the stance, the more power one brought to bear against the opponent and the more readily one might gain an advantage in leverage.

Another popular drill in the confined quarters was the pulling drill, where linemen, most often guards, did not lunge ahead but rather pulled out of their position and ran to the opposite side of the field to block for their back. The more these drills were run the more precise the blockers became and the more they proceeded to work as a coordinated unit.

If the weather remained inclement, the team generally also practiced inside the Field House, and while the blockers continued with pulling drills and lunging after each other, the somewhat larger confines of the Field House permitted the staff to introduce run-throughs of plays and defenses. This accommodation, with its dirt floors, only provided a marginal improvement over the outdoors, a venue that the team utilized as soon as a thaw set in.

Cartier Field, or one of the contiguous lots, might be mired in mud, but if it was free of snow, the coaches often called in practice, which generally meant full intersquad scrimmages. Scrimmages might sound like fun in comparison to boring repetitive drills and walk-throughs, but in reality they were savage affairs. In his first outdoor scrimmage, Jack Lee came up against junior guard Paul Burns, who had at least a few inches on him in height. Burns came out the better in the contact, breaking Lee's nose and making him swear he was back in the North End of Boston.

The more the snow melted, the more Leahy scheduled scrimmages and young men like Jack Lee learned how to better protect their noses. Many others dropped out of the program, never making it to the fall of '51, at least not as a varsity football player.

As painful as Jack Lee's baptism by fire may have seemed, it paled in comparison to John Lattner's experience at this time. Christmas break provided little respite for John Lattner, because the condition of his father continued to worsen. On New Year's, Lattner learned for the first time that his father had cancer, at the time a virtual death sentence, which necessitated his taking time off frequently to travel back to Chicago thereafter to visit his Dad. On one of those trips, teammates Petitbon, Barrett and Mazur accompanied him and Mazur made a promise: "Mr. Lattner, next year John will score a touchdown." Shortly thereafter, Mr. Lattner passed on.

Rather than have the Funeral Mass in Chicago, the services took place in the elder Lattner's boyhood home of Evansville, Indiana. The whole family drove down to the local German church there, where John's parents had met. At the end of the Mass, John Lattner was somewhat surprised to see in attendance his Coach, Frank Leahy, together with some assistant coaches. After expressing his condolences,

Leahy asked Lattner if he had a ride back to campus.

Immediately, Lattner understood that his coach wanted to drive him back to South Bend so that he would not miss too much winter practice. Lattner replied as best he could that he meant to return to Chicago with the remainder of his family, at which time Leahy backed down, and drove back to the University minus his grieving but prized running back.

When John Lattner did return to campus, he not only carried a grieving heart but also the recognition that with his father dead and buried, his family back in Chicago did not have the resources to get by financially, particularly since John's brother had a very low-paying job which kicked up his allergies.

A crestfallen John Lattner knocked on Frank Leahy's door at Breen-Phillips and laid out his family's predicament to his coach, thanking him for the scholarship but proceeding to explain that he might have to leave Notre Dame to get a job and help back home. Leahy listened to this most sad story and expressed his condolences again, and wished his young back and his widowed mother the best.

Fortunately for young Lattner and his family, soon thereafter John's brother received an offer to drive a truck at a much higher rate of pay, which immediately righted the financial boat. The power of prayer can be quite powerful and it is difficult to believe that Frank Leahy did not at least say a quick Hail Mary after talking to John Lattner in his office that day.

May Day

EACH YEAR on May Day, the halls of Notre Dame opened up with the entire student body and a host of priests marching in a most impressive procession to the Grotto. The first day of May held special importance at the University because in past years, Fr. Corby received permission, traditionally through the intercession of the Blessed Virgin Mary, to build a replica of the shrine at Lourdes and then also received the large donation that made construction possible.

The cynical among the marchers might muse that until May 1, it is unsafe to walk and stand outside in the austere weather of the upper Midwest, but miracles are miracles, they do not come too early or too late, and so the freshmen left their rooms for the first procession.

The next day, in spring practice, the Browns' kicker Lou "the Toe" Groza appeared on campus, with Bobby Joseph and Minnie Mavraides eagerly surrounding him for tips. Spring practice had gone well, with Neil Worden taking a leadership role and several of his classmates likewise joining him on the ranks of next year's projected starters.

Joe Heap could be excused for being on a high horse that spring as he tore up the practices. In early April, while the coaches groomed his high school friend Butzi Zimmerman for the back-up quarterback role, Joe chewed up a lot of ground for Coach Leahy's inspection. His longest carry was for 50 yards, but his most spectacular netted 25. Trying to round left end from his right half slot, he was apparently cut off by four defensemen 15 yards behind the scrimmage line. Quickly reversing his field, Heap tore back toward the right side-line and stepped beautifully down the stripe, shaking off three would-be tacklers before finally being knocked out of bounds.

Less than a week later, a *Scholastic* scribe noted that Heap "looked mighty deadly as he churned his way through the line," as he, Fran Paterra and John Lattner pressed the veteran backs, Billy Barrett and John Petitbon. Other freshmen distinguishing themselves during the cruelest month were undersized guard Frank Kettles, linemen Art Hunter and Joe Katchik and fullback Tom McHugh. Even Minnie Mavraides picked up some good press as the most accurate kicker on campus.

The penultimate event for spring football players at Notre Dame for decades was the Old-Timers game, which like its current counterpart, the annual intersquad Blue-Gold Game, draws thousands of students and fans every year into the stadium to see a largely meaningless exhibition, other than to get a football fix before Labor Day.

The Old-Timers almost never won these contests, Leahy had prepared his lads quite well by then and for every returning star like the Bears' George Connor for the graduates, generally two or three out of shape and winded veterans suited up alongside him. Yet in the spring of 1950, the returning Irish had absolutely waxed the varsity, one of the surest signs that the fall campaign might not produce another undefeated team.

As the Old Timers game approached, the coaches coalesced on their probable first string varsity with Art Hunter nailing down the center spot and Dick Hilinski joining the strong and quick Bob Toneff at tackle. At guard, Frank Varrichione seemed locked in with Paul Burns while Jim Mutscheller held down one end position with Joe Katchik and Minnie Mavraides vying for the other assignment. The backfield consisted wholly of veterans, Mazur at quarterback with Barrett, Petitbon and Del Gander joining him in the backfield.

Many of the old reliable alum returned to campus, and since he had never left, Bob Williams started for the Old Timers at quarterback. Leon Hart did not make it this year, but Jungle Jim Martin, Six Yard Sitko and Bill Wightkin did. Many of the stars from 1949 returned to campus, so the game looked pretty even, perhaps even an opportunity to have the Old Timers notch another embarrassing victory over the varsity.

The 1950 varsity team had collapsed mainly under an inexperienced offensive line, with too few Bob Toneffs or Chet Ostrowskis to hold things together. This time, the freshmen augmented the line with such stalwarts as Fred Mangialardi and Joe Bush, while the running back corps had improved quite dramatically with the infusion of Bull Worden, Johnny Lattner and Tom McHugh.

Only an exhibition, the game did provide John Lattner for one a certain release. He had not played a football game for almost a year and a half now and had suffered for much of his freshman year, with his father being so sick and then dying. In this otherwise meaningless game, played before approximately 20,000 fans and students, Lattner scored three touchdowns.

Exhilarating as it might have been for stars like Lattner and Worden to finally display their talents before a large friendly crowd, the exhibition also proved the last hurrah for many other promising freshmen. Zimmerman appeared groomed for the starting QB spot by 1952, but Leahy had recruited a few talented signal callers for next fall, which helped push Joe Heap's good friend to the Boston Red Sox minor league system. Others began to weigh their realistic chances of ever playing much on the Notre Dame varsity and determined that the promise did not warrant the sacrifice. For them the dream had ended.

Once the actual game began, the freshmen dominated even more than expected, as John Lattner not only excelled in scoring on offense but also played a shut-down defensive back. Heap, Paterra and Worden joined Lattner at slicing "through the line or cut[ting] around the ends with what looked like ridiculous ease." Fred Mangialardi distinguished himself on the line with Neil Worden playing a mean linebacker, as the Varsity rolled over the Old Timers 47-20.

Ultimately, the game meant something, a chance for the varsity to at least not get embarrassed, but it served as a useful barometer in charting the program's hopeful rise from mediocrity to competitiveness. It also provided the young men a chance to stand out, an important step for members of the hamburger squad who got punched around all fall by the sophomores, juniors and seniors, only then to endure long, boring and most taxing conditioning drills in the winter and practice in the spring.

After the Old Timers game came final exams, a worry for all freshmen, but particularly for ballplayers needing to stay above a 77 in a course in order to retain their scholarship. For some, this proved the cruelest obstacle after all of their perseverance during the year, establishing a simple truth that Notre Dame had grown more academically challenging in the 1950s. A truth that Leahy appreciated is that some of his stars in the '40s would never have made it at his school in the next decade, but he may have appreciated by this time that a smarter ballplayer made a better one in many circumstances, which may have eased his concerns about the quality of his recruits a bit, but probably not at all.

With the end of school, John Lattner returned to Chicago, missing out on the summer practices that Leahy supposedly never conducted, but in retrospect, he might have preferred to stay on campus because his summer job involved working with asbestos. He once had the opportunity to single-handedly empty an entire train-load of blue cement by himself. Such was the lot of the most talented all-around college freshman in the country in the summer of 1950.

Second Quarter

The Catholic West Point

THE KOREAN WAR, which began on June 25, 1950, had seemed virtually concluded a few months later when an amphibious landing devised by General Douglas MacArthur landed in the rear of the North Korean forces, causing them to retreat back to their Yalu River border with China. Then in November, the Chinese Communist forces overran many of the United States and United Nations positions, causing the war to degenerate to one of attrition along the 38th parallel, the border between North and South Korea, established after the end of the Second World War.

Sensing a potential shortage of football players on college campuses in the fall of 1951, as selective service boards drafted young men across America, the NCAA dropped its ban of freshmen playing on varsity football squads. Whereas John Lattner and Neil Worden and their classmates had to fill out a freshman team which never played games and only served as real life tackling and blocking dummies for the upperclassmen, the newcomers arriving after Labor Day in 1951 would see considerable action in fall scrimmages and in games during the season ahead.

Other events involving the military had a bearing on Notre Dame in the fifties, with one of the largest direct influences arriving as a result of the West Point Cheating Scandal of 1951. Coached by Red Blaik and led by their two Heisman trophy winners, Doc Blanchard and Glenn Davis, the Cadets provided ND with its biggest rivalry throughout much of the 1940s. Army defeated the Irish, demolished them really, by a score of 59-0 in 1944 and 48-0 in 1945, and in one of the greatest games in college football, the rivals tied in their 1946 contest. Even though Notre Dame won the National Championship in '46, years later Leahy often trailed into a state of gloom, bemoaning the fact his team did not attempt a field goal at a crucial point during that game.

Army had ceased playing the series after the 1947 season, supposedly because the Irish by then dominated them, a strange claim to make considering they lost by only a 27-7 score. That aside, the West Point squad remained very competitive until August 3, 1951 when Secretary of the Army Frank Pace announced the expulsions of 90 cadets, 37 of whom were varsity football athletes, due to alleged cheating. On many campuses, the transgressions that resulted in the cadet's expulsions might have attracted little notice, but the West Point Honor Code was sacred, and after the substance of the allegations emerged, a large part of the student body was wiped out.

With the advent of McCarthyism, it seems apropos that the cheating scandal resembled a witch hunt, with guilty and innocent alike affected. Undeniably, a cheating ring did exist, centered around the football team, the members of which already possessed an exalted and favored status at the institution. Since the 1940s, a gap existed between what some cadets received on final exams and their general class work, sometimes quite comically.

Like the Notre Dame football program, the Army team had gotten a bit out of hand, becoming bigger than the school, and most importantly the administration. When a cadet did come forward, the ring quickly became exposed; sadly, a number of cadets received their walking papers based mostly on their association with ringleaders or because they knew about the conspiracy but took no steps to expose it.

Many of the cadets left the school only to begin matriculating at the University of Notre Dame in the fall of 1951, due to the generosity of a then-anonymous donor, now known to be Joseph Kennedy, who graciously paid for many of these young men to enroll at the University. Due to its rigor, Notre Dame had often been called the Catholic West Point, and now a number of former cadets began their experiences at the University not in Beast Barracks but in sunrise morning chapel visits and early evening lights out.

One caveat, none of the cadets were permitted to play football, so when Leahy surveyed his lads that fall, all of them were his own recruits, largely a Catholic group who had never known war or had any military training. As for the former cadets, many of them joined the Air Force ROTC, serving with distinction as military men, but as sons of Notre Dame and not the progeny of the United States Military Academy.

Fr. Hesburgh had a fairly abrupt exchange with one of the transferees on the ban on transferee cadets suiting up for football. The former cadet started his case by saying, "There are about a dozen ex-Army football players here who would be delighted to play for Notre Dame, if you let us. After all, the other schools are letting the ex-Army athletes play."

In part, Fr. Hesburgh retorted, "There is only one difficulty...You were all offered a scholarship here by an anonymous benefactor on condition that you would not compete in intercollegiate athletics. You see, we have a long-standing rule here against transfers competing. It eliminates any temptation of inducing good players to transfer from other schools...I'd like to add that part of the education here consists in learning to live by principle rather than by expediency."

The ex-cadet replied, "O.K. Father...It's your funeral."

Father Hesburgh ended the conversation by saying, "Well, I'm not singing the requiem yet."

That was it. Notre Dame had an honor code as revered as that belonging to West Point, and institutionally the school meant to treat all of its students equally, providing the former cadets their own unique transition to Notre Dame. Preserving antiquity, the administration greeted freshmen in 1951 with the necessity to acclimate to Masses early and often, and for football players, to coaches unlike any most young men had ever seen. And the University retained its rules concerning "lights out" at 11:00 p.m., a policy that students often observed in the breach. Some students sat in their bathroom stalls to study, a risky proposition with patrols going by.

Other midnight crammers resorted to using a high powered lamp or a flashlight. At the risk of sacrilege, some others lit up candles, some taken from the Grotto itself. That was a nice touch. If the young man still had difficulty understanding a topic or had not ratcheted into memory all of the facts and figures required of him, he had a piece of the Grotto in the form of the candle with him, and he might resort to prayer for a passing grade and also recite an Act of Contrition for stealing the candle.

And another small matter never changed, that being Equipment Manager Jack McAllister's attitude toward incoming football players. Before the first frost had come to South Bend in '51, one new ballplayer had the temerity to walk up with hopelessly shoddy shoes to complain to McAllister. Not surprisingly "Mac" sneered at the young man and handed the dilapidated footwear back to him, snapping, "They were good enough for Frank Carideo!" An All-American quarterback at Notre Dame, Carideo had not played for the Irish since 1930, twenty-one years before, and undoubtedly his former shoes had changed a bit for the worse in that interim. McAlllister never changed.

Rather than dutifully act as punishing dummies, or at best weebles who wobbled but did not fall down, the incoming freshmen had the potential with the NCAA exemption, to realistically vie for playing time and even a starting role. Given Frank Leahy's innate conservatism, one might expect an insistence that the freshmen still respect their roles as peons on the club who had to endure a tough first-year weeding out process (slightly more than twenty sophomores remained on the team from the large pool of recruits spearheaded by Neil Worden) before suiting for a game.

Perhaps in the 1940s, when his championship teams teemed with several layers of All-American talent at each position, he may have been so inclined (if given the chance to play freshmen), but since his scholarship battles had begun with the administration, he no longer had this luxury. In partial circumvention of the rules laid down by his superiors, Leahy had stockpiled high school post-graduates, and knew Aquinas Prep stars such as Jack Lee and Frank Varrichione possessed the maturity and experience to win for him. And yet, Leahy also knew quite early that the freshman and sophomore recruiting yield far outweighed his upperclassmen in talent from top to bottom. Leahy would rebuild through the younger classes.

McBride

FRANK LEAHY relied on the Irish tackles coach of the era, Bob McBride, to act as one of the leading architects of his team's return to glory. McBride first came to South Bend as a student in the fall of 1940, lettering the next two falls as a guard, then entering the Army in 1943, along with many other coaches, classmates and fellow players. The type of duty that each ND man completed in the Second World War varied, but Bob McBride's experience proved more harrowing than most.

In Pete Lafleur's superb notes on Coach McBride's experiences, he movingly narrates that McBride served "as a machine gun squad leader in the 106th infantry division. His division quickly shifted to the Belgian front and met the German counter-offensive in the Battle of the Bulge. Almost 7,000 men from the 106th were killed or captured, with McBride taken prisoner on December 21, 1944. While suffering from frozen feet, he was forced to walk 13 days and was placed in two prison camps before a 50-day march during the German retreat. A starvation diet—one-seventh of a loaf of bread per day—resulted in McBride's weight dropping from 212 to 90 pounds, before he was liberated 122 days into his imprisonment (ending 39 months of service). He received three battle stars, a purple heart and the presidential unit citation."

McBride came back to Notre Dame to play on the 1946

National Championship team and then coached successfully at Chicago's Mt. Carmel High School. In 1949, Leahy made him a line coach.

Bob McBride worked his tackles furiously, and after practice, one or more tackles often joined him for some more blocking practice, mano a mano against the coach himself. No one on the team physically conditioned himself into a shape approximating the coach. McBride's secret? Handball or squash games, often as many as three a day.

Coach McBride took a young tackle and screamed at him: "Block me! Block me!" Sometimes he made a player shift left against him or shift right, but each time he had to spring up against the coach, who had not just practiced for two hours, and block him. Often McBride threw an elbow into a player's face, to toughen him up and show him what to expect at game time.

In the one-on-one sessions, McBride always had the advantage. He set himself up sideways and braced for the hit, never acting in a realistic manner of a rushing lineman who had an eye on a quarterback or a halfback and approached the point of attack with a certain sense of abandon. When McBride had his tackles run into him, the player already had endured numerous contacts during drills and scrimmages while the coach approached the post-practice sessions fresh. Finally, McBride possessed the advantage of being a coach and while he might throw an elbow into the face of the student/athlete across from him, that young man rightly feared the potential consequences attendant to popping the coach back.

It is tempting to portray Bob McBride as a Dickensian figure, and yet a polarizing approach does not accurately depict him as a human being. He is an American hero and he coached some of the greatest linemen in college history, men who achieved their stature over similarly talented or potentially great players at other universities, because Bob McBride formed them. Many of his former players became cordial with him after they graduated, having hardly known him while they played for him, and have warm and fond memories of someone they admire and appreciate.

Relatively few people know this, but Bob McBride played a major role in breaking down any racial barriers on the varsity football team through vigorous recruiting and then taking all possible steps at making an African-American athlete feel comfortable and happy with his choice of school. Having tasted all that Nazi Germany had to offer during his imprisonment there during the Second World War, Bob McBride admirably displayed charity with persons of color and helped create bridges and knock down barriers not just in his own program, but in other universities eager to follow Notre Dame's lead.

But for many of the lads, there exists the lingering feeling that sometimes Bob McBride went too far with a player or players, that his coaching techniques exceeded what was necessary to optimize the gifts of a young man at ND. His staunchest defenders invariably point out that he reflected his times and may not have achieved the same level of success had he not acted as he did. Many of the then young men who played under him hated him then and have decidedly mixed feelings about him now, over fifty years later. It is equally valid to ask if Bob McBride was such a great coach, could he have accomplished just as much or more with a more measured intensity?

While Bob McBride tussled with the tackles, a flinty New Englander named Joe McArdle instructed the guards, both on the offense and the defense. Equally tough as Mc-Bride, McArdle did not take on his players physically, but rather relied on cutting remarks, hollering and sarcasm to motivate his players, many of whom called him "Captain Bligh." There were no mutinies under McArdle, and though some quit, many more stayed and worked hard with little hope of receiving a compliment.

Although he never played for Notre Dame, McArdle caught Leahy's eye early while blocking for Fordham, and after a stint in the business world, he returned to his mentor and to football when an assistant's job opened up at Boston College. When Leahy bolted Boston for South Bend, Joe McArdle loyally followed him there.

After he coached one year at ND, McArdle received his draft notice for the Navy, and before sailing off to the South Pacific, he married his hometown sweetheart from Lowell, Massachusetts, Eleanor Sullivan. McArdle served with distinction aboard the aircraft carrier Wasp, nearly being shot dead on the final day of the war when a Japanese pilot made a strafing run of the deck. Upon discharge, McArdle signed up with Leahy again and coached some of the finest guards in Irish history, including Outland Trophy winner Bill Fischer.

A third line coach, Wally Ziemba, won All-American recognition as a center in 1942, playing for Leahy and the Irish. Enlisted into the Marines during the war, he was discharged soon after he reported to Parris Island and became a full-time Irish center coach thereafter.

By far the most popular line coach, John Druze, starred

as one of the Seven Blocks of Granite for Fordham, under then assistant coach Leahy, and even played a year of professional football for the Brooklyn Dodgers. Like Joe McArdle, Druze assisted Leahy at BC and pulled carrier duty in the Second World War. After his discharge from the service, Druze coached the ends and scouted the next week's opponents during the regular season.

Traditionally, the toughness of the Irish line coaches during this period has received more than adequate coverage, but their devotion to technique and insistence on improvement required of each of their players has received less attention. Coach Leahy always stressed constant betterment, and the line coaches marked each young man's development in a written grading card marked for each item on a 1-10 scale:

1. Desire to win
2. Natural ability
3. Off the field representation
4. Loyalty to
    a. Notre Dame
    b. Teammates
    c. Coaches
5. Aggressiveness
6. Tackling
7. Blocking
    a. At line-thrust block
    b. Downfield
8. Pass protection block
9. Rushing passer
10 Pass defense
11. Pass receiving
12. Attitude

If a lineman practiced hard and held a stiff upper lip, he still had a difficult lot, but he certainly had an easier time than someone who provoked the ire of the coaches. That type of person knew no peace unless and until he addressed his shortcomings or took his deficiencies elsewhere.

In addition to the line coaches, the Irish had two backfield coaches in 1951, Bernie Crimmins and Bill Earley. Hailing from Louisville, Kentucky, Crimmins won varsity letters at Notre Dame at three different positions and served on a PT boat in the South Pacific, earning several medals for valor. A contemporary of Crimmins on those early '40s Irish squads, Earley won three letters for football and also earned several medals in the War, serving as a bombardier on a B-24 over Italy.

All of Leahy's assistant coaches played football themselves and served in the armed forces during the Great War, and with the exception of Wally Ziemba, they served harrowing tours of duty. Most had coached college football for several years, with the exception of Bob McBride, who coached at Mr. Carmel High in Chicago in 1947 and 1948, coming to the Irish during their last national championship campaign.

To Frank Leahy's credit, while he demanded loyalty and dedication from his subordinates, he did not require them to make the types of sacrifices he made for the team. No coach slept for days on end with Leahy at Breen-Phillips or the old fire house. They had to watch a lot of film and attend meetings and keep some players late if possible, but if their head coach sat and watched film late into the night, usually the whole staff did not have to stay there and quite often Athletic Director Moose Krause kept Leahy company.

Some even imitated him. If Frank Leahy wore a bow tie, as he quite often did, Bob McBride did too. Crimmins left the staff after the 1951 season to take the head football coaching position at Indiana, but most of Leahy's assistants stayed with him, and after Leahy left Notre Dame, all of them walked the plank with him, either in the year he left or soon thereafter. When Frank Leahy went out of style, so too sadly did his assistants, even though they were all gifted football coaches.

Most of the ballplayers did not establish genuine interpersonal relationships with their coaches while they played at Notre Dame. Leahy acted aloof and many of his assistants did not try to become buddies with their charges, even if they felt so inclined, because they had to execute the boss's orders and make sure the players minimized their mistakes on the field and mastered the plays and proper technique in practices. After they graduated, many of the players asked for and received letters of introduction or recommendation from Leahy, and grew to appreciate and even grow fond of their position coaches. For others, after they graduated or left the University under other circumstances and saw the Golden Dome in the rear view mirror of their car for the final time, that was the last contact they ever had with the coaches.

Googs

AS SOME FOOTBALL PLAYERS had already begun practicing with the team before their future classmates in the Class of 1955 arrived, Grandview High senior Ralph Guglielmi enjoyed a comparatively idyllic spring, playing baseball and dating his girlfriend. He had almost seventy offers for full scholarships to play football in college, and had enjoyed his visits at many schools, particularly those south of the Mason-Dixon Line where hospitality flowed for blue chip prospects.

He enjoyed the attention and the interest but he needed the scholarship offers. Quite young, while still in seventh or eighth grade, Ralph Guglielmi heard from his father, a machinist in a factory, that "I can't send you to college unless you get a scholarship." Sobering words indeed, but by that point, the elder Guglielmi had seen in his son what others had, a prodigy in athletics. Very early, Ralph's father emphasized to him not to engage in any misbehavior which imperiled what the God-given talent might produce for him one day.

If Neil Worden embodied the compelling Drive to improve and ultimately excel and achieve his goals, Ralph Guglielmi had the Certainty. As the only child of immigrants Marino and Rose Guglielmi, who emigrated from their homes in Aquila, Italy, to Columbus, Ohio, Guglielmi always knew that he had the tools to accomplish great things in life. While Marino worked in a plant, mother Rose served as a fraternity house mother at Ohio State University. Ralph not only grew up with doting parents but also had his grandmother around, all of whom not only provided him with love but the knowledge that he had an athletic gift that few other American boys his age possessed.

Ralph had the Certainty but he also had appreciated some very austere facts early in his life and he took the advice of his father to heart and not only worked to improve in sports, but with the exception of one Halloween night of impropriety during his adolescence, he avoided compromising situations. He caught in high school baseball games and scored so many points in a high school basketball tournament that Adolph Rupp from Kentucky came by for a visit.

As he grew older, coaches began to exert their influence over him and for Ralph, his greatest teacher was his baseball coach Chet Hanna, who often intoned, "Great athletes prepare and prepare...Eliminate as many possible things that can surprise you." The maxim became Gospel to young Ralph, and this imbued him with a work ethic centered around not simply pure reliance on athleticism, but on a study of his opponents as well as a keen knowledge of his own teammates' proclivities so that as often as possible, during a game he did not encounter an alien situation. Every play for Ralph Guglielmi became a simple return to déjà vu.

So the Certainty never led Guglielmi to become brash or cocky or uncoachable; just the opposite. The Certainty actually helped remove the stress of worrying if he was good enough and allowed Ralph the luxury to concentrate on improving his game and his leadership skills. Certainty instilled self-confidence, and when his teammates saw Ralph working so hard to improve his game, their belief in him as their leader and their belief in self grew. As one grateful teammate put it, Ralph exuded confidence.

His bearing and his speech suggested refinement, an elegant carriage not unlike Joe DiMaggio, yet Googs never projected aloofness. Like Neil Worden, he communicated well, arguing in a very articulate and forceful way for matters and principles in which he believed passionately. Leahy understood this and he adopted an open-door policy for his talented quarterback, because the Old Man appreciated that when Googs spoke out he did not do so as a malcontent, but rather someone dedicated to winning. As Notre Dame continued to grow as an academic institution, Ralph Guglielmi personified the thoughtfulness and intelligence the school cherished in its student-athletes. All Leahy knew was that this Guglielmi kid could play like hell.

The Certainty that Ralph Guglielmi felt for his ability influenced his inclination to attend Notre Dame, because many recruiters from other schools kept reminding him that Leahy had already recruited Don Bucci, a quarterback from East High School in Youngstown, Ohio. Guglielmi and Bucci had been compared often during their parallel careers in Ohio schoolboy football, so Ralph ignored the warnings of other schools about the presence of Bucci on the roster next year, accepting Bucci's enrollment in ND as a challenge, an opportunity to beat out his cross-state rival for the starting quarterback job in college.

He had also visited South Bend for a game during a blustery November weekend, not the perfect recruiting experience for a young man who had his pick of schools with addresses in the south, with belles as dates and warm weather year round. He had met with Leahy on that occasion, and like many young people before, no matter what the weather was like that weekend and despite the modest South Bend night life, something commanded young Guglielmi's attention.

Guglielmi was the type of quarterback that could turn around a program and after enduring a .500 campaign in '50, Frank Leahy needed this vastly talented young man to attend his school in the fall. That is why on a nice spring day, Guglielmi came home from baseball practice to see three black limousines parked in front of his house. They contained some very eminent personages, Frank Leahy and his "entourage," Bishop Reedy of Columbus and the Mayor of Grandview, Ohio.

Leahy in fact had already commenced a very deep conversation with Ralph's grandmother, even though Leahy knew no Italian and she knew little English. Somehow, Leahy had sold Ralph's grandmother on Notre Dame and when Ralph asked her afterward why, she replied that she trusted the coach, it was something in "his eyes." As devout Catholics and daily communicants, Ralph's parents also valued an education at such a wonderful school as Notre Dame.

What the Guglielmis did not know at the time is that Frank Leahy rarely visited a recruit's home, favoring instead to send a coach to meet the potential player and his family, and then once a young man decided to visit the campus and providing the coaches all liked him, Leahy then generally interviewed him and extended an offer, as if he were the Pope personally extending an indulgence.

Frank Leahy personified power, and certainly hiring

out three limos and taking along a Bishop and a Mayor constituted a show of force, but he no longer could afford to sit back and wait for potential recruits to heed the siren notes of the Notre Dame Fight Song and automatically end there. He either already had, or soon would discover that he had, lost out on an extremely talented Catholic young man, back Alan Ameche, destined to win the Heisman Award in 1955 for Wisconsin. He could not afford too many such defeats for top talent. Simply put, he needed Ralph Guglielmi.

Guglielmi, nicknamed Googs, signed on eventually not only because of the feelings of his parents and his grandmother, but due to the fact he simply did not like the offense that Woody Hayes had installed at Ohio State. Ralph's girlfriend planned to attend Ohio State University and word came to Ralph that if he signed on, she also would get a full scholarship.

Lacking an ability to compete with Ralph's girlfriend, Frank Leahy won out in the recruiting sweepstakes as a result of his potent offense, a system he constantly tinkered with to draw out its maximum firepower. Frank Leahy had not only successfully recruited a star quarterback, but with the earlier successes with fullback Neil Worden and halfbacks Joe Heap and John Lattner, had just assembled what many now consider the finest backfield at Notre Dame, before or since.

It did not stop there. Historically, the backfield of Guglielmi, Heap, Lattner and Worden all were drafted in the first round of the NFL draft; but in 1951, freshman Paul Reynolds received much of the press accolades accorded the running backs. A relative rarity as an engineering student on the team, he hailed from Abe Lincoln's home town of

Springfield, Illinois, where he starred as the captain of Cathedral High School.

Mining the rich vein of talent from Terry Brennan's perennial Chicago champions, Mt. Carmel High, the team recruited teammates Tom Carey, Paul Matz and Dan Shannon. And Leahy did not stop after running through Illinois with scholarship offers from Our Mother. From Gary, Indiana, Gene Carrabine quickly gained repetitions in the defensive backfield.

Up in Toledo, Ohio, Leahy picked up one of his finest defenders ever, linebacker Dick Szymanski. Everyone in the country wanted Szymanski, but even though he entered the recruiting sweepstakes relatively late, the coach offered an iron-clad scholarship to this very tough and agile young man, a person so athletic that he starred at center on offense too. Having endured some austere times recruiting the few players the University permitted him to offer scholarships to, Leahy basked in the relative luxury of securing most of the men he wanted and in so doing hauled in a class as talent laden as the year prior.

Change in Fortune

IGNORING FOR THE MOMENT any extracurricular summer practices or "freshman" football player "early orientation," the formal and official team sessions began on September 4, 1951 for photo day. Paul Neville from the *South Bend Tribune* already anticipated the rather tedious and staged nature of this event by commenting that "Notre Dame's football warriors collect on Cartier Field today to grimace and pose for photographers...Big Joe Katchik, six-nine, is a sure thing to have his likeness transferred to film at least a half dozen times standing beside the team's shortest player."

The photo op proved just as mundane as feared, with Leahy predicting his team would not exceed last year's record although the number of players and their spirit cheered him on. The *South Bend Tribune* reported that 85 players suited up and mugged for the cameras with 25 freshmen out with the varsity; together with the sophomores, they constituted 65% of the traveling team. The *Chicago Tribune* matter of factly described the congregated as "the greenest Notre Dame squad in recent years."

The *South Bend Tribune* voiced a bit of disagreement arising from "Capt. Mutscheller, who rarely says much outside the team circle, offered...'I think we'll do better this year.'" Paul Neville fretted that most of the frosh were a year away from varsity caliber, although he did particularly praise newcomers Carey, Paul Matz, Dan Shannon, Dick Szymanski,

Paul Reynolds and Jim Schenk. He also accorded honorable mentions of sorts to new back Leo Callaghan, end Walt Cabral, kicker Bob Arrix, center Dick Frasor and tackle Bill Hollenback. In his survey, he made no mention whatsoever of backs Ralph Guglielmi and Joe Heap.

Green-eyed Dan Shannon and crew-cut Dick Szymanski roomed together that freshman year. Shannon came up from Mt. Carmel High in Chicago, one of the most consistent feeder programs for ND in that era, while Szymanski hailed from Toledo. Szymanski impressed the coaches early, so the major issue with him became starting him right away at center or at linebacker, there being no real debate about his superior athletic skills.

Shannon impressed few as a starter, but for a kid that supposedly "came from money," or at least a more solid financial family background than most of his teammates, he was probably the most intense player on the field. Having a larger head than most, supposedly McAllister or one of his assistants had to cut his helmet in half and add a leather strap in the middle and then sew it all together so that Shannon had a piece of equipment that fit. Many times it appeared Shannon struck the opposing runner or blocker with his head first and shoulders after.

Tough as he was, Shannon missed his home town sweetheart Kitty Hughes terribly. One night, shortly after 11:00 lights out, Szymanski heard Shannon talking to Kitty and figuring that his roomie was talking in his sleep, he looked over to observe him speaking to and kissing a ring. Curious, Szymanski asked what he was doing, to which Shannon explained that each night at 11:15 p.m., he and Kitty promised to kiss each other's ring and "talk" to each other.

Szymanski sized this up for a moment, and then asked, "How's that working out for you?" Shannon did not really have much of an answer, but each night the ritual continued.

Meanwhile, the writers kept typing away as the coaches began to coalesce around certain prospects. Sophomore "Johnny Lattner—was given considerable attention…in punting." It also became clear early that Lattner had sewn up a starter's job in the defensive backfield, in addition to at least spot duty as a halfback on offense. By this time, Leahy also sensed how to optimize Lattner's efforts for the team, doling out cruel criticism at times, yet measuring it out with often public praise, such as proclaiming him the club's "ranking football athlete," and telling the press that "I believe that Lattner really excels as a tackler…Lattner does everything well." In exchange for this high praise, John Lattner sacrificed all for the Fighting Irish of Notre Dame.

Others had a more difficult time of it. In the very chilly autumn, the Irish held their first intersquad scrimmages on the first Saturday of the whole team's return to campus. Last year, the Old Man carefully scheduled his scrimmage due to lack of healthy manpower, but on September 8, 1951, he relished his chance to return to his favorite training method. His starters wore green jerseys, the reserves settled for blue, with the Greens led by quarterback John Mazur, halfbacks John Petitbon and Billy Barrett and fullback Neil Worden. The starting line consisted of ends Jim Mutscheller and Joe Katchik, tackles Bob Toneff and Joe Bush, center Art Hunter and guards Chet Ostrowski and Paul Burns.

For the Blues, quarterback Tom Carey "displayed a world of poise," leading backs Joe Heap, Fran Paterra and Del Gander. The Greens won by a 28-16 margin, led by linebacker Dick Szymanski intercepting a Carey pass for a touchdown, while Worden ran for one of his own on offense. But troubling spots emerged in the ranks of the starters, as Blues' Dick Frasor and Bill Gaudreau intercepted Mazur for 45- and 35- yard touchdowns respectively. Bob Arrix missed only one kick all afternoon, serving on both sides.

The two-a-day practices officially ended on September 14, with the commencement of classes. By mid-week, Leahy and the coaches tinkered with the starters' assignments: Minnie Mavraides shifted to tackle and Frank Varrichione took over guard duties. At the next team scrimmage, on September 15, the reconstituted Irish starting eleven defeated the second team Blues 28-0.

John Petitbon ran for a touchdown and also snared a 60-yard TD reception, but Paul Neville offered his highest praise for John Mazur: "Perhaps the biggest reason for the sharpened Irish play was the work of Quarterback John Mazur...reminiscent of Notre Dame's long line of great signal callers." Five "first-year men," Jack Lee, Dick Szymanski, Gene Carrabine, Sam Palumbo and Dan Shannon started on defense for the Greens.

For the beleaguered Blues, John Lattner departed early due to injury, Fran Paterra replacing him in the backfield with Joe Heap, fullback Tom McHugh and Tom Carey at QB. Al Petranick also sustained neck injuries, with the expectation and hope for a rapid return. Compared to the previous year's team, which contained too few players and too many injured ones, the 1951 group thrived.

Abruptly, early the next week, Wilfrid Smith of the *Chicago Tribune* felt confident enough to jettison any hopes for the

Irish varsity for 1951, citing inexperience and lack of depth in the ranks as the largest cause for concern. He knew Frank Leahy spouted pessimism as a way to lessen expectations and perhaps make opponents overconfident and yet, Smith indiscriminately quoted the coach as lauding Bob Williams and Jerry Groom from the previous year's edition, while intimating without them the result might prove "catastrophic."

Leahy accurately observed that "Notre Dame will use more freshmen than any other school," but what the Coach knew, and Smith did not take enough effort to divine, was that many of his players possessed potential All-American caliber talent. Smith did concede that Neil Worden, John Lattner, Joe Katchik and Art Hunter "unquestionably will aid the Irish in their 10-game schedule," and yet left an overall impression of hopelessness.

With Worden for example, Smith asserted that he and quarterback Mazur had had a "disappointing" fall and that Worden might not start at fullback over Del Gander, an observation probably fueled by Leahy for motivational purposes. This period marked an ebb in his devotion to Notre Dame, and when a talented young fullback from a Wisconsin high school came down to South Bend for a recruiting visit, Worden talked him out of enrolling at Our Lady's University, which is how Notre Dame lost out on recruiting Alan Ameche, the 1954 Heisman Award winner and later star with the Baltimore Colts.

For years after, his teammates kidded Worden that he only talked Ameche out of coming to ND because he wanted to retain his starting job at fullback, but Worden's critique emanated from a profound feeling he had at the time.

Significantly, even at his lowest point at Notre Dame, Neil Worden did not transfer out, because as much as he missed his freedom and the availability of girls, he knew he had made the right choice for himself.

As harsh as the *Tribune* scribe had been with Worden, he saved his more cutting analysis for end Joe Katchik: "For an inexperienced big man, Katchik is a good blocker. Critics insist he lacks coordination and the coaches point out that he never competed in handball, tennis or other sports calling for coordination."

This is the silliest critique of all because there were few "critics" at that juncture of the pre-season to critique Katchik. Smith did not know what he was talking about, and with the exception of Joe Doyle and Paul Neville of the *South Bend Tribune*, no one outside of the ND sports establishment did either. Of all the athletes who participated in the Notre Dame football program at the time, almost all of them list their high school sports as football, basketball, baseball or track. Neil Worden had an extensive training in gymnastics, but few others even had access to any other sports (or facilities) than the basic high school ones, never mind handball or tennis.

Internally, the Irish brain trust could not figure out Joe Katchik. Any time he spent at the campus handball courts, he invariably participated not in spirited and sweaty contests, but rather worked on blocking drills. Very few of his teammates growing up generally in either very rural areas or industrial hubs in the Midwest or Massachusetts had ever seen a tennis court. The "critics" were his coaches who thought they had recruited the next Leon Hart, but did not understand how to inspire him to approach the level of performance of the great Heisman winner, and current Detroit Lions All-Pro. Dumping on him in the press was the worst thing they could have done, but they did it indiscriminately and Smith enabled them.

If Katchik struggled, guard Jack Lee quickly became one of the most popular players on his squad, earning the appreciation of his coaches for his hard work and prodigious organizational talents, while earning the respect and friendship of even upperclassmen like Bob Toneff. Possibly the only player on the team who had played high school hockey, Lee did not so much love to hit as he seemed impervious to the punishment inflicted upon him by his coaches and his teammates during exhaustive drills.

In fact, during one of the fall scrimmages, Lee had sustained a heavy hit in the mouth after blocking Toneff, causing many of Lee's teeth to loosen. Thereafter, he lost tooth by tooth in subsequent sessions until after he had lost his third one, he briskly strode right up to his coach Joe McArdle, protesting loudly, "What the hell, this has got to cease!" Eventually, Notre Dame provided him with a plate, and although team trainer Hugh Burns once lost it on him, Lee wore it proudly as he submitted to the smash mouth football of his practices with good nature, which only increased the admiration and affection his coaches and mates already possessed for him. He made the Irish eyes smile.

Shifting from an analysis of the linemen, although Smith had quoted Leahy's useless moaning about the team's prospects as if he were serious, he did pick up a scoop in that Leahy had decided upon young Tom Carey as the team's second string quarterback, spelling starter John Mazur. In the wake of Smith's bombshell column, the Irish staff scheduled a third large scrimmage for the last free Saturday before the regular season began, preparing the team for this final exhibition. But before it began, Ralph Guglielmi very vigorously made his dissatisfaction with his station well known.

Having turned down offers from every major football program in the nation with the exception of Notre Dame, Ralph Guglielmi found his first few weeks of August practice most frustrating. Rather than taking snaps and drilling running and passing plays with the other backs, Ralph merely held up tackling dummies for other players to run into. He learned nothing about the plays or the players or proper quarterbacking technique. Invisible during the scrimmages to date, he seethed, certain he could outperform his competition if only provided some drives down the field.

Seven other quarterbacks stood above him in the depth chart, with senior John Mazur starting. Developing a slow burn, he began to think about his girlfriend back at Ohio State University, and how he had passed up so many other opportunities to watch others on his squad perform a job he frankly thought he could perform better. Talks home to his parents did not seem to help much, so one day he decided to force the issue and have a direct talk with Coach Leahy himself.

No player ever did this, approaching the great Leahy, and nobody ever seriously considered doing so. Leahy existed in the pantheon, this great coach surrounded by subordinate position coaches who did his bidding and dealt with the players at the direct level. Leahy operated though his staff, often referring to a player in vague, impersonal ways, and directing the coach to ask this player to not commit the same mistake again.

This mattered little to Ralph Guglielmi who marched into the Old Man's office at Breen-Phillips Hall and met the head coach's secretary, who unsuccessfully attempted to prevent the unscheduled meeting from occurring.

Leahy let him in, "Yes, lad, what can I do for you?"

Guglielmi got right to the point, "You don't even know who I am, do you? I'm the best quarterback here, I can see it, but you can't see it because you have me holding blocking dummies!"

Leahy never let a player talk to him like this before, but he allowed it this time. He offered Guglielmi playing time in the next inter-squad scrimmage, a perfect opportunity to let his assertive young QB either get creamed by the upperclassmen, or less likely, back up his boast. But with Ralph Guglielmi, Leahy broke a lot of his own policies; he almost never traveled to a recruit's home, but to secure Guglielmi, he did. With Bob Williams having graduated, and Mazur only a one-year solution as a senior, Leahy had to evaluate the future of the position and concluded that if his prized freshman recruit did not succeed he may have a problem winning national championships in the near future.

For his part, Googs' initial sense of exhilaration gave way quickly to an almost sick feeling. He had just lectured the great Frank Leahy and had gotten a shot, just like he wanted; and while holding up blocking dummies held no allure, now he had to produce. He calmed himself with one thought: if things did not work out he always had a chance to return to Ohio to play for Woody Hayes and see his girlfriend every day. Once he placed matters in this perspective, he calmed down and returned to the advice that Coach Hanna had given him back in Columbus, prepare and prepare.

At the penultimate September 22 scrimmage, at least one player's fortune was secured while another saw his position with the team virtually eliminated. All this because the reserves defeated the starters 14-13.

Guiding the Blues, Ralph Guglielmi aced his opportunity to demonstrate his preeminence at quarterback, with help from a 20-yard touchdown run by Joe Heap and a two-yard plunge by Bobby Joseph. The Blues defense even sacked starter John Mazur in the end zone. Elated, Ralph Guglielmi for the first time began to feel with conviction that "I belong here!" The result of this scrimmage profoundly changed the way that Leahy saw his team, perceiving the value of giving Ralph Guglielmi more snaps from center, while also shifting a largely ineffectual Joe Katchik from end to tackle.

It was worse than that. Leahy went to the press, "making no effort to hide his disappointment over his football team's shoddy performance in a game scrimmage in the Irish stadium," according to Paul Neville. Neville himself opined that the "subs made the first stringers look bad in the process." The *Tribune* accompanied the article with two photographs, one of Joe Katchik and the other of Chet Ostrowski, and informed its readers that Ostrowksi had replaced Katchik at left end, due to the latter's failure "to develop as rapidly as was expected." It got stranger, as soon thereafter, the team announced that Minnie Mavraides had supplanted Ostrowski at end.

The public roasting of Katchik was unnecessarily humiliating, serving to mask many mistakes the coaching staff had made in evaluating talent. Wisely, they promoted Guglielmi to the varsity "as a reward for piloting the subs to victory over the regulars," and yet the fact that it took the young quarterback himself to summon the courage to get in the game at all, reflected quite badly on Leahy and his backs coaches.

Guglielmi could be motivated by poor treatment; Joe Katchik could not, and his very public humiliation accelerated the destruction of his collegiate career. With the positional shift came the transfer of Katchik from the kindly Coach Druze to the stern taskmaster Bob McBride, who had little patience for Katchik. Maybe Katchik was never going to be the next Leon Hart, but he had played end in high school back in Plymouth, Pennsylvania with John Mazur, and could have contributed to that position at ND with him. Instead, Joe Katchik had entered the Twilight Zone.

In part, Leahy's laments to the press presaged his own attempts to motivate his players for their opener against Indiana, a squad he had built up to levels never seen before in intercollegiate ball. He promised a week of a return to "fundamentals," expressing disdain for the starters' blocking, tackling and deficiencies in scoring and defense. Commenting on kicker Bob Arrix's twisted knee and necessity to replace him, Leahy stated that Minnie Mavraides would handle the kicking, "If we make any touchdowns."

And still the shuffling of the deck continued. John Lattner felt thrilled to learn in the fall that he had secured a starting position as a defensive halfback, but now with days approaching before the first game, Coach Earley informed him that he also was going to get a number of hand-offs on the offense, behind halfback Billy Barrett.

As for Ralph Guglielmi, fortunately he passed the audition. Having earned the confidence of his coaches and the respect of his peers, his days holding blocking dummies had ended and as a freshman he dressed for games. Ralph Guglielmi would will himself to become the next great quarterback at the University of Notre Dame.

Opening Day

PATIENTLY, QUARTERBACK JOHN MAZUR had waited his turn for three years, watching Frank Tripucka and Bob Williams star for the last two great Irish teams of the 1940s and then suffering helplessly as 1950 unwound. With Williams having graduated the previous spring, Mazur had just the one year opportunity to return the Irish program to prominence and he naturally wanted to maximize his opportunities. He had just one chance.

The Korean War had opened up the varsity to the incoming freshmen and rather than plug gaps as best as possible with veterans playing sixty minutes a game, Frank Leahy embarked on a youth movement, with "30 of whom had never before performed on a collegiate gridiron." The promising core of freshmen and sophomores now held the predominant positions on the depth charts of the Irish offense and defense, with a sprinkling of upperclassmen like Bob Toneff hopefully poised to hold the whole operation together.

Traditionally, the Indiana University teams did not measure up to the talent arrayed against them by the Irish, but in 1950, the Hoosiers had defeated ND and in doing so, reinforced the fear of Frank Leahy that his varsity was in for a very long and frustrating year. Frighteningly, the Hoosiers supposedly improved since the previous campaign and although the rules now permitted them to suit up freshmen like every other team in the nation, they intended to field only three frosh at most against an Irish club replete with them.

Leading up to the opening game of 1951, the Irish coaching staff virtually every day preached the greatness of the Hoosiers, in particular to the underclassmen that had never played against this foe before. As a result, once the game began, the Irish linemen went after their opponents with singular ferocity, slapping them in the helmet, elbowing them in the face and constantly hitting them, so that quite suddenly most of the Hoosiers had blood running down their faces.

Joe Bush had awaited the game in sheer dread, fearing that the Hoosiers meant to administer a drubbing just like last year, but this time on a bunch of neophyte Fighting Irish. He reasoned that if they had manhandled the defending national champions the previous year, what chance did a batch of rookies have against them? A few plays into the game, Bush relaxed a bit as he saw his line dominating the opposition and after one fierce exchange on a play, one of the Indiana players actually pleaded a bit stating, "Hey, cut that out!"

Certainly dominating the line pleased the coaches, but more importantly, Coach Druze had diagnosed the Indiana offense and had decided the key for the Irish lay in shaking up the Hoosier quarterback Lou D'Achille. "Don't worry about the pass, hit him [D'Achille]! We want to soften him up a bit," preached Druze. Not only did the Hoosier linemen get beat up early in the game, but their quarterback had been thoroughly tenderized by the end of their first possession.

In addition to scaring his players silly and having them come out ferociously attacking their foe, Leahy had also secretly modified his backfield at times from a T-formation to a solid I with quarterback Mazur backed up like dominoes by backs Billy Barrett, John Petitbon and Neil Worden. They ran a sustained drive from their own 25 yard line for their first touchdown, highlighted by a forty-yard pass from Mazur to end Jim Mutscheller, and the ultimate score on a Billy Barrett run.

Early in the second quarter, Harry Warren wrote that "Mel Beckett, Indiana center, passed wildly to Ray Petrauskas, who was back to punt and the ball sailed 5 yards over his head," to turn the ball over to ND, culminating in a six-yard run for touchdown by Neil Worden. The Hoosiers tried to reorganize, but they lost possession of the ball again, which led to Worden plowing into the end zone, this time from one yard out.

Reeling, Indiana on their next possession coughed up the ball on a fumble to Notre Dame's rookie linebacker, Dick Szymanski. His mates on the offense exploited the situation almost immediately, with Worden rushing for yet another touchdown. Error compounded on error as Indiana regained possession, this time to lead only to another mishap as their quarterback Lou D'Achille found his Achille's heel in Irish defensive back John Lattner who intercepted one of his passes. Predictably, Neil Worden exploited the situation for his fourth touchdown of the afternoon, this time on an eleven-yard romp for his final six points of the day.

John Lattner demonstrated his considerable offensive prowess moments later to score a touchdown of his own on a run, and after kicker Minnie Mavraides kicked his sixth extra point of the half, the teams went into their dressing rooms with the Irish way ahead, 42-0.

The team had just broken an all-time record for scoring points in one quarter with 35, shattering the mark attained against Tulane in 1946. During half-time while the bands played on, Carol Mitchell, an Indiana University co-ed and runner-up for the Miss America crown in '51, philosophically analyzed the game and promised, "We've always had a second-half team."

In the second half, with each team appreciating the ultimate outcome, their offenses seemed to slow down a bit. The level of defensive intensity did not, with Bob Toneff tossed out of the game. On the same series, the opposing linemen got sick of the Irish' physicality, so on one play a Hoosier player took a swing at right tackle Bob Ready, who turned around and said, "You SOB…" and promptly tried to return the favor. The referee did not see the first punch and only saw Ready's effort, which did not even connect; the flag went up and Ready went down for the game. On the bench, Ready and Toneff heard an earful from Leahy, who "put on a Barrymorean display of tongue-lashing technique" about how "we don't do that at Notre Dame," as the game continued to get out of hand.

Deprived of the services of Toneff and Ready, the Irish defense finally relinquished a touchdown, which the press attributed rightly to the "two roughing penalties on the ND defense, a group determined to the end to rub the Hoosiers' noses into the sod in retribution for last year's humiliation."

Determined to get in the last word, back came the Irish, starting with a long kick return by Billy Barrett. Quarterbacking by then, Tom Carey initiated one last drive, punctuated by reserve fullback Del Gander shattering the plane of the opposing goal line, as Leahy emptied the bench to get every player in the game. Had he kept the starters in the action longer, the Irish probably would have surpassed 70 points.

Besides Lattner and Worden and some of the other young starters, Ralph Guglielmi, Joe Heap and Tom McHugh saw their first game action that afternoon. Frank Leahy let Googs run some late plays but placed one very strict restriction upon his young quarterback: "You cannot pass the ball." Leahy issued the command because he did not want to cause Indiana any more embarrassment, a likely result if the young gunslinger started firing passes down the field. Guglielmi followed the orders and at the end of the game, jubilant Irish players carried Frank Leahy off the field, with big Art Hunter leading the charge.

Talent and toughness tipped the scales in the Irish favor that afternoon. The Hoosiers not only had to face Bob Toneff, they now had to account for exciting new backs like Neil Worden and Johnny Lattner and linebackers like Szymanski. Minnie Mavraides could hurt you with his kicking and blocking, and while most of the Irish lacked intercollegiate experience, the starting players had the skill and toughness too often lacking in several instances in 1950. They had to be good, and on this opening day, Leahy's lads were very good.

And yet some did not appreciate it fully. While Neil Worden had gained the instant adoration of his classmates and coaches, he did not believe he had done anything truly special until after the game, when some fans lined up outside the stadium and asked him for his autograph. The Polish kid from Milwaukee, who had done nothing but practice for a year and a half, had become a star.

And yet he still had a day or two to savor his accomplishments in his own way before he permanently became part of the public domain. After he signed his new found fans' autographs, he "just went for a walk...and then stopped at the chapel for a few minutes and came home." After that Ed Sainsbury from the UPI news service interviewed him and, as was his custom, Worden modestly deflected attention from himself and onto his teammates, maintaining that "I think I could do better...I say that because our line was wonderful. Anybody could have run through the holes they opened up."

The Irish began to prepare in earnest for their next opponent, the University of Detroit, by the Tuesday after the Indiana game. All that week, Leahy drilled his defense to combat a very potent shotgun attack by the opposing offense, or so he said. It is one of the oldest maxims in sport that a team never looks beyond its next opponent, but unbeknownst to the Irish defenders, Coach Leahy was doing just that.

Even though his lads had played .500 ball the year before and despite the fact that he habitually overworried about even the weakest of foes, Leahy had clearly decided that Detroit had no chance of defeating his team; and in fact, very early after the Indiana game had ended, he had begun to prepare his men for the shotgun formation and its master, quarterback Fred Benners at SMU. The extremely strong ND national champions of two years ago had barely scraped by Kyle Rote and SMU by a score of 27-20, and Leahy had already leapfrogged over Detroit to effectively provide his men with two weeks of practice in anticipation of the much stronger Mustang team. Of this he told his players nothing, as they primed for the non-existent shotgun formation/aerial show that supposedly awaited them up in Detroit.

Of most importance to Leahy, the Irish had to practice under nighttime conditions for their first night game in history. On Wednesday evening before the game, they worked

under the lights of South Bend's School Field and they arranged to work out Thursday night in Detroit to also get ac-
climated to Briggs Stadium.

The team traveled by train up to Detroit on Thursday
morning from nearby Niles, Michigan with Frank Leahy
showing his deep concern for the upcoming game by sleeping for an hour and a half while Coaches McArdle and
Earley played gin rummy in their car. Although he did not
attend the game, Joe Doyle had recently received congratu-
lations from his many friends and fans due to his promotion up from his reporter's position at the *South Bend Tribune*.
Doyle had worked as "a farmer, a gasoline station operator
and a newspaper reporter," and with Paul Neville shifting
up to managing editor at the paper, Joe now had become the
Sports Editor, effective October 13, 1951.

Once the train arrived in Detroit, former Irish players
Leon Hart, Jim Martin and Gus Cifelli met the team at the
station. From there, they jumped on two buses for their trip
to the Whittier Hotel, with four police motorcyclists escort-
ing them there with sirens screaming. Meanwhile, Detroit
coach Dutch Clark conceded, "[w]e're way out of our class"
against Notre Dame.

To celebrate the 250th anniversary of the founding of the
city of Detroit, Michigan, Notre Dame traveled up there for
its first scheduled night game in history on October 6 against
the Titans (a previous game against North Carolina in
Yankee Stadium ran long enough for the lights to go on). The
game itself effectively ended long before the moths found the
giant game lights surrounding the field.

This time it was senior back John Petitbon, the fastest
man on the squad with the possible exception of Joe Heap

and Dave Flood, who paced the team, scoring three touchdowns in the first period. Amazingly, ND scored a fourth touchdown in the first period on a thirty-yard pass from Mazur to Mutscheller. In the second half, the Titan players, somewhat like the Hoosiers the week before, composed themselves in their locker room and then began to play better, even managing a touchdown of their own. Wrongfully believing that they had gained some momentum, on their next possession their quarterback Ed Gornak threw a pass which defensive back Lattner intercepted and ran back thirty-two yards for a touchdown.

Freshmen Walt Cabral and Paul Reynolds made their first significant marks for the Irish that evening, Cabral with a fumble recovery and Reynolds with some good runs as an offensive back. Taking over the controls from Mazur late in the game, quarterback Ralph Guglielmi ran a sneak from one yard out for another touchdown.

John Petitbon garnered most of the headlines with his 85-yard kickoff return, 73-yard punt return and his almost ten-yard average from scrimmage as a halfback, but the young men on the team continued to perform well as a unit that had not quite gelled. Compared to the ferocity they displayed toward Indiana, the Irish revealed a mellower side, not having any grudge against Detroit, a team that they had played only once before in their history.

After the game, Irish and Detroit alums shared the general good feeling together in a joint party, with the promise that these two Catholic schools soon would partake in an annual series, a match-up that fortunately never came to fruition, because ND always wisely chose not to play other Catholic schools much, preferring not to split the loyalty of the faithful. They would not always be so careful. Still, a good time was seemingly had by all, and with the Irish up in Michigan anyway, the entire team was awarded tickets to the Michigan-Stanford game in Ann Arbor the next day. All except for Coach Druze, who bought a ticket to view upcoming opponent Michigan State and Frank Leahy, who flew down to Dallas to scout Southern Methodist University with Coach McBride.

Against a much more skilled and powerful Southern Methodist team coming up on their schedule, Frank Leahy needed his lads to continue to mature on the fly.

The Shortest Yard

THE POOR FRESHMEN who stormed into their dorms in the fall of 1950 had little fun, what with three early church services a week, bed checks and practices for games in which they would never play. Of course, in 1951, newcomers like Ralph Guglielmi and Joe Heap worked themselves into varsity ball games, but this year the walk-on freshmen, and those deemed in need of a pinch of seasoning, also had the opportunity to play on the B team.

In 1950, with freshmen ineligible and few uninjured varsity players, the Irish had a difficult time fielding an eleven for these B games, but this year with the infusion of several sophomores and the clearance to play freshmen, the B's flourished. The concept of a freshman team had not vanished, it had evolved with the Korean War and the shifting rules of the early NCAA. Late '30's legend Benny Sheridan disappeared, but law student and late '40's star Bob Lally coached, along with Gene Smith and Dick Cotter. Smith and Cotter had played their senior year with the varsity in the ill-fated 1950 season and had returned to help out training the backs.

Joining the freshman hopefuls were a number of "B" upperclassmen, players who stood little chance of seeing much time in the varsity games, but who might blossom in the future. The young men practiced every day, and while they

151

still served as scrimmage victims for the varsity, they did get in a few games in the fall.

Against Illinois, strong efforts by quarterback Bob Martin were not enough as the B's lost 21-7. The Irish then played Purdue to a tie, as Martin threw a touchdown pass to Steve Gomula in the pouring rain at Cartier Field.

Notoriously, the Irish traveled down to Tennessee, allegedly in a contest with their B team, but to this day, most of the players who took the trip believe they played that day against the Tennessee starters, a contingent that went undefeated that year. Backs Bob Rigali and Bobby Joseph did their best, and Joseph actually scored a touchdown, but the B's went down like stalks of hay in an Indiana cornfield 38-7.

The B's had a couple of more games scheduled but they were canceled due to snow, which demonstrates most teams' devotion to the underlying B team concept. Jim Bigelow got some playing time, as did non-freshmen such as Jim Dunlay, Joe Caprara, Jim Weithman, Art Nowack and Ed Buczkiewicz. Jim Dunlay served as one barometer of how things had changed so much in one year; in 1950 he was pressed into service for the varsity, but in '51 he was relegated to B team duty as freshmen and sophomores thrust themselves into starting positions.

As an adjunct to the scheduled games against other college B teams, some of the Notre Dame players were treated to a game against inmates at the Indiana State Penitentiary at Michigan City, a game scheduled in part perhaps to make the normal practices back at Cartier Field look easy in comparison. Before the game started, all of the collegians had to have their equipment checked thoroughly by the guards and once they entered, they started tossing the ball and stretching in a prison yard of nearly all hard ground and very little grass. The Irish coasted early to a 35-0 lead against a group of slow and mean prisoners, led by a silver-haired quarterback. The most noteworthy item about the contest is the beating some of the inmates tried to dole out against the young Fighting Irish, with a number of broken noses resulting.

The spectators by and large rooted for the ND men, but at one point, some of the inmates nearly rioted after a disputed call went against the prisoners. The referee summonsed the Irish coaches and players and advised them not to score any more points during the game so as not to stir the restive opponents and their associates, a piece of advice immediately taken as Gospel. The game ended with the Catholics defeating the Convicts, with the Catholics scurrying home on their bus with stories galore for their friends back in the residence halls.

Few of the freshmen on the B team did much for the Irish in the years ahead. Unlike the first scrimmage the previous fall, in which a number of the freshmen starting eleven against the Irish varsity vanished soon after, Leahy had figured out early who had the most talent among his freshmen. The B teams served little purpose in retrospect, but to this day, the stories of a hopelessly overmatched squad taking on the undefeated Tennessee varsity team or the Convicts drew laughs, and for those who know football, an admiration for the guts of the B's those days.

The true Killer B for Notre Dame in the fall of 1951 was not their reserve squad, but rather Fred Benner, the quarterback of Southern Methodist, who came to South Bend on October 13, 1951, and threw the ball to his receivers and backs on his team's first 26 plays.

Like anything else unpleasant, Leahy never forgot the experience of his narrow escape against SMU in 1949, and rather than reason that fortunately neither Kyle Rote nor Doak Walker still suited up with the team, having both become professional football players, Leahy saw only the negatives. After he returned from his scouting trip to see SMU play, Leahy stated that, "That's a fine S.M.U. team...I didn't know S.M.U. could run at all." Apparently neither did the SMU staff, which no longer had its greatest 1-2 punch in the backfield (before the much later arrival of Craig James and Eric Dickerson), and it had installed a shotgun formation in part to protect its quarterback, Fred Benners, as he searched downfield for receivers.

Certainly Leahy had decided correctly to look past Detroit and prepare his men for the then fairly unique shotgun, but having started work in that direction, the Coach then overdid matters, starting with personally flying down to watch SMU play. It was a self-defeating trip as Bob McBride certainly knew enough how to scout a team and transmit his report to the other coaches and players. All Leahy did by shooting down to Texas was indulge in over-worrying, the worst feeling to have and then convey inadvertently to his team of relatively young players. They needed to play loose, plus even after SMU won the game which Leahy scouted, the Mustangs' record was only 1-2.

But Leahy, after 1949, equated the Mustangs to the White Whale.

Instead of taking Monday off as usual after the Detroit game, the team began to practice as a whole that day, concentrating on pass defense. Since the Irish had played on Friday night against a weak team, they still had their customary two days off after a game to refit, so the scheduling of the Monday practice made sense. The team listened raptly as Coach McBride delivered his verdict on Fred Benners: "stands back seven or eight yards to take the pass from center... and no lineman can catch him. He roams all over before he throws."

The practices revolved around pass defense, although running back Fran Paterra apparently upset Leahy or one of the other coaches as the player missed practice for late afternoon instruction. It is likely that Paterra experienced difficulty walking after the early evening drills required of him, but little else was written about this week and little is remembered, most likely because Paul Neville had not completely handed the reins over to Joe Doyle as sports editor of the *South Bend Tribune* yet. What most people later recalled was that it seemed as if the preparation entailed getting to Benners and putting the hurt on him, rather than neutralizing his passing options.

Describing the day of the game, in a letter home, tackle Bob Taylor wrote: "Before the game all of the players go to Mass and communion in Dillon Chapel. After the Mass we all received a special blessing and some holy medals." They needed all of the divine intervention they might get.

What developed was an aerial show between SMU quarterback Benners and John Mazur, who traded long throws and touchdowns all afternoon. It was worse than the scouting report—not only did Benners take his hikes in the shotgun formation, he invariably then dropped back another five or ten yards before looking for receivers. One of the Irish linemen admitted that he exhausted them that way, as the Irish stayed with a five-man front, rather than drop more men back.

Benners fired away while Leahy did not adjust quickly enough or did not have some contingency plans laid out beforehand. Part of the frustration lies in the general defensive alignment of the early '50s, with five linemen, at least three linebackers and two to three defensive backs. There were no nickel or dime packages, as known today, but the rules did not restrict defenses to such an extent that a Fred Benners was handed a blank check before the game and could score at will.

Indeed, in their next game SMU lost to Rice, due mainly to Rice's coach, Jess Neely negating the strengths of the opposing offense. As Joe Doyle analyzed it: "Neely sent three linemen charging in, not to tackle the Mustang ace, but rather to see to it that he didn't run. The other eight? Ok, they dragged back to cover the five eligible Southern Methodist receivers." At the end, Rice had shut down Benners and won 28-7, dropping SMU to a 2-3 record. While most teams used their linemen in a very orthodox way, Leahy almost always instituted change, and with no running game of note from SMU, he only had to shut down the pass. To do that, all he needed to install was three men on the defensive line, with everyone else dropping back in coverage, which a far less acclaimed coach like Jess Neely did with great success.

The SMU coach, Rusty Russell, admitted as much, stating, "We didn't feel we had the power to run over 'em like we did Missouri, so naturally we stressed passing."

And yet, SMU came into Notre Dame stadium having previously lost two out of three of its games, so somebody had adjusted to the pass-happy offense. Leahy might have rotated his offensive linemen more, or, more importantly, conceded points on defense while figuring out ways to out-score the Mustangs.

Forced into a passing contest, John Mazur never was going to match Fred Benners; the only quarterback Leahy had in his arsenal to match Benners as a passer was Ralph Guglielmi. With improved Irish passing, the overwhelming advantage they possessed in the running game should have tipped the scales in their favor. Instead, they moved fullback Del Gander into the defensive line where he rarely if ever played, figuring his speed might place more pressure on Benners.

After the Mustangs had passed over twenty-five times and had scored their third touchdown, Leahy finally "moved its linebackers a few yards farther from the scrimmage strip, and SMU immediately switched to a running attack," according to Arch Ward. The move was long overdue, as Irish could have contained the weak Mustang running attack all day. One of the Irish stars years later concluded that Leahy had been out-coached during this game, a point hard to rebut.

With the Mustangs on a later drive deep into Irish territory, the adjustment paid immediate dividends. Dave Flood planted a Mustang runner for a two-yard loss and Walt Cabral dropped another rusher for no gain. On third down, Fred Mangialardi made another key stop and on fourth down, hard-nosed nose tackle Jack Lee drilled a Mustang back for a two-yard deficit, with ND taking over on downs at its own 8 yard line. The Irish would have won the game in the trenches, instead the coaches permitted the Mustangs to negate this advantage with an air show. Having spent the better part of the game playing the other team's game, ND lost 27-20.

Prior to the SMU game, Frank Leahy displayed his first public doubts about John Mazur as his starting quarterback, alternating Mazur, Guglielmi and Tom Carey behind center during practice that week. During the game itself, he pulled the string on Mazur at one point, inserting Ralph Guglielmi into the fray late in the game, with mixed success, causing the Southern Methodist athletic director Marty Bell to acidly comment, "If those Notre Dame coaches make a great a quarterback out of that fellow, they will have done a tremendous job." In two years, Bell had completely altered his opinion of Guglielmi, immortalized today while Fred Benners barely merits a memory, but Googs did not yet have the experience to carry off a come-from-behind rally against a strong team like the Mustangs.

Marty Bell's views clashed with Joe Doyle who opined, "Most heartening note of the afternoon was the showing of Frosh Quarterback Ralph Guglielmi who clicked on four of six passes in the early part of the fourth period." Statistically, Bell's statement does not possess the solid ring of truth, as Mazur went 14 for 35 in his pass attempts, in contrast to young Guglielmi who completed 4 out of 6 throws. Arch Ward, too, gave the young man a "salute" for his exertions.

Despite a mismanaged game plan, the lads did not surrender, with John Lattner running in for a touchdown to restore his team to within one touchdown of tying. After another gallant defensive stop by their defense, the Irish got the ball back and Mazur passed to Neil Worden, who brought the ball down to the SMU 27 yard line. No two-point play existed in college football at that time, but ND had a realistic chance of tying the game; but then they incurred a fifteen-yard penalty and the Mustang defense dropped Mazur for another fifteen yards as he took a sack, and time ran out with the Mustangs victorious.

Like many of his peers, freshman Dave Metz walked back to his hall as if he were walking through an endless snow bank. Back in his room at Farley Hall, he opened his third floor window and sat on the ledge, pondering the unfairness of it all. A passing SMU fan hollered, "Don't jump, it's only a game!"

Not to Dave Metz. Not at Notre Dame.

"Swim, Damn It, Swim!"

ON MONDAY, OCTOBER 15, Leahy listened to scouting reports from John Druze and Wally Ziemba concerning their upcoming opponent, the University of Pittsburgh, while experiencing acid reflux viewing the game films of the recent SMU debacle. Glumly, Leahy had to digest reports of the passing excellence of Pitt's quarterback, Bob Bestwick, a possessor of an unreal .792 completion percentage. Bestwick loved throwing the ball to his favorite receiver Chris Warriner, and after facing the deadly Flingin' Fred Benners, the Irish now had to defend against a Pitt QB with what was believed to be the highest completion percentage record of any quarterback who ever opposed Notre Dame.

Even with pessimistic Frank Leahy, hope does spring, and word began leaking out that Bestwick had a sore wing and Warriner did not feel so hot either. Also, whereas Leahy had shifted from respecting an opponent to fearing one with SMU, he hopefully had the better sense of appreciating that mighty Pitt had not won a game all year; they had just lost pretty convincingly to Iowa by a 34-17 margin, causing Joe Doyle to quip, "the Panthers as usual are trying to play a $2 schedule with a $1.25 ball club."

Additionally, Joe Doyle noted that five scouts from upcoming ND opponents had witnessed the SMU game, with Pitt and Purdue among those represented, so obviously a temptation existed among the upcoming teams to throw the

161

ball all afternoon against the Irish. In trying to solve the team's perceived defensive backfield woes, the coaches had to face the likelihood that they had permanently lost the services of lineman Paul Burns who had sustained a severe shoulder separation in an earlier game.

Tom Seaman replaced Burns, but then it also appeared that the other guard, Frank Varrichione, might have to sit out the next game or more, so all week the coaches had to borrow players from other positions like Bob Taylor and Chet Ostrowski and convert them to guards to provide depth at that beleaguered position.

Injuries aside, Leahy loved scrimmages so on the Wednesday leading up to the Pitt game, he had Ralph Guglielmi directing the first team offense, while tellingly John Mazur directed the second team offense against the first team defense, using Pitt's plays to train the first team defenders. During the scrimmage, Frank Varrichione jogged around Cartier Field while Petitbon, Barrett and Tom McHugh all scored touchdowns. On days like these, the great Leahy often stopped to comment on the performance of runners like McHugh or Fran Paterra, saying, "You'll be playing a lot on Saturday." But first the Irish had to fly out that Friday to Pittsburgh for their upcoming game.

On Friday evening, many of the players dispersed from their hotel rooms to enjoy a night away from their normal clerical supervision. Some younger linemen went out to dinner at a restaurant together, among them Sam Palumbo and Jack Lee. Palumbo had ordered a steak and was about to slice up his first piece when Lee reminded him that tonight was Friday, back then there being a Church requirement that the Faithful not eat meat on that day, although they were encouraged to dine on fish. Thus reminded of the fish on Friday stricture, Palumbo dumped his glass of water on the steak, yelling at it "Swim, damn it, swim!"

Approaching game time, Pitt finally announced that stars Bestwick and Warriner had not recovered sufficiently from their injuries to play, although once the game began, Warriner did attempt an appearance or two. Alliteration aside, for Notre Dame Bestwick would be no Benners. To replace Bestwick, Pitt called upon Blair Kramer, who like Huck O'Neil for the Irish, had to transfer schools once Duquesne dropped football. Learning of the Panther's injuries, the bookies made the Irish two touchdown favorites.

The odds makers had it all wrong as Leahy's lads rebounded by shutting out Pitt 33-0. Everyone got in the act. Early in the game, after their first possession stalled deep in their own territory, Pitt punted but lineman Sam Palumbo, by now extremely hungry for red meat, bolted past all Pitt men in his way to block it. ND did not take advantage of the turnover and Pitt regained possession of the ball, albeit deeper in its own territory.

Deprived before the game of the services of their passing and receiving tandem, the Panthers went nowhere again and punted away, with John Petitbon returning it to the Pitt 32 yard line. Moments later, John Mazur threw to wide open Bill Barrett who scored the first touchdown. By this time, what passed for the Irish special teams department had begun experimenting with Minnie Mavraides as a kicker, and although he missed this extra point, he continued to kick for the team in the future, most notably in 1953.

Pitt threatened in the second quarter, marching as far as the ND 46 yard line, until defensive back John Lattner jumped on a loose ball, recovering it for his mates on offense. Mazur led the team downfield masterfully, culminating in another unmolested touchdown pass to Barrett, this time for 28 yards. Mavraides converted on this kick for the 13-0 lead.

Again Pitt answered with a decent drive but then their substitute quarterback Blair Kramer whipped a pass to his receiver just over midfield, only to be intercepted by John Lattner, acting as the team's defensive stopper that day.

In the glory days of the 1940s Leahy loved to stockpile star running backs and then dip into his depth each game by alternating fresh backs all game until the opposition invariably cracked. In 1950, he did not possess much depth and once Petitbon, Gay and Barrett went down for spells that year, he basically had to rely on Bob Williams' passing to salvage each game. In 1951, the coach had some of his veteran backs back and healthy, but he also had Lattner, Heap, Worden, Tom McHugh, Fran Paterra and a fellow named Paul Reynolds to send into the breach.

Little known today, Paul Reynolds was then an eighteen-year-old freshman halfback from Springfield (IL) Cathedral High School whom Frank Leahy began to call upon with increasing frequency. By the end of the schedule, he ran the ball with the second greatest frequency with 93 carries, with only Bull Worden surpassing him with an ungodly 181 rushes. Reynolds had only one less carry than John Lattner, Fran Paterra and Tom McHugh combined.

In a good way, there was always something different about Paul Reynolds. During Reynolds' young adulthood, Leahy and the assistants recruited scads of players from Illinois, mostly from Chicago's rich Catholic High League, but Reynolds came from downstate. It kept him a bit distant from the Chicago boys and in doing so, kept him out of any clique and, like Don Penza, popular and welcome with everyone.

When many of his teammates and classmates savored every bit of sleep they might get, Reynolds quite often arose at 5:00 a.m. to begin his studies. He laughed a lot despite his somewhat unassuming demeanor, and genuinely felt heartened every time one of his mates succeeded, whether in the classroom or before Leahy and the coaches. Once one of his teammates asked Reynolds if he had received any money on the side to attend Notre Dame, or received some type of reward during the season, to which Reynolds replied, "Only from one of these young kids in Springfield who sends me $10.00 every time I score a touchdown." Knowing Reynolds, he probably sent the money back to the youngster at the end of the year.

During his freshman year, he promised to make Lattner and Heap and the rest of his backfield mates the truly forgotten backs, running deceptively in scrimmages and in games. He darted past would-be tacklers who never got a direct tackle against him, only an arm or a leg. He had the ability to stop on a dime and accelerate back up again, another device to make defenders run past him and around him. Later on, Leahy placed him more on defense and then severe injuries marred his career; but in 1951, Paul Reynolds had the potential to win a Heisman or, at the least, cop All-American honors somewhere along the way.

With time running down in the second quarter, Reynolds redeemed the faith that the coaches placed in him by slashing for 11- and 20-yard runs to bring his team within twelve yards of another score. On the next play, quarterback John Mazur found Mutscheller who caught the pass and made it to the one yard line, after which Mazur sneaked it in for the touchdown and Mavraides kicked in his second extra point just before halftime.

John Petitbon fumbled the opening kickoff of the second half and after Pitt recovered, their offense drove the ball right down to the Irish 12 for a first down. There Leahy's lads held for three downs and when the Pitt quarterback Kramer faded back to pass, Huck O'Neil almost ripped his head apart, sacking him on the 20 yard line, as he left the field to his teammates on offense, as the Irish took over on downs.

The game see-sawed for a couple of possessions, until Mazur engineered an 80-yard touchdown drive, mosly through runs by Neil Worden and Paul Reynolds. Mazur plunged over the line of scrimmage for the team's fourth touchdown of the day. After that Mazur sat for the afternoon as talented freshmen Ralph Guglielmi and Tom Carey substituted for him.

Pitt could not get out of its own way and one of their last drives disintegrated after their quarterback threw another interception, his fourth of the day, this time to freshman linebacker, Dick Szymanski. Carey directed a garbage time drive for the final touchdown of the day, a thirteen

- yard dash by Joe Heap for a final victory margin of 33-0. Although the game had taken place in the afternoon, many of the Notre Dame players, even those who grew up in industrial areas, were surprised how dark the surrounding pollution made the field, with the waste of the steel mills creating a nocturnal atmosphere.

The win marked the high-water mark for John Mazur as the quarterback of his team. He had decimated a Pitt defense, seemingly at will, directing sustained and repeated drives into the end zone. Undoubtedly Pitt contributed mightily to its own demise, with its multiple turnovers, due largely to the absence of its starting quarterback. Now Mazur marched back as the Big Man on Campus, with Ralph Guglielmi and Tom Carey seemingly relegated to apprenticeship status with their game minutes coming only after victory had been assured. Leahy felt it was Mazur's finest game ever.

The victory brought the team into 12th place, slightly behind Cornell, in the UPI poll. Unfortunately, Varrichione became dinked up again, this time with a chip fracture in his ankle, so the guard position continued to plague the still very young team. Nursing some player injuries, the club took it easy as the week began, and on Monday, Coach Druze shared with the other coaches the fruits of his scouting of Purdue, a team that had lost some of its key backs to injury.

The scouting reports meant little to the seniors, players who had contributed to the National Championship team of 1949, only to lose the team's first game in over four years in the second game of the '50 season to Purdue. The players all knew about the wild celebrations in Lafayette, which rapturously ignited after the Irish's humiliation had come. This year's edition needed no Knute Rockne speech to prepare for Purdue, their motivation coming from within. Purdue also drilled their players hard, faced with the possibility that quarterback Dale Samuels might have to operate in the upcoming game with three new backs due to injuries to the starters.

In some ways the preparation for the Purdue game resembled that for Pitt, as the Irish again set up a hard scrimmage with the first team offense against the second team defense and vice versa after the relative peace of the film-viewing and team meeting at the Law School Auditorium (now the "Lounge") on Monday.

Although Leahy and his lads bitterly recalled losing to Purdue to end the unbeaten streak and reading about how the campus in downstate West Lafayette went berserk after mighty ND finally fell, the rivalry had taken on a whole added dimension. Other forces came into play, including the presence of many Chicago players from Purdue who nursed ancient grudges against the native city lads who, at their expense, won scholarships to ND instead of them. South Bend and Notre Dame authorities estimated the forthcoming arrival of 10,000 cars to the stadium parking lot, with several trains set up to wheel in fans from Lafayette, Indiana, not to mention the many centers of the ND subway alumni.

Even the Irish band director, H. Lee Hope joined the fray, introducing for the first time the Irish bagpipe players, explaining that he had gotten the idea of suiting up these performers after he saw some of Eire's own bagpipe players in the ranks of the British fusiliers, contending that Ireland had as much a claim to the bagpipes as Scotland. Correct or not, no Scotchmen came forward publicly to disagree with him, although strangely enough a minor controversy did briefly flare up, this is no joke, concerning what the bagpipers would wear under their kilts, but it quickly died away.

The student body also conspired to whip up a frenzy, scheduling a giant bonfire on the south side of campus, coinciding with the sophomore cotillion. Then came the contest itself, when the teams met again for an anticipated pay-back for last year's debacle.

Even with an eager squad, Leahy could not get his men to score in the first period, with Purdue similarly blanked. In the second period, the Irish drove the ball from their own 25 yard line mostly on the running efforts of Paul Reynolds and Neil Worden. Adjusting to the Irish running the ball down their defenders' throats, the Purdue coaches parked nine men on their front line. Making a small change himself, Mazur completed a pass to end Chet Ostrowski, who ran it all the way down to the Purdue nine yard line.

On successive runs, Reynolds and Worden drove the ball for six more yards. On third down, Mazur faked a hand-off to fullback Worden and then slid the ball to Reynolds who ran the ball into the end zone for a touchdown. Minnie Mavraides P.A.T. increased the score to 7-0, which is where matters stood until halftime.

In the third period, taking advantage of an ND fumble, Purdue attempted a field goal from the Irish 41 yard line, which their kicker Jim Reichert very surprisingly made, this in an era when very often even chip-shot extra points did not go through the uprights. After Notre Dame fumbled again, Purdue's star quarterback Dale Samuels exploited the situation by promptly throwing a 43-yard touchdown pass to his receiver, Darrel Brewster. Typically, Dale Samuels failed to convert, yet still Purdue led 9-7.

Minnie Mavraides put the Irish in front soon thereafter, with a field goal of his own, memorable for being the only field goal scored by the Irish that year (they failed to make any in 1952).

The redoubtable Samuels guided his Boilermakers right

back, but committed a critical error when Dan Shannon intercepted his pass on the ND 26 yard line. Mainly through runs by Lattner and Worden, the Irish then marched over mid-field. There the drive seemed to stall on the Purdue 40 yard line on fourth and inches. Here, John Mazur handed off to John Lattner who found a huge hole in the line opened up by tackle Bob Toneff and end Jim Mutscheller and, after fighting off three Purdue tacklers, ran for a touchdown.

Uncharacteristically, Purdue seemed to die rather meekly. Joe Heap had some more good runs late in the game, after he "replaced" Paul Reynolds at left halfback. Billy Barrett ran for a touchdown and Mazur completed a pass to Mutscheller for another as the Irish cruised to a 30-9 defeat of the Boilermakers. The universe made sense to coaches and players, alumni and subway alumni alike. Jerry Groom, captain of the '50 Irish, was avenged.

Sid and Doyle

FEDORA IN HAND, chain-smoking Charlie Callahan charged into the Sports Information office at Breen-Phillips to complete another week's press release for the Fighting Irish football team. A tall drink of water with slicked back black hair, he resembled nothing as much as a walking ironing board. Each Monday evening, Charlie and his staff assistants folded 1,800 copies of his media releases for writers and newspaper editors throughout the United States, sending the whole collection out by mail that evening in order to build up the public's interest in the team and provide a lazy writer enough of a start for a column or article in his paper.

Although Charlie passed Boston, Massachusetts, off as his home town and affected a broad Boston accent when called upon for effect, he actually grew up in the country in Lexington, the location of the first battle of the Revolutionary War, where someone, either a nervous minuteman or a British soldier, fired the "shot heard around the world." Charlie's upbringing had more in common with fishing all day by the local brook than a street-wise adolescence on a bustling street in a quaint urban neighborhood.

Yet whether he came from an urban Irish neighborhood or a quaint Yankee enclave, Charlie's life seemed to start at the University of Notre Dame, where he enrolled as a freshman in 1934.

Terrific writers such as Arch Ward, Ray Fitzgerald and

171

Joe Doyle trained at Notre Dame en route to careers as newspaper columnists, yet Charlie wanted to stay on the campus he loved, spreading the gospel of Elmer Layden or Frank Leahy or whoever else happened to be coaching the football team at the time. Assuming the position of the Director of Sports Information in the late 1940s, his proselytizing began at the pinnacle of the Leahy regime.

A disorganized soul, Charlie used to scrawl his notes and reminders to himself on an envelope, which he shoved in his pocket and rarely scanned again. His best work occurred in bars and taverns, where he might sit down with a writer, become his friend and preach the news of his beloved school. He only drank Miller beer, in honor of Fred Miller, the president of the brewery and frequent visitor to Cartier Field.

Unfailingly polite, he found equal time to speak to a reporter from a small Indiana town as well as the head writer in the largest dailies in New York, Chicago, Washington or Los Angeles. He loved to talk, could not write very well and often spoke to people late at night, always calling collect. He once called Cleveland Browns' quarterback and former Notre Dame reserve George Ratterman collect and after Ratterman accepted the charges for the call, Callahan informed him that "I am glad you took my call, because John Lujack didn't take my call to him and you are now the greatest quarterback in history."

Even Charlie Callahan could not make George Ratterman the finest signal-caller ever, but he did approach his SID duties passionately. It was his dream job and Charlie Callahan was living the dream.

Similarly, at the *South Bend Tribune*, Joe Doyle had grad-

uated from Notre Dame in 1949 and walked right into the
Trib's news room as a sportswriter, a job he still has not
relinquished over sixty years later. Born in Shullsburg,
Wisconsin, Joe had farmed, helped run a gas station and
navigated air planes during World War Two before he got
paid for what he enjoyed doing—writing about sports. Doyle
came to Notre Dame almost by accident, much like Frank
Leahy himself, but unlike the Old Man, Doyle never left
South Bend.

With one exception. In the early 1980s, Joe left to work
in Florida, a move that seemingly segued into a retirement
eventually for him. Trouble was, Joe Doyle was not the re-
tiring type and Florida did not suit him long term. He had a
home and to South Bend he returned, still penning columns
well into the twenty-first century.

Although a loyal alumnus of Notre Dame just like Charlie Callahan, Doyle's first loyalty was to the *South Bend
Tribune*, a fine paper in a city on the brink of becoming a rust
belt casualty. He might root for the Irish to win, but he had
to comment upon people, places and things he did not like
and could not let the paper serve as a propaganda rag for
Notre Dame. It was a more interesting job than Callahan's
anyway, because Joe could write about the Cubs, or Big Ten
football or the local high school sports at any time he wished.
An interstate rivalry such as Purdue/Notre Dame allowed
him to kill two birds with one stone in his sports coverage, but in the upcoming game against the Naval Academy,
Doyle focused on his Irish.

Having avenged themselves against Purdue, the Fighting Irish drilled intensely on Wednesday and Thursday

before their next game against Navy. Notre Dame officially had no classes on November 1 in order to observe All
Saints Day, a Holy Day of Obligation on the Church's cal-
endar, and to honor this sacred day, Frank Leahy scheduled
an "earlier and longer" practice than the day before.

The school had chosen this game to let its students take a
road trip to see a game, so five hundred young men and the
Marching Band got on a train for Washington, D.C., presumably to give the voyage at least the veneer of a field trip to
the nation's capital before arrangements were made to see the
game in Baltimore. On Friday at 9:00 a.m., the team itself
flew to Baltimore for the game and a respite from the recent
practice drudgery.

The games between the Naval Academy and Notre
Dame during this era vaguely resemble the contests of today,
gentlemanly affairs in comparison, at the conclusion of which
the Irish players salute the contributions that the Middies
make to protecting our country. In the early '50s, they more
closely resembled slugfests. At one of the Monday afternoon
team meetings at the Law School one year, Leahy warned
his lads, "Navy plays gutter football, they can get down and
are not afraid to get dirty," and he never changed his mind
while he coached. Adding to the mayhem, it had rained for
three days before the game, causing Joe Doyle to rechristen
Babe Ruth Stadium the "land of a thousand puddles."

Few coaches at Our Lady's University had issues with
their football players hitting the opposition hard and frequently, but there was an aversion to assignments not producing the desired results and no scoring occurring on
offense. The coaches had to endure many such lapses until

nearly ten minutes had elapsed in the second quarter. Starting just shy of midfield, the offense kicked in a bit, and then Neil Worden ran a "delayed buck" that bailed out Mazur and resulted in a 36-yard touchdown. Lost in the statistics of a very successful first year at fullback was the fact that Worden had not scored a touchdown since his four-score effort against Indiana to start the season.

Mavraides' extra point failed, but soon after Navy regained possession of the ball on the kickoff, they coughed up the ball to Irish defensive halfbacks Dan Shannon and Dave Flood. With time running down in the half, Billy Barrett ran the ball all the way down to the Navy one yard line, and on the next play Mazur bootlegged it in for another touchdown. This time Mavraides converted and the teams dispersed into their locker rooms at halftime.

The Irish played stellar defense in the first half, with Navy massing "a minus three yards in rushing and only two first downs." Under these circumstances, the Irish should have been rolling up the points, and yet they stalled too often, relying on the Worden run and the fumble recovery for their points. Navy made up for its lack of talent with some brutal defensive hitting, paying particular attention to roughing up John Mazur.

After one series on offense, quarterback Mazur returned to his team's sidelines with his face shrouded in blood. Frank Leahy went right into action, yelling out, "Hughie, get me the smelling salts, get me the smelling salts!" The team trainer, Hugh Burns, darted right off to rummaging for the smelling salts, sensing an urgency in Leahy's voice to assist his battered starting QB, and as soon as he located the magic restorative, he ran it right over to Leahy who thanked him. Rather than administer the smelling salts to a woozy Mazur though, Leahy unscrewed the cap of the bottle, stuck it under his nose and snorted in the strong vapors until he felt better, all the time with Mazur lurking about and continuing to bleed.

It might warm some hearts to think that Leahy tore into his lads at halftime, and thus inspired, they demonstrated to Navy all the intricacies of the split-T with lethal intent and results. Instead the Navy defense continued to shut them down. In fact, Navy turned up the pressure with a new quarterback in the second half. On one drive the Midshipmen ran the ball down to the Irish 10, but on the next play their back fumbled and Irish junior linebacker Jack Alessandrini jumped on the ball to kill their drive.

Nothing much else happened in the third quarter, while in the fourth, ND scored for the final time that day, when Billy Barrett ran back a punt from his own 24 yard line for a touchdown, aided greatly by a "crushing block thrown by Shannon." Navy made one last ditch drive late in the fourth, thanks to a successful fake punt, but the Irish defense stopped them one foot short of a touchdown at game's end.

The game marked the final highlight in the career of John Mazur. Even with a superbly talented Ralph Guglielmi vying for increased playing time, Mazur to date was well on his way to being immortalized, like later quarterbacks such as John Huarte and Kevin McDougal, as one of the greatest "one year" signal callers in team history. With four games left in the season, he stood poised to lead his men back from a .500 record to national championship recognition, with a little help from some losses from other programs.

Sporting a 5-1 record, the Irish contingent flew out of Baltimore and girded for a game in East Lansing against powerful Michigan State.

Who Forgot the Holy Water?

EVEN BEFORE THE NAVY GAME, bad blood began to flow between Leahy's staff and the Michigan State Athletic Director, Ralph Young. As part of a continuum involving controversies surrounding the Irish football program, the Spartans' AD asked Johnny Druze to leave the press box before a game between MSU and Pittsburgh. The uncomfortable confrontation sprang from an interpretation of the rules both schools subscribed to concerning the number of occasions a team's official representative might scout a future opponent.

Under the Western Athletic Conference rules adhered to by both universities, a limit of three official scouting trips during one season existed. Clearly, before the incident occurred, Druze or a colleague had made two official trips up to the press box to see the Spartans and in one game had bought a ticket and viewed a game from the stands like any spectator, in what the Irish termed a "busman's holiday."

Ralph Young disagreed, figuring Frank Leahy did not let any of his staff take holidays to watch a game during the season and that since he ruled the roost, he made certain that Druze watched his fourth game against the Irish rival from the stands.

Moose Krause protested immediately and loudly, and considerable logic backed him up. If Young let Druze watch

179

the fourth MSU game of the year from the stands, then by extension it was okay to watch a game from the stands and not the press box. If it was fine for Druze to watch a game from the stands, then he could have done so every game MSU played that year, and Young had no argument in opposition. The three games for a scout only counted if the game was viewed from the loftier perch of the press box.

On a legal level, Druze should have been permitted to watch the last game from the press box, but legalities increasingly meant little to Leahy or his opponents. Jealous of his success and suspicious of his motives, opposing coaches and ADs had for years suspected that Leahy either broke rules or bent them beyond recognition. A phrase that accelerated off the lips of Leahy's detractors with each year was "the spirit of the rule."

In that more nebulous area, Leahy might argue he did not violate the regulation while members of the press or the opponent's administration increasingly argued that he did. Sending Druze on a "busman's holiday" fooled no one, it simply provided him with the occasion to potentially see the other team over and over. Young overreacted, but in his frustration, he spoke for many who came across Leahy, and in the '40s when Leahy won all of the time, the complaints largely elicited little empathy, dismissed as the whining of the defeated, loser's laments. Once Leahy started to lose, his interpretation of the rules became more of a public issue, an issue not helped when some of his players quit the team and transferred to other programs across the country. They took with them the play book and the bag of tricks.

Of course calmer administrators prevailed, mainly because each university wanted to keep the series alive, but it did nothing to staunch the flow of folks complaining about Frank Leahy and the spirit of the rules. After so many trips to see the Spartans, the Irish should have had a good report on them and come prepared to systematically defeat them. The reports may have passed muster, but the execution did not.

The team went from the land of a thousand puddles to blizzard conditions back in South Bend for much of the week. The practices unfolded almost exclusively indoors with some of the team at the Field House while others went to the Navy Drill Hall and quite literally walked through practice on the cement surfaced Drill Hall floors.

Biggie Munn and his Spartan players had to practice under similar conditions, but their team needed the practice a lot less, having a much more veteran-laden roster and having already humbled Michigan by 25-0. The most impressive work of the week may not have been conducted by players or coaches, but rather the Michigan State student body, who had to clear the stadium and field of almost a foot of accumulated snow.

As described by Ed Burns of the *Chicago Tribune*, "Hundreds of students and a paid crew of 150 worked throughout last night and into the day to shovel 11 inches of snow off the playing field and stands of Macklin Stadium." ROTC candidates and Physical Education students got time off from class to pitch in, while at some point bulldozers came into play to clean up the mess before the game.

None of the Notre Dame players witnessed this as they blissfully prepared for the game. Or as Bob Taylor observed more eloquently, "We flew to the Navy and Pitt games. What a way to travel, comfortable chairs and good looking stewardesses...Tomorrow in the game, I sure hope we win it.

We have Mass at 7:00 Saturday morning and then at 9:00 we leave for Lansing on the train."

Once in East Lansing, the team was transported from the station to the stadium, where they entered the locker room and prepared for the game. In addition to attending Mass before games, the team also brought along Holy Water to away tiffs, and each player and coach dipped his fingers into the blessed water and generally made a Sign of the Cross on his chest before running out onto the field.

Except this week someone forgot the Holy Water and apparently they did not have a priest in the vicinity to bail them out, a point made by a frazzled Coach Bill Earley, who whisked Frank Leahy into a bathroom to deliver the bad news. The coaches both thought they were alone, but unbeknownst to them, Minnie Mavraides had seated himself in a stall and overheard their entire animated conversation.

Pondering the unfortunate situation for ten or fifteen seconds in silence, Leahy finally spoke. "Ooooh Coach Earley," Leahy said in his half-brogue, "get a pail of tap water and tell the lads it is Holy Water, they'll never know the difference!" Which is what Bill Earley proceeded to do, and initially only Mavraides knew the better, and he kept the secret until after the game.

The ruse did little good as a flat squad went out and got shut out 35-0, for the "worst defeat ever suffered by a Frank Leahy-coached football team," and one of the half-dozen worst drubbings in past school history.

The game ended early. In the absence of Holy Water, one of the Irish assistant coaches had a more concrete instruction to make to one of his players, middle linebacker Dick Szymanski. On the sidelines, just before kick-off, the coach sidled up to the linebacker and grabbed his shoulder pads, ordering him, "On their first offensive play, I want you to smash the center in the mouth as hard as you can. AS HARD AS YOU CAN, UNDERSTAND!" Szymanski understood, but pointed out to his coach that if he did so, the referees might eject him from the game. "Do it," the coach replied, "or I'm benching you."

After Michigan State ran back the opening kickoff only to their 12 yard line and brought their offense on, Dick Szymanski lined up against their center, and after the ball was hiked, threw a punch so hard against the center that Szymanski almost fell down from the follow through of the blow. When Szymanski peered heavenwards, he saw only sky as MSU's back, Dick Panin went right past where the Irish linebacker was supposed to defend, on his way to an 88-yard touchdown run from scrimmage. Safety John Petitbon, the fastest Irish player with the possible exception of Joe Heap and Dave Flood, doggedly scooted after Panin and made a last desperate unsuccessful dive at him.

Parenthetically, later that week, back in South Bend, the entire student body was treated to a Movietone film clip of the play, and Bob Toneff kept yelling, "Get him John, get him!" In the film version, John Petitbon did not catch Dick Panin either.

The game just got uglier, with Notre Dame never getting past the Spartans' 30 yard line, then only on a late drive engineered by Ralph Guglielmi, who sometime during the game overtook poor John Mazur as the number one quarterback on the Notre Dame depth chart. Indeed, the *Scholastic* concluded that "One of the few bright spots for Notre Dame was the emergence of Guglielmi as a topflight quarterback.

The first-year signal caller put on the best display of the afternoon for the Irish as he led the team during the third and fourth periods."

It was not all Mazur's fault. Spartan coach Biggie Munn had planned all week to run trick plays and shifts and his players executed them to perfection, accumulating a remarkable 465 yards of total offense and 21 first downs. Still, had Irish offense answered back effectively in the first half, the rout might have been partially contained, and when Guglielmi played well in the second half, he played better than Mazur had. If only Bill Earley had remembered to bring the Holy Water.

By the beginning of the next week, Frank Leahy had begun to openly question retaining John Mazur as his starting quarterback. In a conversation with the *South Bend Tribune*'s Joe Doyle, Leahy lamented, "Oooh Joe, what are they saying about us?"

Doyle got right to the point, "If Mazur has a bad day, we're going to get the hell beat out of us!"

Leahy figured as much. Mazur had waited patiently for his turn and had never given anyone trouble, but he simply did not possess the leadership skills and the same level of natural athletic talent as Ralph Guglielmi. Googs needed seasoning, but after the Michigan State debacle, he need never worry again about getting experience, starting with the team's next opponent, the North Carolina Tar Heels.

Guglielmi Promoted to First String by Leahy

DAYS LATER, Frank Leahy was still nonplussed, moaning, "I'm still at a loss as to why we did so poorly against Michigan State." In part this was just Leahy being Leahy, as he had begun to lose faith in his starting quarterback, a feeling he tangibly acted upon during the following week as Ralph Guglielmi and Tom Carey began to work out with the first team on a very pronounced basis.

The practices reflected Leahy's frustration, with an offense/defense scrimmage on Tuesday and a particularly rough Wednesday scrimmage, causing at least one significant Irish casualty, Billy Barrett. Certainly, Barrett put up with a lot and during this practice, backs coach Bill Earley called out a play "43 on 3" which featured the small back going through the line at a certain point. Since everyone on the defensive side of the ball had heard the play, Barrett got clobbered at the point of attack. Again and again Earley rang out the same play and on each occasion the back predictably got hammered. Finally, on the fourth call of the same play, Barrett got crushed under a heap of defenders and this time he did not get up.

Emergency workers came onto the field and a number of Barrett's teammates, George Hubbard being one of them, helped lift him onto a stretcher and then into the ambulance for transport to the hospital. Hubbard did not believe that Barrett had been knocked out, he simply felt that his teammate had reached his limit and had no stomach for running into a meat grinder any longer.

The press reported that Barrett "was taken to St. Joseph Hospital for the X-rays, then returned to his room on campus..." The doctors officially diagnosed an ankle sprain, certainly not the type of injury to warrant an emergency trip. The coaches seemed to conclude that they had a gold brick on their hands. By the time he returned to his room, Barrett may or may not have appreciated that fact—that his career at Notre Dame had just ended.

Barrett had his problems but a healthy John Mazur had issues of his own, and as the team flew from South Bend to Carolina for the next game, Frank Leahy had decided to start Ralph Guglielmi at quarterback, this despite the absence of banged-up veterans Barrett and John Petitbon in the backfield.

At Chapel Hill on November 17, the new-look Irish made their debut with Guglielmi and Tom Carey taking most of the snaps from center and John Mazur gaining cameo credits, almost completing the way for the Irish to introduce their youth movement against the then 2-6 North Carolina team. One subtext had the Tar Heels revved up to save the job of their beleaguered coach Carl Snavely with the other being the Irish attempting to revive from one of their worst losses ever. Or as Arch Ward of the *Chicago Tribune* put it, "Tar Heels are determined to win for their gray haired, dour faced leader, Carl Snavely, who is under alumni fire." Winning one for the "gray haired, dour faced leader" hardly had the inspirational ring of "Win one for the Gipper."

The game itself, a dull affair with moments of terror, had the Irish tallying touchdowns in the second quarter on a run by Paul Reynolds and in the third with a four-yard rush by Neil Worden. Ralph Guglielmi and Tom Carey each orchestrated a scoring drive while John Mazur had much less luck in his stints, completing only one of six passes with one interception. Sam Palumbo and Dick Szymanski won kudos from the media for their tackling prowess.

Poor Mazur actually came off worse than even these weak statistics indicate, as he killed one drive in which Tom Carey had led the Irish down to the Tar Heel 15 yard line, most recently having just completed a pass to Paul Reynolds. Inexplicably, Leahy interrupted this momentum by inserting Mazur back in as quarterback, and the senior threw three straight incompletions; after Mavraides' field goal attempt failed, the Irish ceded the field to their opponent. On another occasion, Ralph Guglielmi had led the Irish to the North Carolina 18 yard line, at which point Leahy trotted Mazur out again. The senior quarterback promptly threw an interception that the opposing back ran to the ND 46 yard line. From there, the Tar Heels then marched the ball into the end zone to cut the Irish lead to 12-7.

As prophesied by Joe Doyle, the Irish were getting the hell beat out of them by allowing Mazur in there on a bad day. Late in the game, the Tar Heels almost made Leahy pay for his unusual coaching decisions with their offense driving down to the Irish 7 yard line. Underrated back Gene Carrabine intercepted the pass by UNC quarterback Connie Gravitte. But the Tar Heels were not finished and with less than two minutes left in the fourth quarter, they regained possession and had again driven the ball deep into

ND territory. Fortunately, Johnny Lattner intercepted another Gravitte pass on his own 29 to save the day. The Irish
had survived.

Approximately five hundred fans came from South Bend
to see the game, and captain Jim Mutscheller received an 88-
foot telegram before the game expressing the student body's
best wishes with the name of each student typed in. Largely, when the Irish defense had to step up, it did, and "[t]he
44,525 spectators saw a preview of the Irish squad for the
following two years." With one exception, the *Scholastic* had
the wrong back of the future joining Lattner and Worden,
in Paul Reynolds.

As soon as the team's DC 6 landed on the tarmac back
in South Bend, Frank Leahy went about bemoaning the fate
of his team, which after all, had just won a game away from
home the week after a terrible shellacking: "You know, by
now everyone knows that we can be had," proclaimed Leahy
to the assembled press.

Having just dispatched with a Tar Heel team led by a
head coach on the hot seat, the Irish faced another such situation the next Saturday against Iowa and its own dead man
walking, Coach Leonard Raffensperger. Leahy ran the lads
hard on Tuesday, but went relatively easy on them the remainder of the week, including Thanksgiving Day. For the
first time in a half dozen years, the Irish faced a home game
with the possibility of empty seats.

The key implementation this week by Leahy was a
4-7 defense, whereby the front four practiced chasing the
Hawkeye quarterback while the other seven defenders
drifted back with the receivers. Had Leahy installed this
defense against SMU, the Irish may have won, but against

Iowa, the coach realistically feared a loss so he instituted this defensive change. He also elevated sophomore back Bobby Joseph to the first team kicker slot.

Had Bobby Joseph made a compromise here or an allowance there, he might have become the Ziggy Czarobski of the 1950s, a beloved Irish comedian who made Leahy's demanding practices a bit more bearable and even managed to burrow a small area into the aloof head coach's heart. Sadly, it was not to be, Bobby could needle people with the best of them, but somehow lacked Czarobski's rare wit and ability to make people laugh at themselves with good humor.

Plus, he tended to get on Coach Leahy's nerves. On one occasion Joseph had just made a nice tackle or had run off a number of yards on a run and Leahy raced across the field to see who had accomplished the feat. Generally, on those types of plays, Leahy complimented the player or at least excoriated the other players who had not executed their assignments properly. When an assistant told Leahy that Bobby Joseph had performed brilliantly in the play, the Old Man simply said, "Oh," clicked his heels and walked away.

Yet when the Irish returned home for their then annual game against Iowa, it was Bobby Joseph whom Leahy called upon on two critical occasions to save the team from their third defeat of the year. On November 24, 1951, it was the small back's day to wake up the echoes.

The Hawkeyes were not a good team in 1951, and yet they always played ND tough, and this year proved no exception. Iowa offensive stars Burt Britzmann and Bill Reichart ran rings around the Irish defense so much so that by halftime, the Hawkeyes led the Irish in South Bend by 14-6.

The Irish, utilizing some changes on defense suggested

by their coaches during halftime, instituted the 4-7 alignment on defense and they began to slow Iowa down, but not
enough as the Hawkeyes shifted from the pass to the run
and closed the third with an even wider lead, 20-6. Only a
Bob Toneff block on the extra point try kept the game within
two touchdowns for the Irish.

It seemed to matter little in the fourth quarter until Ralph
Guglielmi began throwing passes all over the place, reinvig-
orating the offense with a 31-yard bomb to Paul Reynolds
and a 44-yard completion to Lattner to the Iowa five yard
line. Lattner then broke through for the score with Bobby
Joseph making the crucial extra point.

Iowa took over after the kickoff but the ND defense held
them, forcing the punt. Guglielmi came back in but took
two quick sacks, causing Leahy to bring back Mazur, who
completed a 15-yard pass to Lattner, bringing on a fourth
down and long. At this juncture, time running down and
ten yards to go for a first down, Leahy ordered John Lattner
in to punt the ball away. In general, Leahy did not run his
team as a democracy, but once the team huddled up, Bob
Toneff voiced a dissenting opinion concerning what Lattner
should do, instructing the young punter, "You aren't gonna
punt!"

Now there was a Catch 22 if there ever was one: either
disobey the coach and potentially lose his scholarship or flout
Toneff's wishes and risk having his head ripped off. Captain Jim Mutscheller made it a little bit easier, opining, "We
might as well try it John." That was all John Lattner had to
hear. Taking the long snap from center, he held the ball behind his back and faked the kick. Seeing Mutscheller free,

he lobbed the ball to him, with the pigskin not flying in a perfect spiral, but rather floating end over end to the open end. Mutscheller secured it and ran it to his own 45 yard line for the first down. When Lattner ran back to the sideline, Frank Leahy said nothing to him about disobeying a direct order.

Interestingly enough, in his syndicated column the next week, Leahy (or more likely his ghost writer) actually appropriated credit for making this gutsy call: "It was the first time that we used this play and Lattner...[carried] out his most important assignment of a very busy day." Of course, had Lattner not completed the pass to Mutscheller, Frank Leahy never would have taken "credit" for making the call and John Lattner would have suffered greatly in the week ahead.

From there, Leahy alternated Guglielmi and Mazur on the last drive and both quarterbacks contributed to driving the ball down the field. Mazur saw end Chet Ostrowski in the end zone and telegraphed the ball to him, even though he had to battle double coverage. The pass failed, but the referee called interference on one of the Hawkeye defenders, which brought the ball down to the Iowa 1 yard line. From there, Lattner rushed it in and Bobby Joseph punctuated the comeback with another successful extra point kick to bring the Irish to a 20-20 tie with Iowa, which is how the score stood as the game ended.

It had been a close call, with Notre Dame lucky to have pulled out the tie at home against a less talented club. Iowa almost always played well against the Irish during this era, and while Bobby Joseph saved the day, Frank Leahy did not leave the stadium a happy man, although he intimated that Bobby Joseph "may have gained travel accommodations to California Saturday because of his dramatic kick."

Frank Leahy was not the only dissatisfied person in the football program. Ray Bubick, the genial tackle from South Bend Riley High School, had taken more than his expected lumps as a developing tackle. He fervently felt that Leahy embarrassed one of his lads in front of his peers as a motivational technique, and in many cases it worked as desired. In other instances, like Bubick's own, he did not respond to pointed and open criticism in a positive manner and his game suffered as a result.

Not that he got into many games. The Irish coaches had settled on a youth movement, as on the interior defensive line for instance, transfer Huck O'Neil anchored a contingent of first year players, Fred Mangialardi, Sam Palumbo, Jack Lee and Bob Ready. On offense, Bob Toneff set the tone for talented youngsters Frank Varrichione, Jim Schrader and Joe Bush.

The lack of playing time did not bother Bubick the most though. He started having nightmares of his line coach Bob McBride, with increasing frequency, not surprisingly since his waking hours after practice became noteworthy for the punishment he sustained trying to block his coach. Trying to tough it out, he told no one of his problems with the exception of the popular end Don Penza.

As much as McBride bothered him, in the end Frank Leahy himself pushed Bubick too far, with his chewing him out in front of the team and the seeming lack of any compassion for him.

Finally when he felt overwhelmed and no longer

equipped to endure the stress, he checked himself into the campus infirmary. He had not slept at all for several nights, and his lack of rest only worsened his performance before an ever-demanding coach; it interfered with everything. Football wasn't fun, nothing was fun. The spell in the infirmary temporarily made matters better, but the issues that created the necessity to get away did not go away. The season had nearly ended, but that never provided an athlete under Leahy a nine-month reprieve. At most, one got the time between the final game ending and the Feast of the Immaculate Conception on December 8 for a respite. Then, for Bubick at least, the winter practices began, with plenty of blocking at the hand-ball courts with Bob McBride in charge.

1953 Notre Dame Undefeated Football Team

FIRST ROW, left to right: Fred Mangialardi, Art Hunter, Tom McHugh, Rockne Mornasey, John Lattner, Bob Rigali, Art Nowack, Capt. Don Penza, Neil Worden, Jim Schrader, Bob Martin, Paul Reba, Merril Mavrades, Armando Galardo, Joe Buzz. SECOND ROW: John Jamol (Mgr.), Tom Gaffney, Bob Taylor, Gene Kapish, Jim Mense, Dick Keller, Nick Raich, Ralph Guglielmi, Don Shannon, Dick Frasor, Paul Matz, Tom Carey, Dick Szymanski, Joe Heap, Walt Cabral, Sar Hammer (Associate Mgr.). THIRD ROW: Charles Keller (Associate Mgr.), Wayne Edmonds, Leo Callaghan, Bill Tiazzo, Bob Teach, Ed Cook, Dick Hardrick, Don Zujaski, Tony Pasquesi, Sam Palumbo, Dan Bucci, Frank Varrichione, Pat Bisceglia, Joe Lee, Bob Ready. FOURTH ROW: Gene Morrell, Joe Markowski, Don Schaefer, Jim Bigelow, Mike Regan, Bill Schellena, Dick Washington, Jack Bumo, Ray Lemee, John McMillan, George Nicola, Don George, John Kegoy, George Wilson.

1953 Team photo.

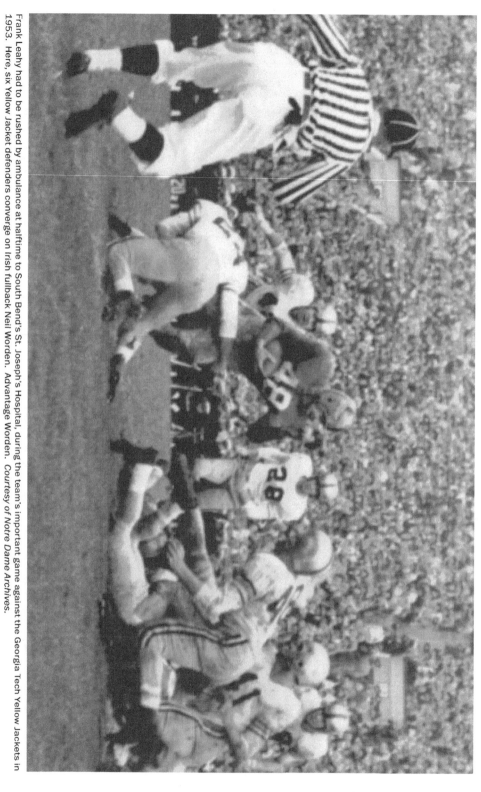

Frank Leahy had to be rushed by ambulance at halftime to South Bend's St. Joseph's Hospital, during the team's important game against the Georgia Tech Yellow Jackets in 1953. Here, six Yellow Jacket defenders converge on Irish fullback Neil Worden. Advantage Worden. *Courtesy of Notre Dame Archives.*

Frank Leahy. By his mid-forties, Leahy had noticeably aged beyond his years, causing most of his lads to call him the Old Man. *Courtesy of Notre Dame Sports Information Department.*

Dan Shannon is about to catch his second touchdown pass of the afternoon as he helps preserve his team's undefeated record in the closing seconds of the 1953 Iowa game. At the extreme left of the photo is teammate Wayne Edmonds, who was brought in to replace one of his "injured teammates." *Courtesy of Notre Dame Archives.*

Tackles Coach Bob McBride. A tough taskmaster, McBride developed some of the most talented linemen ever to don a Notre Dame jersey. *Courtesy of Notre Dame Archives.*

Fr. Charles McCarragher, who became the Prefect of Discipline at Notre Dame in the early '50s. Some of the young men at ND got along with him, but for most, "Black Mac" seemed like a fellow who enjoyed his job a bit too much. *Courtesy of Notre Dame Archives.*

On the Texas sideline in 1952, Frank Leahy looks like the Man in the Yellow Hat while speaking to Neil Worden, as teammate Ralph Guglielmi keeps on his game helmet while others, like Tom Carey in the lower left hand corner wear their pith helmets, purchased that morning. *Courtesy of Notre Dame Archives.*

Senior year roommates John Lattner (l) and Tom McHugh (r) enjoy a laugh in their dorm room. *Courtesy of Notre Dame Sports Information Department.*

Little remembered today, Paul Reynolds in 1951 carried the ball more than any other back except Neil Worden. On defense in 1952, he knocked down Oklahoma's final desperation pass to the end zone to preserve the Irish upset. *Courtesy of Notre Dame Sports Information Department.*

The starting offensive line-up in 1953. The backfield is the only one in collegiate history to have all of its backs develop into first round NFL draft choices, while the line formed the nucleus of a group that produced six players who had subsequent NFL careers of nine years or more. *Courtesy of Notre Dame Sports Information Department.*

Sensing doom, Fred Miller and Bernie Crimmins recruited Neil Worden to Notre Dame in the spring of 1950. He could not play in 1950, but he formed the keystone arch to the rebuilding of the program after the disastrous '50 campaign. *Courtesy of Notre Dame Sports Information Department.*

Jack McAllister headed the Notre Dame football team's equipment division and zealously protected damaged gear so that it could be recycled year in and year out. His quick thinking during half-time of the Georgia Tech game in 1953 may have saved Frank Leahy's life. *Courtesy of Notre Dame Archives.*

Although Roger Valdisseri is the best know. Sports Information Director in Notre Dame history, Charlie Callahan made the position perhaps the most effective source for projecting a positive image of Notre Dame and its athletes. With him is his secretary Jo Papa and student assistants Tom Welly (holding phone) and Jack Sand (sitting in the back). *Courtesy of Notre Dame Archives*

Woody Hayes wanted Ralph Guglielmi to be the starting quarterback at Ohio State, as did most of the major football programs in America, but Frank Leahy got him, in part because Guglielmi's grandmother trusted the Old Man. *Courtesy of Notre Dame Sports Information Department.*

John Lattner, All-American. Perhaps the most modest of Irish superstars ever, Lattner's body was a coordinated whole which could permit him to do virtually anything he wanted to on the football field, a symphony of athleticism. *Courtesy of Notre Dame Sports Information Department.*

At the Champions' Fete at the conclusion of the 1953 season, Don Penza to the left and Neil Worden to the right seemingly ignore their dates as they undoubtedly recall some of the critical moments of the past season. *Courtesy of Notre Dame Archives.*

Only two players in the history of Notre Dame football have ended their careers with at least 1,000 yards in rushing and 1,000 yards in pass receiving. Rocket Ismail is one of them, the other is Joe Heap, pictured here. *Courtesy of Notre Dame Sports Information Department.*

John, Paul, George...and Pete Best? In this photograph, taken circa 1951, the future Forgotten Four backfield is almost in place with, from left to right, Ralph Guglielmi, John Lattner, Paul Reynolds and Neil Worden. This looked like the backfield of the future until Reynolds' engineering degree commitments and injuries marred his career, as Joe Heap ascended in his stead. *Courtesy of Notre Dame Sports Information Department.*

Hollywood

WHILE RAY BUBICK sat in the infirmary, wondering how something once so rewarding had developed into a miserable job, his teammates learned whether they would travel with the team to Los Angeles to play Southern Cal or stay home and try to find a television to watch the first coast to coast live college football game broadcast. For those flying west, those lucky young men received tickets to an event akin to a paid vacation to see the stars in Hollywood, or at least catch some sun.

Not all of the usual suspects made the trip out west. Billy Barrett, the back who had battled ailments all year, had seemingly recovered from the most aggravating of his injuries and had even played well in the scrimmage leading up to the final game. He had every reason to anticipate having a wonderful sunny trip to California, punctuated hopefully by a last great game as a graduating senior, only to learn that he had not earned a spot on the travel team. The starting halfback for the Notre Dame Fighting Irish at the beginning of the season, a monogram winner and member of a national championship team, Barrett seemingly had to spend his last day as a player back in South Bend, Indiana, cheering on his friends from afar.

Everybody on the team buzzed with the news concerning the absence of Barrett: one commonly heard, "Where's

Billy? Why didn't Leahy put him on the travel team?" The travel teams in the early 1950s, especially in airplanes, stayed relatively low in numbers and Leahy had calculated that his young backs stood a far better chance against SC's defense than little Billy Barrett, and even if they did not, they represented the future. So Jack McAllister did not include a jersey for Barrett, as budding star Joe Heap packed his bags and headed out west.

There was another reason, many suspected. Some of the freshmen and sophomores regarded Barrett as fragile, a deadly reputation to tag on a player. Undoubtedly, little Barrett had sat on the sidelines or the infirmary with tweaks and bruises throughout just about every area of his body, and Leahy may have concluded himself that his back was injury prone, or worse, not tough enough. The *Chicago Tribune* had reported as recently as November 29 that Trainer Hugh Burns had pronounced Barrett "ready" for the upcoming game.

If Leahy and his staff felt that Barrett lacked guts, they missed a great part of the past two years, when few of the offensive linemen blocking for the small back rose to the caliber or experience-level of the great linemen of the '40s, meaning that Barrett absorbed a lot more shots from the opposition than the legendary Irish backs who preceded him. That, and with fewer players, Barrett probably took a lot more dives into the line of scrimmage than anticipated.

Fair or not, he was staying home. Until, that is, someone took up a collection on his behalf and bought him a ticket out to Los Angeles, a partial consolation to a most loyal and misunderstood Irish player.

Much had changed in two years, with ND on the very

pinnacle of the collegiate football ranks when it last visited Southern Cal. Back then, the Irish traveled by train, and they almost always came back with a win, with Leon Hart leading them to a 32-0 victory during their last visit. Since then, Frank Gifford had led the Trojans to prominence, while the thinning of the ranks for the Irish had caused them a reversal of fortune. Few expected them to steal a win over the heavily favored Trojans.

The trip portended at best a potential gallant loss for the Irish. They had played well at times, but Michigan State had exposed their deficiencies, primarily their inexperience. Playing Southern Cal in LA, with the Trojans sporting a veteran team. did not lead to overconfidence on the part of the Irish. And perhaps this cool-headed analysis played into the visitor's favor, because while the Trojan players prepared for a serious game, their counterparts saw the weekend in California as more of a tourist excursion and this certainly contributed to their playing loose.

Not that everyone flying from South Bend saw the flight out west as a glorified school field trip, for Frank Leahy and his assistants scheduled a work-out on Friday in LA. And then the field trip began, as after practice Bobby Joseph suggested that some of his teammates take a tour of one of the studios; so the more adventurous Irish, led by Lattner, Worden and Heap joined him in a cab to RKO Studios, where the young woman at the front gate informed them that they could not enter.

Not one for taking no for an answer, the resourceful Joseph went to work on the young woman, "we are a bunch of Notre Dame football players, you wouldn't think of turning us away without a tour would you?"

"Oh my God," the young woman exclaimed, "my brother Ed Pucci is a linebacker on USC, let me see what I can do!"

Next thing, the four Irish are touring around the studios, being invited to meet all of the stars, including Robert Mitchum and Barbara Stanwyck.

Then, Joseph sees a very attractive woman and asks, "Who is that good looking blond?"

"It's Marilyn Monroe," the guide reported.

"Can we meet her?" persisted Joseph.

The answer came back, "yes." At that point, the various accounts of what happened next diverge. Joseph recalls that his friends went one way and he went to Marilyn Monroe's dressing room, where he finagled five autographed pictures of her with her phone number on them, two for him and one for each of his friends, who eventually showed up to gawk.

Lattner, Heap and Worden have different reminiscences of the event, believing they all sat around with her and made what conversation they could. All agree she was an extremely attractive and congenial person, on the verge of superstardom, but not at a point where she had become a legend yet.

She even gave them each a kiss before they left, but she had to turn down their generous offer for tickets to the football game because she was going to meet up with an old baseball player, by the name of Joe DiMaggio. Having to get back to their hotel, the Irish indicated they needed a ride and the good-natured Monroe drove them there. She even patiently smiled and greeted a bunch of Irish at the hotel, who stopped their meal to run out and see the star, an act that made the coaches none too happy. One could almost hear Coach Leahy telling Joe McArdle to put some extra saltpeter in the lads' corn flakes. When Monroe had to leave, she gave them all quick kisses goodbye, except for Joseph, who to this day insists he kissed her for a full three minutes.

Upon reflection, he will always concede, "I might be exaggerating, it was probably only two minutes."

If Joseph puffed up the story a bit, others bent it out of any conceivable resemblance to reality. One of the linemen, over a half century later, fondly recalled kissing Monroe and then having to explain it to his girlfriend, later his wife. "I told her that she kissed better than Marilyn Monroe," the former player relates with a wink, "and she believed me." The only problem with the story is that this player was a couple years away from enrolling at Notre Dame, never mind suiting up for the varsity against Southern Cal, and was nowhere near the scene of the story.

But some of the guys did come back with signed studio photographs from Monroe to prove that they did meet her, and most of the guys kept them for decades afterward until invariably a basement flood or a jealous wife consumed them.

But the Monroe story was only one encountered by the Fighting Irish in the City of Angels that weekend. Several of the players attended a party that weekend at the home of former Michigan halfback great Tommy Harmon and his actress wife Elyse Knox. During the war, Harmon had parachuted into battle in the South Pacific, and at their wedding, Knox dutifully wore a bridal gown made out of one of the parachutes. Either at this party or somewhere else in the city, the boys witnessed Jack Bush dancing with star Ann Blyth.

Fortunately, amidst all of this revelry and star-gazing, the team had not let their focus drop from the game itself. Having weathered a .500 campaign in '50, the Irish still had some points to prove, an emphasis the coaches never let the players forget.

The game itself marked probably the first intercontinental live broadcast of a college football game, an event not lost on Father Ted Hesburgh, who before the game exhorted the players to win for all of the Catholics watching throughout the country. Ralph Guglielmi listened to Fr. Hesburgh's speech, but a moment later Coach Bill Earley came up to him with a piece of information that more directly affected his fortunes: "Ralph, I hope you understand, we have to start John [Mazur], we owe this to him."

Ralph took it well, walking over to Mazur and wishing him good luck. He felt considerable empathy for Mazur that year, and he wondered if he could have been so gracious had the situation been reversed. Mazur was a really nice guy that year, not saying an ill-word at all to the young Ralph Guglielmi, demonstrating the class expected of a Notre Dame man.

In the madding crowd of parties, studio tours, kisses from Marilyn Monroe and last-minute pep talks, the game itself finally started. Neither team scored in the first quarter, not a shocking occurrence for two groups of young men playing in this nationally televised contest. Certainly talent would win out and in the second quarter, Frank Gifford carried his team on an eight-play drive from his own 38 yard line for the first touchdown, which he scored on an eight-yard slant. He also completed a pass on the drive, although his attempt at an extra point kick failed.

Although John Mazur had started at quarterback for the Irish out of consideration for his dutiful service, Ralph Guglielmi relieved him early, and he led the Irish on a 13-play drive from his own 22 yard line to counter Gifford's efforts of a moment ago. Bob Toneff opened up the hole for John Lattner to score the touchdown from one yard out, the extra point attempt missing. And that is how matters stood when the half ended.

Early in the third quarter, Guglielmi threw a pass to end Chet Ostrowski which hit his hands and then bounced out, with the ball intercepted by Trojan defensive halfback Dick Nunis. With Southern Cal in possession and operating from the T-formation, their back Dean Schneider flipped a screen pass to Jim Sears who took off, tackled eventually on the ND five yard line. On the next play, operating from their customary I-formation, a phalanx of blockers escorted Sears in for the touchdown. Even though Gifford again failed to kick the extra point, Southern Cal led again.

Thereafter, an Irish loss seemed inevitable. On a later drive, the Trojans had begun to walk over the Irish and as a coup de grace one of their backs had thrown a pass deep into Irish territory. Unfortunately for the home team, the ball landed in Irish defensive halfback Gene Carrabine's hands for the interception on his own 27 yard line.

Into the fray again came Ralph Guglielmi, who directed his team with precision for another score, on an eight play drive, noteworthy also for the fact that Notre Dame's greatest backfield gained all of the yardage on the drive, with Heap, Lattner and Worden starring together for the first time ever. On the eighth play, the *Scholastic*'s Bill Riley noted that "[w]ith the Trojan defenders pulled in,

Guglielmi placed two flankers out to the right, gave the ball to Worden, who cut to his left, slanted off-tackle, and raced 39 yards down the sidelines without being touched." The P.A.T. failed. 12-12.

In the fourth period, Guglielmi again rose to the pantheon of great Irish backs by throwing the ball from his own 39 to John Lattner, who "dodged, whirled and plunged to the Trojan 30." Lattner then ran the ball for another 14 yards, with Worden chipping in another six, to place their team on the Trojan 10 yard line. Maybe Frank Leahy had a drop of sentimentality in his veins because he kept back John Petitbon in the game, and after Guglielmi handed off to him, the senior ran ten yards for the touchdown. Bobby Joseph converted the extra point, to bolster the Irish lead to 19-12.

Guglielmi never lost his cool. Late in the game, he tried to run out the clock and the referees called a delay of game penalty against Notre Dame, marching the ball back five yards; after doing so they did not restart the clock as the rules at that time required them to do in the absence of any other delay penalties in that quarter. Ralph Guglielmi shouted out, "Start the clock! This is our first delay penalty!"

"Put the ball in play first!" shouted back the ref.

So Googs ran a useless quarterback dive in the line, seemingly unwilling to let one of his teammates get hurt due to the official's missed call. At that the game ended with ND scoring the huge upset. The players threw Leahy into the showers and Coach Bill Earley showed the referee that section of the rules that proved his quarterback right.

While Guglielmi is justifiably remembered for leading his team that day, Leahy started Bob Toneff on defense that day and the future '49er and Redskins' All Pro tackle stuffed the Southern Cal runners. The coaches had ridden Toneff for four years, and by the second half of the '51 season, he had developed into one of the greatest linemen in Notre Dame's proud history. Still, it was Guglielmi's day.

The composure that Guglielmi displayed in challenging a veteran referee exemplified his play that entire afternoon. As an eighteen-year-old freshman quarterback who went into the last scrimmage before the Indiana opener as seventh on the positional depth chart, he had reached the summit in this game, calling all of his own plays while passing for 161 yards on eight passes of thirteen thrown. Fans always remembered the USC game as the event that thrust Ralph Guglielmi into the ranks of great Notre Dame quarterbacks. Ralph Guglielmi had conquered the Trojans at the Coliseum, but now he had to face a much sterner test when he returned home to scale Mt. Carmel.

Mt. Carmel of course was the high school that quarterback Tom Carey and so many other Irish teammates attended, and where Bob McBride once coached. Arch Ward of the *Chicago Tribune* lavished praise upon young Guglielmi after the Southern Cal game as "the leader Notre Dame has needed all season," and as a general "showing all the poise of a Johnny Lujack or Otto Graham…"

But a day after canonizing Guglielmi, Arch Ward had these more cautious words to impart: "Guglielmi can't afford to rest on his laurels, because there's a classmate behind him named Tom Carey…Carey has all the attributes of Ralph Vincent [Guglielmi] except height." In 1952, Ralph would find just how steep Mt. Carmel was.

Once the team returned home from their monumental victory, a few house-cleaning chores remained. On December 12, 1951, as customary, the Notre Dame Fighting Irish announced the selection of their team captain for the following year, this time the honor flowing to linebacker Jack Alessandrini. A stout defender from Charleston, West Virginia, who could double on the offensive line if needed, Alessandrini possessed the toughness that the coaches craved.

That evening, approximately 1,200 guests attended the annual football dinner at the Dining Hall. Last year of course, Father Cavanaugh had saved the affair from descending into morbidity with his stirring return to glory exhortations, and this year proved even more exciting as Ed Sullivan flew in from New York to emcee the event. Not yet at the zenith of his powers, he had after all not yet introduced the Beatles to an American audience, he still possessed the star power associated with Notre Dame football of the not so distant past.

Besides invited speakers from the Western Athletic Conference and the University of Pennsylvania, Executive Vice-President Fr. Theodore Hesburgh made some remarks, as did Athletic Director Moose Krause, Frank Leahy and former Irish All-American Terry Brennan, then the coach at Chicago's Mt. Carmel. Philosophically, Fr. Hesburgh asked, "What's good, not just about football, but what is good about the fellow who makes football, the player. If we are right about him, we are right about the game. If we are wrong about him, no game in the world can justify what is hurting him, and neither can gate receipts, nor TV, nor anything else."

Ceremoniously, departing captain Jim Mutscheller handed over the captain's shillelagh to Jack Alessandrini, while both young men made brief remarks to those assembled. The team formally said farewell to senior substitutes Del Gander, Jack Bush, Joe Caprara, Tony Zambroski, Bob Kapish, Byron Boji and Jim Hamby, together with senior monogram winners Mutscheller, Bob Toneff, Chet Ostrowski, John Mazur, Bill Barrett, John Petitbon and Paul Burns.

Of this group, John Petitbon and Bob Toneff later played in the College All-Star game with Toneff and Mutscheller gaining All-American recognition. In the NFL draft, seven players heard their name called, the '49ers drafting Toneff in the second round, while Petitbon (Yankees), Ostrowski (Redskins), Mutscheller (Yankees), Flood (Steelers), Burns (Giants) and Barrett (Packers) received their call as later selections.

Statistically for the season, Neil Worden led the team in rushing with 676 yards and scoring with 48 points, while Jim Mutscheller again led in receptions. Beleaguered Billy Barrett led in kickoff and punt returns, while John Lattner paced the team in interceptions (5) and playing time with 401 minutes.

With few exceptions, no Notre Dame football players came so close to transferring without actually doing so than Ralph Guglielmi. Almost as soon as the gun went off to conclude the great victory over USC, Woody Hayes from Ohio State recommended his wooing of the young quarterback.

Woody knew how badly the young man wanted to play for the state school and be near his friends and girlfriend. During the off-season, Woody again went after Ralph

Guglielmi, a pursuit that never ended until the great Notre Dame quarterback played his final down. Googs stayed put. He did not come to his love for Notre Dame as a child nor did it come easy for him during most of his time there as an undergraduate, but it did come. When it did, it proved a more profound and lasting affection than that possessed by most other students who graduated from the school.

During the ensuing winter, while Ralph Guglielmi heard the siren song from Woody Hayes and Ohio State, John Lattner heard a more immediate and closer one emanating from Irish varsity basketball coach John Jordan. Like Leahy in the fall, Jordan had run short of spare parts, so he enlisted Lattner to practice with the team, and in appreciation let him travel with the team during an east coast swing of three games.

Lattner did not simply suit up and warm up and take a seat on the bench, he actually got into action against a then formidable NYU squad, netting eight points. More than that, in overtime, John threw in a buzzer beater to give his mates a one point victory. A few nights later at Penn, he tried another last-minute shot which rolled around the rim twice before falling to the floor as his new team narrowly lost. Leahy probably would not have allowed Lattner to take much more of a part with the varsity cagers, since his prize runner had fictitious winter track/conditioning commitments, but it does demonstrate the superb athleticism of the modest John Lattner.

Milk Riot

THE GREAT MILK RIOT happened on February 28, 1952, in the Dining Hall.

Traditionally, Notre Dame men were allotted five glasses of milk each day from ten ounce glasses, two at breakfast, one at lunch and two at dinner. The practice stopped on February 28, at dinner, when the students began to receive their two dinnertime glasses from eight ounce glasses for the first time.

Why the change? The University later stated that the administration had decided that the students had wasted too much milk during the day drinking from the large glasses, so borne out of a concern for conservation, the slightly smaller glasses were purchased and introduced to the students. It is difficult to believe this, because at that time Notre Dame had not reached its financial status of, to excuse the pun, becoming a cash cow. It was on the verge of realizing millions of dollars from nouveau riche alumni donations and from the sale of every Fighting Irish novelty in creation, but at the time the school more closely resembled the Depression era college that had almost folded, but for the introduction of the Naval courses and training during World War Two.

As an economic measure, the smaller glasses proved a bust. Quite spontaneously, students figured out that their finite allotment of milk had shrunk even more, and the hated glasses began to get smashed against the floor of the

dining hall by the angered students. The shorter and squat-
ter glasses did not break as easily as the older glasses, so the
University's bowlers began to stack the glasses up at the end
of the long varnished wooden tables, pyramid fashion, only
to be busted up by a single glass whipped down the table like
a bowling ball. No one kept count but apparently few gutter
balls resulted and hundreds of broken glasses began to frag-
ment on the floor of the venerable dining hall.

Feeding the rage were rumors that the administration
had added saltpeter to the milk to lower the amorous ardor
of the young men, and when some claimed their milk poured
out foamier than the previous day's fare, this apparently confirmed their most deeply seated fears. Satisfied that they not
only had received less milk, but also tainted sex-inhibiting
liquid, one of the ringleaders yelled out, "We're not going to
drink this shit!" which of course prompted a hail of glasses
smashing against wall and floors.

The revolt continued outside when several students
palmed the glasses and removed them from the dining hall,
only to smash them against the rust-colored exterior brick.
As many as 800 glasses shattered that night. Black Mac Mc-
Carragher most likely went into meltdown that evening but in
order to squelch the insurrection, he most likely would have
had to dismiss over 90% of the student body who resided on
campus. He would have done it too, but cooler heads, like
that of Fr. Ted Hesburgh prevailed.

The *South Bend Tribune* picked up the story and soon the
New York Times ran a piece. To curtail the embarrassment to
the University, Fr. Hesburgh met with the students to address two pressing concerns: the smaller milk glasses and the
lack of toilet paper in dorms. Fr. Hesburgh did not defend

very strenuously the glass issue, but he did point out that since toilet paper had been thrown as streamers at football games, not much was left over to meet the purpose for which the paper was intended.

Since the football season had long since concluded, the toilet paper was not likely to be thrown around the stadium for at least another seven months so that issue easily rectified itself. Because the eight-ounce glasses had largely and almost completely disappeared from campus, the University had little choice but to restore the larger glasses and the revolt was quickly suppressed through almost total abdication by the administration to the student body.

It is tempting to ascribe too much significance to the milk riot, that it constituted some deep seated revolt against the strictness of the University and the Faith on the cusp of Vatican II. Mostly, it began as a spontaneous revolt more likely directed against the quite long and harsh Indiana winters, a rage less against the machine and more against nature itself. Perhaps it had something to do with the Leap Year, as more and more ND young men figured out that the woman of their daydreams did not intend to ask for their hand in marriage that year.

Whatever the cause, the students had won a small and immature battle, one they never forgot. It proved to be the last one for some time.

The student body may have erupted, but at Breen-Phillips, Frank Leahy still reigned unchallenged over the football team, at least in all matters concerning student-athletes. With the oncoming spring, two big events captured the attention of most of the freshmen on campus, the upcoming Class Dance on Friday, May 9, 1952 and the Old

Timer's Football Game the next day. In virtually every other college in the country, no conflict would have existed in events held on separate days, but Dan Shannon knew that he did not attend most colleges and he figured Coach Leahy demanded his players' undivided loyalty and focus on the annual scrimmage.

Competing with this near-certainty was a profound desire to invite his girlfriend Kitty to the Class Dance, so expecting little, he and his old Mt. Carmel teammate Paul Matz screwed up the courage to visit Leahy at his office and ask permission to attend the cotillion. Courteously, Leahy greeted the two young men and asked the "lads" what he might do for them.

Shannon gulped, and then started his prepared spiel, "Coach, there is a big class dance on Friday and some of the guys wanted to know if..."

At that point, Leahy jumped out of his seat and bolted right up. Both Shannon and Matz figured they were finished. "I want you and every other Freshman," bellowed Leahy, "to attend that dance and to be perfect gentlemen to your dates!" With that, the two friends profusely thanked their coach and told their girlfriends and all of their teammates what Leahy had ordered.

Fortunately for Shannon and Matz, the Varsity walloped the Old-Timers, 33-6, keeping alive the hopes of future dancing football players for the years ahead. The lop-sided score reflected not only a resurgent Irish eleven, but also regretfully a rather sudden and irreversible decrease in ardor for the contest on behalf of alumni. In part, the trend may have reflected a disdain of professional coaches to potentially sacrifice the health of their stars in a meaningless exhibition, but in two short years since Leon Hart and his friends insisted on winning, the match had fallen on difficult times.

Jungle Jim Martin returned and many of the soon-to-depart seniors helped field a reasonably competitive line-up, with a number of unheralded sophomores such as Ed Sarna, John Darago, Frank Kettles and Ray Bubick joining them, and hopefully enhancing their prospects for the next fall with a good performance. The varsity starting lineup still reflected some experimentation by the coaching staff, as Dan Shannon started in the backfield with Guglielmi, Lattner and Worden and Joe Katchik at least temporarily returned to the staff's good graces with a start at end.

Neil Worden dominated the game, rushing for 132 yards on 12 carries, with touchdown runs of 25 and 46 yards. John Lattner also won kudos for his running and receiving and Ralph Guglielmi and Tom Carey handled the quarterback chores well. The Varsity also played quite well on defense, holding the Old-Timers to negative ten yards of offense.

Dances and football exhibitions were nice, but on another spring day that year, Neil Worden and a gaggle of his friends decided to tempt Mother Nature herself. The St. Joseph's River divided South Bend and with the onset of heavy rains, the relatively swift river became quite treacherous to anyone who fell into it. Naturally, Neil Worden sized up the challenge and decided that jumping in provided a suitable test of one's mettle and a shot of adrenalin to boost the spirits.

Quickly a dare formed, with some of the more adventurous lads such as Bobby Joseph sizing up the situation and deciding not to risk their lives by diving off the bridge into the torrent below. The most swashbuckling souls, led by the intrepid Neil Worden jumped in, followed by reserve back Lee

Getschow and end Joe Katchik. The decision soon proved an unwise one, with the water much colder and deeper than first thought, as the river yanked the young men around like so much flotsam.

At one point, Worden looked around in horror, able to spot Getschow bobbing along the waves, but frighteningly unable to see the 6'9" Katchik anywhere. Where had he gone? Had the swift undertow pulled down and clutched his massive teammate?

Terror quickly abated when Neil saw his friend ride to the surface again. Once they all negotiated themselves out of the river and sat on its bank, Worden asked Katchik what had happened, how his friend disappeared from sight. He wasn't drowning or struggling against the undertow, explained Katchik, he simply had lost a shoe and had taken a dive to see if he could locate it. The retelling of this event made everyone laugh, but it underscored how strong Katchik was, not only able to navigate a swift current but also quite willing to dive to the bottom of a body of water to retrieve a shoe.

If only Bob McBride had seen it.

Around the time that Neil Worden and his friends were traveling by sea, Joe Heap and his roommate John Darago were venturing by land in pursuit of mischief. In back of what is now the Joyce Center once stood a farm; so one nice day the two roommates rented a couple of horses and rode around South Bend, crossing the highway at one point and then riding around their ultimate destination, St. Mary's College.

Girls all over the place started yelling to them and a ride or two might even have been arranged had not the nuns caught wind of it and chased the two cowboys out of the college grounds. The two roommates enjoyed the laugh and rode back to return their steeds to the farmer from whom they rented them.

On a much more sober note, that spring marked the last time about a half dozen young men played varsity football for Notre Dame. During the summer, some of the coaches telephoned players at their houses and informed them that they no longer had scholarships at the University and, no matter what, would not be invited to try out for the team in the fall. Or so they said.

No one exactly knows what happened, whether the University had run out of scholarship slots and wanted to keep them open for freshman recruits with upside, or that the coaches had wearied of the particular players, but not everyone took the counseling out of the program sitting down. At least one player spoke to Moose Krause, who had little influence over the micro issues in the program, but some of the men came back to the campus in the fall, just not as Notre Dame football players. The Class of '54 continued to shrink.

Third Quarter

Exodus Off Campus

GENERALLY, BY JUNIOR year at Notre Dame, a student at least had to consider the possibility of lodging off-campus, in South Bend or a neighboring suburb. For some, the choice did not realistically exist, if for example parental disapprobation for such a course precluded it from ever occurring. Oftentimes, parents wanted the security of knowing that their son resided in a nice safe dormitory with priests watching over their loved one and making him go to Mass frequently.

Another faction, Frank Leahy and the Notre Dame Fighting Irish football staff, positively insisted that their boys remain on campus. Ballplayers had enough temptations luring them away from the goal line, living off of the University grounds jeopardized everything, so it simply did not happen. The ballplayers remained under lock and key.

In one way, the exodus into private living quarters reflected the inability of the University to guarantee housing. As the campus yearbook the *Dome* put it in its 1953 edition, "The influx of freshmen this year was the largest in the history of the school. Unfortunately, however, campus living accommodations have been unable to absorb all of these members and such circumstances have forced many to find quarters elsewhere. Over one thousand and three hundred...or roughly one-fifth of the student body, live off-campus."

217

If you resided at home and commuted in, you were a "villager." Presumably, Mom and Dad monitored your progress and your moral compass and the University needed to mind very little what you did in your free time. The University made one major concession to off-campus students, allowing them to drive a car around.

If a student intended to reside with a non-family member off-campus, that young man must first obtain the permission of the Dean of Students to do so, and then choose his lodging from only a pre-approved list furnished by the University. The school, of course, had presumably screened the landlords properly and had a previous working relationship with them, because the landlord had to enforce the rules of Our Lady even though their tenant no longer resided in a student hall: in general, "[t]he same rules apply to the off-campus students that apply to campus students. They must be in by midnight every night, they must register with the Dean of Students' Office before leaving for a weekend, they must notify the Dean of Students of a change of address, and the like."

Many of the landlords lived exemplary lives. One of Notre Dame's most enduring legends was Mrs. Hoover, a sainted widow who leased her basement apartment to a couple of most fortunate law students each year, helping them adapt to the sixteen-hour days of studying they had to endure while providing them with a true home at the end of the day. She ceaselessly provided them with encouragement, citing all of the students that came before them that lodged with her who had also faced great obstacles, but who obtained their degrees and passed their bar examinations.

Not all house mothers (and fathers) were created equal.

Some cared less about the University or its rules as long as the rent came in at the first of the month. Others manifested peculiar personal quirks, with one house mother rifling through the students' clothing drawers and closets while they matriculated during the daytime, a practice that only ceased when one of the young men under her charge began to leave notes in his underwear drawer asking "Mrs. K" if she were having a good time checking out his dainties.

Living outside of one of the halls had other disadvantages, particularly if one did not have a car. The trek to campus consumed time, the camaraderie of hall life was lost, and the move did not necessarily provide the student that much more personal liberty, particularly if an individual or group of guys rented space from an elderly couple or a single person who continued to reside in their home and expected the renters to keep reasonable hours and quiet.

The lure of relocating still proved intoxicating, according to a Department of Journalism guidebook, as it afforded "somewhat less stringent obligations and regulations, away from the paternal egis of the good Fathers, and usually the off-campus student is given first consideration and priority on course schedule arrangements." No one kept lists to ensure a student went to early morning chapel three times a week for instance, an instant appeal to non-Catholics who aspired to obtaining an excellent education while reducing the nearly constant reminders of the religious core of the University. It also appealed to late sleepers.

Given its student housing shortage, the administration certainly provided incentives for a student to "move out," better course selection, for one. Often residing with a landlady did not prove that much less personally restrictive than a dorm, but renting an apartment or staying at a non-owner occupied home (assuming the landlord lied to the Dean of Students) pretty much furnished a young Notre Damer unfettered leeway to do what he wished in his free time. If you wanted to drink beer or have girls stop in, or even better, have girls with beer stop by, no one stopped you.

Shortly after Labor Day in 1952, Ray Bubick for one, had permanently moved off-campus, choosing to reside in South Bend as a villager with his mother and brother. Precipitating this decision, he had sustained a knee injury and a bruised clavicle at practice, and after visiting the infirmary, received a prescription which mandated he stay on the sidelines for awhile, until he recovered. So Ray went out to practice as a spectator, a point not lost on Coach Bill Earley, who immediately started chewing him out and insisting he suit up and go to work.

At one point, Ray tried to explain about the nature and depth of the injury to his clavicle, causing Earley to roar, "What's a clavicle?" Ray Bubick quietly walked away, simultaneously leaving the team and his free financial ride to the University of Notre Dame.

Because he had quit the team and lost his scholarship, he had to work in the Studebaker plant at night for tuition money and to defray expenses. The drudgery of working in a factory and keeping up a full load of academic courses and fulfilling his ROTC commitment fortunately was outweighed by Ray's separation from Leahy and Coach McBride and from the watchful eyes of the Holy Cross Fathers.

In time, his home became a refuge for frazzled ex-teammates and since Ray had grown up in South Bend, he knew a lot of young women and he often arranged dates with them and his former teammates.

Other students left for blissful reasons. John Darago, Heap's horse-riding sidekick, had not played with the team his junior year and, before his senior year, got married and found a place off campus. To help pay the family expenses and school tuition, he worked at the local A & P grocery store. Excepting students from Vetville, married men either lived away from school or resided in their hall away from their new bride.

Back on campus, some of the students, football players included, received some lightening of their burdens and a bit more responsibility and perks on the occasion a hall rector requested that they serve in leadership capacities. Some players also remember that juniors got a couple nights out until midnight, because the rules had changed for them and some more worldly priests had let them have an extra night out. It might not seem like a huge concession, particularly since many of the Irish players lined up against teams filled with guys who stayed up late every night with their friends or a young co-ed, but the leeway at Notre Dame did seem to prop up spirits a bit. With age came slight privileges.

So the rules eased up a bit for the students at their halls, but for the athletes under Frank Leahy's supervision, the practices remained demanding. Behind their backs, the football program had changed in the late-forties with a cutback in scholarships, and although this had apparently eased somewhat, the University faced new realities with a more vigilant and militant NCAA looking over them.

Most importantly therefore, the new school year ushered in the long reign of Fr. Theodore Hesburgh as the President of the University of Notre Dame. Having barely survived the Second World War, the University chose the right man to bring it to the forefront of the great universities in the world. During his tenure, the endowment went from a paltry $9,000,000 to $350,000,000 and the number of students almost doubled.

Construction occurred seemingly everywhere, from a new Athletic and Convocation Center to the Hesburgh Library with all of its majestic stories and the Touchdown Jesus mosaic with arms raised triumphantly over the Stadium. The students in the early '50s saw most of these changes when they came back years later as alumni, but the impetus for change accompanied the elevation of Fr. Hesburgh to the top position.

No one embodies the rapid growth in both the physical plant expansion and the establishment of the University of Notre Dame as a top twenty academic institution in the United States more than Fr. Ted Hesburgh. In fact, whoever might conceivably challenge him is not even close to his stature in this regard.

His imprint on all matters pertaining to the school and athletics was immediate and permanent. In the 1953 school yearbook *The Dome*, the editors observed that "like his predecessors, [he] is limited by Canon Law to no longer than two terms of three years each." Someone must have altered the sacred Canon Law a bit because Fr. Hesburgh served at the helm of the school for thirty five-years.

In the sphere of athletics, a triumvirate of men dominated Notre Dame in the post-war years right through the mid-1980s, with President Hesburgh joined by Fr. Edmund Joyce and Athletic Director Moose Krause.

Had Fr. Joyce not chosen the priesthood as his vocation, he easily could have dominated courtrooms across the country as the finest lawyer in America. He possessed a clear and logical mind and could out-argue anyone; married to a commanding presence and a stentorian speaking voice, he might have never lost a case, but he chose a much more challenging position as a chief administrator at the University.

Born in 1917, the same year as Fr. Hesburgh, Ned Joyce came to his vocation in a much different fashion than this great friend. Born in Belize, he attended Spartanburg High in South Carolina and although he graduated from Notre Dame, he went right to work as an accountant.

He did not even begin studying for the priesthood until eight years after graduation, with his ordination coming at Sacred Heart in 1949. From there he rose meteorically, his star fixed to the rising one of Fr. Hesburgh, and he became Executive Vice-President in the fall of 1952. Having studied a year at Oxford, he undoubtedly saw in which areas Notre Dame might improve and become truly great, and he shared his friend's vision concerning how to get there.

Although Fr. Hesburgh subsequently dwarfed him in fame and national influence, Ned Joyce became a commanding voice in the NCAA and helped nudge intercollegiate athletics closer to the ideals expounded by his own university. He did not see how Notre Dame had to sacrifice its athletic greatness, but he, like Fr. Hesburgh, had a vision for the future and that common dream embraced their alma mater as not only a preeminent sports school, but also a leading research and academic center.

At first blush, the third leg of the triangle pushing Notre Dame to greatness on all fronts after the war was a most unlikely source, Director of Athletics Edward Krause. Edward Krause served as Director of Athletics at the University of Notre Dame, starting in 1949 and ending in 1982. Nicknamed "Moose," Krause's ascension to the post in part was designed as a means to decrease the pressure on Frank Leahy, the previous director, who then could hopefully focus on football and relax a bit more. The shift only accomplished the former of these objectives.

One of the central myths obfuscating any analysis of the University in the late 1940s and early 1950s is that Notre Dame, in attempting to become the "Catholic Harvard," somehow deemphasized football and left poor Leahy to twist in the wind. This view is nonsense of course, as the University continued to win National Championships long after Leahy left, and certainly Moose Krause made certain of this. And in any event, anyone who knew Fr. Hesburgh during these years sensed he did not want to make Notre Dame the Catholic Harvard. He wanted Harvard to become the Eastern Notre Dame.

Unlike Frank Leahy, Krause never played under Knute Rockne, as Moose only suited up for games just after Rock died. In addition to obtaining All-American honors in football and basketball, Moose also earned a track monogram. The answer to a trivia question, Moose Krause indeed was the man responsible for the institution of the three-second rule in basketball because of his dominance in the paint.

Whatever his personal feelings, Krause first and foremost served his university loyally, and followed the orders given to him by Frs. Hesburgh and Joyce. If Notre Dame had to stiffen up academic and admission requirements for athletes and non-scholarship students, he did not oppose this development, at least not outside of the University's board rooms. Frank Leahy experienced issues hewing to the tougher standards the school demanded in the post-war years, while Moose Krause took an opposite tack, rising to the challenge of achieving athletic excellence simultaneous with an increased emphasis on academic preeminence. Moose Krause could change with the times, Frank Leahy either could not or would not.

For the more secular, at Notre Dame under Fr. Hesburgh, there was a balance of power that needed to be upheld at all times, like the executive, legislative and judicial branches of the United States Government. If one branch becomes too powerful, the country loses out. Hesburgh saw this, and unfortunately by the late 1940s Frank Leahy and football reigned supreme.

We Have to Improve

SHORTAGES BEGUILED the Irish again as September, 1952 dawned, particularly on the line with sophomores Mike Torrelli and Len Cyterski (both hailing from Cathedral Prep in Erie, Pennsylvania) not appearing for practice. As the Notre Dame Fighting Irish kicked off their official fall varsity football sessions, Leahy and his coaches immediately had to shift around their linemen in response to the personnel issues, while ensuring that those who did return to the team quickly worked themselves into shape. Of course, many of the players had engaged in some type of preparation for the season ahead during the summer, a fact not advertised by Frank Leahy.

The *Chicago Tribune* reported that the "biggest problem of the coaching staff is the development of an offensive line," in the absence of alums Bob Toneff, Chet Ostrowski, Jim Mutscheller and Paul Burns. To reinforce the interior of the line, the staff shifted Minnie Mavraides from end to guard and Joe Katchik from end to tackle.

True to form, Leahy had his lads scrimmaging from virtually the outset of the formal commencement of practice, when on the 6th Joe Heap paced the backs with 30-, 35- and

60-yard scoring runs. Typically, Neil Worden scored the hard way with a two-yard plunge into the end zone, as did Ralph Guglielmi with a one-yard quarterback sneak. Paul Reynolds bolted for 45 yards and quarterback Tom Carey added the other score with a 65-yard gallop around left end.

Unbeknownst to Guglielmi and Carey, they would play virtually the entire season to come as co-quarterbacks. At no point did the staff tell them this, and Leahy and his assistants themselves probably did not plan this to happen, but that is precisely how the situation developed. Googs had worked hard mixing mud and carrying hod all summer for $1.80 an hour, and then as soon as he got home and showered, he worked out all night at his old high school, repeating this routine each day. Tom Carey too worked hard and had expectations of playing that year, so he and Guglielmi competed for the starting position until the final gun sounded at the conclusion of the final game that year.

In that September 6 scrimmage, Bill Gaudreau "departed early after getting jarred by a surprising block by big Joe Katchik." Joining Katchik at the event were some other little-used players such as Ray Bubick, Ed Sarna, and Tom O'Brien; within the month all of these players fell off the roster, although O'B did return years later to play for the Irish after completing a stint in the military.

Having shifted Joe Katchik away from end, Frank Leahy engaged in one of his favorite pastimes, that of incessantly and loudly criticizing his tall lineman, with the *Chicago Tribune* quoting him on September 12, that Katchik has "been a disappointment at end" and that "he still has not shown ability to play tackle." It did not stop there, as the Notre Dame student's football preview for the year opined, "Big Joe Katchik,...was a disappointment last year and played only a few minutes. Despite his height, six-nine, he has never been particularly adept in the pass-catching department."

Leahy did not restrict his critiques to the media, delivering one of his most withering comments to his least favorite lineman during a blocking drill: "Ooooh Joe Katchik, we could put eggs underneath your shoulder pads and you wouldn't even break them."

It is likely that sometime within the next few days, Joe Katchik's career at Notre Dame concluded. Ray Bubick had just walked off the team and away from campus, sacrificing his scholarship and his opportunity to room with his friend Don Penza that year. Similarly, Katchik reached his limit with Leahy one day when the Old Man began to chew him out for some perceived transgression in front of his linemates, including Jack Lee. Finally, Joe took off his helmet and said, "Fuck it," and exited Cartier Field for the final time, thereby signaling the end for the "next Leon Hart." While Bubick remained a Notre Dame man and after graduation even played in an Old-Timers Game (to his surprise lining up against O. B. O'Brien who by then had returned to play for the Irish varsity), Joe Katchik left campus never wishing to return.

Fall practice had caused a handful of juniors to leave the team, but for those who endured, tedium often followed these strenuous two-a-days. Awaiting their regular room assignments, the ballplayers stayed in three different dorms, with Joe Heap and Art Nowack for instance rooming temporarily at Sorin Hall. An avid gun enthusiast, one day Heap displayed to Art, Neil Worden, Lee Getschow and Bobby Joseph one of his prized possessions, a German Lugar. Deciding to have some fun, Heap pointed the pistol toward where

Art Nowack was straddling a chair, at which point the trigger somehow touched off, Heap not realizing the fact that a single bullet rested in the chamber.

The gun fired and the bullet passed just a silly centimeter away from what would have given Art Nowack his worst groin injury at Notre Dame. The gun's percussion made such a deafening noise in the confined space of Neil Worden's dormitory room that it temporarily deafened everyone in attendance, but it mattered little to Art Nowack who took it in good humor, as it could have been so much worse. It took him fifty years, but he finally thanked Joe Heap for being such a lousy marksman, on behalf of his wife, three daughters and most importantly, himself.

Fortunately, neither Frank Leahy nor Black Mac McCarragher ever found out about the incident, as bodies began to drop on the gridiron during two-a-day practices. On one day alone, Johnny Lattner came up lame with a pulled leg muscle and William Gaudreau hurt his leg while Dave Flood bruised his shoulder. Flood recovered but Gaudreau did not, and his latest injury, when totaled with the hurt placed on him in the past year, spelled the end of his football career. Now in addition to the false worries that plagued Coach Leahy, he had a real one: the realization that he now had to replace a starting safety.

Lattner was the indispensable man in the eyes of the *Chicago Tribune*'s Wilfrid Smith, who waxed, "[Lattner] stands as one of the best—perhaps the nation's best—players. Lattner is the Johnny Mohardt, the George Gipp, the Marchie Schwartz of this generation…[he] must play full time, and an injury could shatter Irish hopes."

Less certain at quarterback, the coaches alternated Guglielmi and Carey almost equally in snaps at practice and scrimmages while they tried out for the first time Huck O'Neil, Walt Cabral, Art Hunter and Paul Matz at end. Officially, Notre Dame did not encourage transfers from other schools to enroll and join their football team, but the Irish made a most fortuitous exception to their rule when they accepted end Huck O'Neil from the recently defunct Duquesne team. One tough nut, O'Neil fit in immediately and helped alleviate some of the line woes.

The Irish made another vital addition to their program in the off-season, after the departure of Bernie Crimmins to take over as head coach at Indiana, with the return of Johnny Lujack, the school's Heisman trophy winner in 1947, as a backfield coach.

A class act, Lujack came from Connellsville, Pennsylvania and starred in many of the great Irish backfields of the 1940s. After copping the Heisman in '47, Lujack went on to a very successful career with the Chicago Bears both as a defensive back (at quarterback, Sid Luckman still started many of those years) and then as the quarterback, winning All-Pro recognition in 1950 and 1951.

In 1952, Leahy offered Lujack a coaching position, and in the framework of the team with young and developing quarterbacks, in essence Lujack became the *de facto* quarterback coach. Still a young man himself, the new coach loved challenging the players to races, fifty and one hundred yard dashes. Initially, he tried too often to teach by demonstrating how he might punt or pass, an impossible task for most players who simply did not have the experience, or in some instances talent, to replicate Lujack's feats. In time, he conveyed his knowledge in a more nuanced and effective way, with an emphasis on maximizing the considerable potential of one Ralph Guglielmi. He could also be quite funny: after back-up Bob Martin had just completed a practice toss, Lu-jack yelled out, "Martin, you just threw that ball like it was a bag of shit and you were worried about getting it on you!"

Lujack worked very hard at mastering his new position, meeting with the quarterbacks each evening in his office at Breen-Phillips and quizzing them all on how they would re-act each time they saw a certain defense. He did not devote his time just to Ralph or Tom Carey though, choosing to educate and challenge even the lowest man on the positional depth chart. He might have made a fine head football coach at his alma mater, had the invitation arisen.

Having once played under Leahy, Lujack knew how to run each practice, drilling the quarterbacks in order that not a wasted moment occurred while the men stood on the field. Although he expected much from his charges, Lujack did not run into the same problems the linemen in particular often had with their coaches, that of working them beyond endurance.

He also endeared himself to the team managers by let-ting them have the occasional use of his car, a huge oppor-tunity at that time at Notre Dame. But while the managers drove around, Leahy openly worried about Guglielmi, la-menting, "We can only hope...that Ralph may again equal his performance against Southern California." All this after only about one week of practice had transpired, yet Leahy had no coronation planned for Guglielmi, meaning to make him earn the starting spot. And if he did not, Tom Carey waited in the wings, taking as many snaps in practice as the presumptive favorite to lead the Irish.

Googs had saved some games the previous season as the understudy for John Mazur, but lost on many fans and football scribes was the fact that the young man had only limited college experience entering his sophomore campaign and had to continue to practice and absorb the T-formation, all the while operating with a line and backs with not much more experience or maturity than he had. The Chicago papers loved it of course, because Mt. Carmel's Tom Carey provided much of the challenge to Guglielmi, with Don Bucci and Jim Bigelow vying for the third string QB position. The team also suffered from depleted ranks, which also made it difficult for young quarterbacks to run their plays with the comrades who would go into the games with them.

No longer able to recruit the massive classes of years past (and having run so many others off the field), Leahy had about 46 men on the roster; his ceaseless practicing and scrimmaging left even these ranks decimated and a mid-September scrimmage had to be cut back "because of minor injuries and a siege of colds which left barely enough players to form 2 teams." Neil Worden made a 35-yard touchdown run but Tom Carey starred with a 25-yard pass to Lattner, a 30-yarder to Joe Heap and his own five-yard plunge, all good for touchdowns. In the midst of shortages, Joe Doyle did note a small gleam in Leahy's eyes as he saw the freshmen players, fresh from their physical exams, marching into the stands to see the scrimmage.

So desperate had the team become, that Bob Arrix, perhaps the team's smallest back with Bob Rigali, started receiving attention as a back-up for Neil Worden at fullback. Arrix could run, but he lacked the muscular framework that the Bull brought to the point of attack on every hand-off, and as early as 1951 had undergone his first leg operation. Fortunately, the young man also kicked the ball well, and this skill undoubtedly kept him away from several maulings by both his own teammates at scrimmages and from opposition tacklers. As Arrix evaded linebackers, his head coach boldly strode into the landmines of national politics.

Having recently seconded the nomination of Dwight Eisenhower for President at the Republican National Convention, Leahy was visited by Ike at South Bend in a rather obvious ploy for Catholic voters in the upcoming general election against Adlai Stevenson. Perhaps the visit shifted Leahy's focus away from the field as he extended mercy to his team by emphasizing "dummy scrimmage work, with the intense heat again cutting down on planned heavy conditioning."

The latest class of freshmen provided Leahy with some hope amongst the bumps and bruises of his veterans. Everyone wanted crew-cut halfback Dick Fitzgerald on their varsity along with fullback John Gaffney, both Chicago Catholic school products.

Notre Dame had recruited two African-American stars from Pennsylvania, halfback Dick Washington and lineman Wayne Edmonds and unlike years past, both players stood a very good chance of earning one or more monograms apiece during their time at the school.

Other future stars joined these prominent recruits, namely linemen Jim Mense, Patsy Bisceglia, Ray Lemek, John McMullan, Jack Dumas, John Kegaly, Robert Lasch, Gene Martell, Pat Nakfoor and George Nicula; and backs Dick Hendricks, Dick Keller, Joseph Markowski, Nick Raich, Don Schaefer and George Wilson.

The most experienced recruit, Patsy Bisceglia, was a few years older than his classmates, having served in the Navy during the Korean War. He had played enough service ball well enough to attract the attention of Frank Leahy, through his vast network of contacts in the military, and the Old Man invited the sailor to Notre Dame for a tryout.

Trouble was, Bisceglia had no leave, an issue he brought to the attention of his commanding officer. "No problem," his superior assured him, "we will get you the leave." "There's one more problem, sir," the young sailor offered. "What is it?" "I don't have the money to get out to South Bend and back," replied Patsy.

No problem, his commander gave him $200.00 for his train fare and meals and lodging for his big try-out. Despite his protestations of poverty, Patsy pocketed the $200.00 and hitchhiked across the country for free, only relying on mass transit when he arrived in Terre Haute, Indiana, at which point his luck in thumbing a ride ran out.

Once at the campus, Patsy had to get dressed in sweat pants and a tee shirt and meet line coach Bob McBride for the first time, at which point Patsy learned that as part of his audition, he had to demonstrate proper blocking form. The first time up from his stance, he received an elbow to the face and fell to the floor, a situation that repeated itself on his second attempt at blocking Coach McBride.

Dusting himself up for his third blocking attempt, the potential recruit heard McBride snarl, "What's the matter, can't you block?" Preparing for the next contact, Patsy balled up one of his fists and when the coach barked out "block," Patsy wheeled his fist back and then fired it straight into McBride's scrotum with extraordinary speed and prejudice.

Coach McBride dropped to the deck faster than Bambi's

mother, barely able to breathe. Audition over.

Patsy immediately felt bad, not so much for the coach's condition, but because he impulsively blew his one chance to earn a scholarship to play football at Notre Dame. He figured his interview with Frank Leahy, later that day, constituted a formality on his way back to base with the Navy, never destined to play intercollegiate football.

When the time came for this meeting, Leahy mentioned that he had heard about the work-out with Coach McBride, and just as the young sailor prepared to profusely apologize, Leahy cut him off and offered him a full athletic scholarship. Hitting Bob McBride south of the border sealed the deal, demonstrating to all of the staff that this Bisceglia kid was tough, a war veteran just like themselves and the great players of the '40s like Jungle Jim Martin and Ziggy Czarobski. Bisceglia was in.

As the new freshmen established themselves, Ralph Guglielmi and Tom Carey carried out a public battle for the starting quarterback position, a challenge undoubtedly leaked by Leahy to ensure a sharp competition between the two young men. One of the lads theorized that since Carey had run the split T so much in high school, Leahy and the other coaches had begun to favor him. For his part, Guglielmi stormed back to practice after a four-day rest for a sore arm and Frank Varrichione shifted from guard to tackle and back to McBride's tutelage.

Having welcomed the freshmen, Leahy threw them at the varsity for a full-scale scrimmage the Saturday before the Penn game, and the frosh acquitted themselves all too well. Before 4,000 spectators, mostly students but with a small gaggle of horrified coaches and disgusted sportswriters, the freshmen held their elders at bay most of the day, earning a sub-headline the next day in the *South Bend Tribune* of "IRISH VARSITY UNIMPRESSIVE AGAINST FROSH."

Leahy commented that the team had "receded" to spring practice levels in the execution of the plays, and no one wrote the comment off to his habitual pessimism.

Much of the chronic problems stemmed from the lack of healthy personnel, with Art Hunter out with an injury received the day before in practice, thus joining backs Worden, Heap, Reynolds, Arrix and Joseph on the injured list. Fullback Tom McHugh got himself kicked out of the game by the Big Ten officials for violating the new rule against "use of elbows," leaving Lattner as one of the few healthy backs.

Lattner did not disappoint, scoring three times, twice on runs and once on a pass from the newly healthy Ralph Guglielmi, but the lack of team depth had reached alarming levels. Purely as a band-aid measure, Leahy remembered that Lattner had served on the basketball team the previous winter when they needed healthy bodies, so he enlisted cagers Joe Bertrand and Junior Stephens, with Leahy reasoning, "One thing a basketball player learns is to ignore the faking and play the ball."

Bertrand did not stick after a try-out, but Junior Stephens did, quickly impressing the coaches by defeating all backs, with the exception of the still-recovering Heap, in a 100-yard dash race. Sarcasm and injuries had pruned the squad to levels not seen since 1941 and by necessity, Stephens stuck. The thinning Irish ranks did not escape notice with one Philly scribe, Art Morrow of the *Inquirer,* who previously had handicapped the Irish as 3-4 touchdown favorites over Penn in the season opener, altering his prognostications to calling the game even after seeing Leahy's lads. Against the odds, the club continued to prepare for their opening game.

In anticipation of the single wing offense of their first opponent, the University of Pennsylvania, the team ramped up its defensive schemes and alternated Neil Worden, Dick Szymanski, Dave Flood, Dan Shannon and Jack Alessandrini at linebacker. Art Hunter remained injured for the better part of the week and Huck O'Neil replaced him on the line. The team also practiced field goal kicking quite a bit, with emphasis on blocking kicks and making their own kicks. It seemed unusual to review and fine tune this element of the game at the expense of others with no games under the still young team's belt.

The men on the line had talent, but still not enough game experience, with some very tough teams on the schedule for the year. The *Chicago Tribune*'s Arch Ward did not like the Irish offensive line, a point he made before the season commenced, and held out little hope for his alma mater for 1952, which he maintained had "too little material, too much schedule."

Leahy did not underestimate Penn, a proud program in the midst of irreversible deemphasization, because he truly feared every opponent. And yet his practices leading up to this first game reflected almost a finessing of the kicking game at the expense of shutting down the opposition's main threat, running back Ed Bell. Perhaps even Leahy began to recognize this as his team arrived in Philadelphia and checked into the Hotel Warwick.

Ominously too, in the games in both 1950 and 1951, the Penn Quakers had more Catholic players than Notre Dame, a fact that startled some of the Fighting Irish when they saw each other at Mass at the Cathedral in Philadelphia each year. Even Frank Leahy would have encountered difficulty praying for the intervention of Saint Mary against a team carrying more young men fervently reciting their "Hail Marys" than his own. It was an illusion of course, Notre Dame had a small squad and only took a portion of their team to away games, so many of their Catholic lads sat back home rooting for their teammates and wishing they were there.

More concretely, the Away/Away series those two years clearly did not work in ND's favor and the 1952 game should have kicked off in South Bend, but since Franklin Field seated about 75,000 fans, each game ended up in Philadelphia instead. At the game itself, almost a full house shuttled into Franklin Field, which Arch Ward estimated "was the largest crowd that has ever seen an opening game in the east." Pretty much everyone left perplexed at the end of the contest, an alternately boring and frustrating one which culminated in a 7-7 tie. It started well, when Penn fumbled on the ND 36 yard line and Fred Mangialardi recovered, sparking his team. Unfortunately, the Irish promptly fumbled the ball back to Penn. Thereafter the game largely devolved into a defensive battle.

Ward again blamed the Irish offensive line, slapping his own back for his pre-season prophesying, but he neglected to dollop any blame for the unsatisfying result on the coaching staff, which unwisely alternated Tom Carey and Ralph Guglielmi at quarterback. The club had two talented signal-callers from which to choose, but the coaches did not make a choice, and the lack of continuity hurt the squad.

And yet it was a drive jointly engineered by Carey and

then Guglielmi which produced their team's sole score. When the Quakers began to key on Carey and the option, Googs came in with a fourth-down-and-seven situation and completed a first-down pass to Heap. After that, Googs drove his team to the promised land as John Lattner punctuated the drive with a one-yard touchdown "buck."

To the extent that momentum might have helped any team, the fates shifted back and forth too often, too quickly. In the third quarter Penn's star back Eddie Bell sprinted free in the Irish secondary and caught the tying touchdown pass as linebacker Dan Shannon vainly tried to chase him down the last forty yards.

Guglielmi did engineer a strong march down the field in the last couple minutes of the game, completing a pass to Lattner at the Penn 26 yard line, but at that point Eddie Bell, playing defense, stripped the ball and a Penn teammate recovered it in mid-air. On offense, Penn dove into the line until time expired, the teams having tied.

Comically, Neil Worden's efforts got short shrift from the television announcer, who had not received word that the Bull was not wearing his usual number, but rather the "44" of reserve fullback Bob Arrix who had not traveled with the team. Arrix started getting calls about his "performance," causing him to quip, "I only hope my folks back home in Teaneck, NJ are listening [to the game]." That small item of levity constituted the only break the press cut for the team that week, with the Monday morning quarterbacking starting almost as soon as the final gun sounded. After the game, someone asked Ralph Guglielmi why he did not throw more jump passes, to which Googs replied, "Well sir, if I had from Saturday until Monday to think about it, maybe I would have."

Arch Ward lambasted the team and many of its players,

picking apart Dan Shannon for mechanical "mistakes," particularly in backpedaling on defense when Penn's Eddie Bell ran forward on a pass play, claiming Bell "could have run all the way to Camden without a Notre Dame hand touching him." He expressed his disdain for the offensive line again and did not much like Worden and Heap as running backs, although he did praise Lattner. Ward predicted 3-4 losses for the Irish in '52 due to their offense.

Notre Dame should have defeated Penn, and Leahy definitely should have gotten the ball to his "hot hand" Lattner more, but Ward missed the development of one of the greatest offensive lines in college football history, a line that by 1953 carried six young men who in the future played at least nine years apiece in the NFL. For this still young and developing Irish squad, an opening game against a patsy might have served their interests better than scheduling a strong Penn contingent away for its opener, but it took almost another half century to learn that lesson.

More embarrassment followed with the publication of *Life* Magazine at the beginning of the next week, purportedly showing the photographs of four Notre Dame football players with significant amounts of their respective front teeth missing. The publication got it mostly wrong, misidentifying players and apparently showing a picture of Dan Shannon with no teeth when he had his originals still inside his mouth. Similarly, a snapshot supposedly of Tom Carey missing his front teeth actually depicted Jack Lee. Three of the players identified in the story still had their teeth intact, causing the editors headaches and creating a situation where SID Charlie Callahan vowed never to speak directly with the publication again.

Hot off the heels of the Penn debacle, the missing teeth

controversy, part of a larger story about the return to prominence of the football program, culminated in one more black eye against the Irish.

Controversy aside, the team still had a game against Texas, so on Monday, September 29, the varsity conducted a dummy scrimmage, instead of letting the starters have a day off, a concession to the fact that the team had not prepared itself that well going into the Penn game with their overemphasis on kicking and punting. The next day the team emphasized passing drills, not a bad idea for a team that scored only one touchdown a few days earlier, yet the coaches had still not settled on a quarterback, dividing the snaps between Guglielmi and Carey with Huck O'Neil and Don Penza pulling down most of the receptions.

Tragicomically, the team did not even review the Penn tapes to diagnose their mistakes and correct them as the film had been destroyed during development and Penn did not have time to send a duplicate copy to the Irish between the beginning of the week and Saturday, when the Irish had to play the very deep, talented and highly rated Texas team. The type of depth that allowed them to rotate 50 players into their opening victory against LSU and 48 in their next game, a win against North Carolina. Notre Dame did not have that many players healthy on their entire squad.

With so much to worry about, Frank Leahy still had commitments to keep, one occurring in the middle of the week as he kicked off the inaugural Quarterback Club luncheon at South Bend's Hotel Oliver before 350 people, impressing them with what many considered his finest speech ever. He took time out to defend Carey and Guglielmi when questioned about why the team did not pass more often on first down, stating, "Undoubtedly we should have but that's our fault. It's hard to blame a pair of 19-year-old quarterbacks."

Accompanying these noble sentiments, Leahy also made some gratuitous and petty observations. When questioned about what happened to Joe Katchik, the coach offered: that "We made the mistake of telling our squad how tough the schedule would be, so Katchik and three others dropped out of school." Just because Leahy no longer had Katchik to kick around anymore did not mean he meant never to kick him around again, and it is exactly that strain of mean-spiritedness that drove Katchik, Ray Bubick and others off the roster, not strength of schedule.

The gathering may have taken Leahy's mind off of Texas a bit, but hearing news that Art Hunter had received clearance to play had more of a salutary effect on him. One of the positive developments that occurred in the wake of Hunter's absence was a shift in practice, as the club started to run passing plays not only to the ends but also to backs Joe Heap and John Lattner, much better natural receivers than Hunter.

Another development that helped the Irish to not fixate on Texas was the counterreformation conducted against *Life* Magazine for its September 29 toothless Irish story. Fr. Joyce led the attack, charging the publication with "gross misrepresentation," specifically "Two of the players pictured have never participated in Notre Dame games. Three of the falsely identified players are still smiling with their own front teeth....Ninety-four percent of our varsity squad have never lost a tooth playing football at Notre Dame."

Captain Jack Alessandrini joined the fray, observing,

"One picture correct out of four...is a pretty poor average. I know our team couldn't operate on the 25 percent level of efficiency." The *South Bend Tribune*'s Joe Doyle deadpanned that the magazine's editors should inventory their own dentures as "there are just as many incomplete sets of teeth in the publishing business as there are in the sport of football."

The magazine article and photos upset a lot of people in South Bend, but a smart chap like Frank Leahy probably thanked Mary in his prayers each day that the article had come out, as it drew the team together and deflected scrutiny of their recent shortcomings in Philadelphia against the University of Pennsylvania. It was hard to criticize developing talents like Ralph Guglielmi and Tom Carey when everyone just wanted to talk about missing teeth.

Down in Austin, the Texas coaches ignored dentures and plates and misidentified players and wisely did not provide Leahy and his coaches with any more locker room bulletin board fodder to fire up the Irish. Few gave the Irish any chance as they flew down to Texas for their October 5, 1953 game, and most odds makers, who cared nothing about hurt feelings, had the Irish down as two- to three-touchdown underdogs.

Frank Leahy had the Longhorns right where he wanted them.

Deep in the Heat of Texas

RANKED NINETEENTH in the nation, the Irish picked one of the hottest days in their history, in temperatures exceeding ninety degrees, to defeat the staunch Texas team. To stay cool, the players along the sidelines wore pith helmets bought by Joe McArdle in Austin on the day of the game, and their coaches uncharacteristically advised the lads to stretch and take oxygen during the game, rather than simply toughing it out. Frank Leahy looked like the Man with the Yellow Hat pacing the sidelines back and forth.

Relying on (hopefully) superior conditioning and whatever edge he might obtain for his players, the Old Man set out to exhaust the opposition into submission in their own stadium. Being Frank Leahy, he of course did more than that. Before the game began he had the Notre Dame players doing their warm-ups in tee shirts, a trick he picked up from Purdue's coach Stu Holcomb, while the Longhorn players limbered up in their pads and helmets. Leahy intoned to his lads, "Don't exert yourselves!" This accomplished two things: it prevented the Irish players from dehydrating and otherwise using up their energy before the game and it made them look like little guys in the eyes of the Texas players, who ran by them with all of their gear on.

And he did not stop there. Leahy also asked the Texas Athletic Director, Dana Bible, if his team could share the same sideline because of the extreme sun on the visitor side of the gridiron, a request that was graciously granted. The Old Man then followed it up by asking for a certain half of the sideline for his men and that too seemed reasonable, so he got what he wanted. This became important because in the second half, Leahy's side became shaded by the "towering" press box while the home team Texans sat with the sun beating down on them. At one point Texas coach Eddie Price saw the Irish lounging in the shade and yelled out, "You son of a bitch, Leahy!" But by then Leahy had outfoxed another opponent.

Nearly 68,000 fans purchased tickets for the game, a then-record crowd for the no. 5 ranked Longhorns. Disaster struck Notre Dame almost immediately, when on its first possession, back Joe Heap fumbled on his own 43 yard line, Texas recovering. The Longhorns drove the ball down to the 27 yard line, until the Irish held, and rather than try a field goal, they decided to punt instead.

In 1952, of course, few kickers stood much of a chance of hitting a field goal from that distance, owing mostly to college coaches paying scant attention to the kicking phase. However, Texas should have tried for a first down, a point underscored when its punter, a poor soul named Bob Raley, attempted to drop a "coffin corner punt" deep in Irish territory, only to have the ball bounce up the field in the wrong direction to the 17 yard line. A ten yard net punt!

Still it seemed like a wise coaching move when Ralph Guglielmi fumbled the ball on his own 22 yard line shortly thereafter, Texas recovering. Texas then drove down to the 13, and with fourth and one facing them, their coach Eddie Price this time decided not to punt but ran a play by Jim Jones, who himself fumbled, with the Irish' Albert Kohanovich recovering on his 15 yard line.

The odd playing and play calling continued once ND recovered. Not making much progress on offense, Leahy sacrificed a down by having John Lattner "quick-kick" on third down, with the ball settling on the Texas 49 yard line. Although the Irish had given up an offensive opportunity, at least when they punted the ball did not roll back on them. Unfortunately, the Longhorns then went on a very effective sustained drive of their own, until their left halfback Gib Dawson coughed up the ball, and Gene Carrabine recovered it for the Irish on their own 7 yard line.

To this point, poor play calling and inexcusable fumbling characterized the contest, not the ungodly heat the players slaved under. Still the Irish failed to capitalize on their opponent's hospitality, and as the second quarter began, Lattner had to punt from his own end zone. While he kicked the ball almost to mid-field, the Longhorns returned the ball well and then staged another good offensive set. The Irish defense once again met the challenge and stopped the drive with fourth down on the three yard line. This time, Dawson came in to kick the field goal, successfully, as the Longhorns gained the first lead of the game, 3-0.

The Irish continued to stall on offense, never crossing mid-field, and Texas did not relinquish the lead as the teams went into their dressing rooms at halftime. During the half, the two teams staged a ceremony to honor one of their joint heroes, Jack Chevigny, who died during the Battle of Iwo Jima. Chevigny had served in the ND backfield from 1926 through 1928, and later coached Texas from 1934 through 1936.

Chevigny did not post a very good record at Texas, although he did coach his team to a 7-6 defeat of his alma mater, after which he received as a gift in honor of this victory a pen with the inscription "To Jack Chevigny, a Notre Dame boy who beat Notre Dame." Legend has it that after Chevigny died, the next time anyone saw the pen occurred as the Japanese delegation prepared to use it to execute the surrender documents at the close of World War Two. As part of the ceremonies, the Japanese delegate returned the pen, which found its way back to the States, this time re-inscribed, "To Jack Chevigny, a Notre Dame boy who gave his life for his country in the spirit of old Notre Dame."

During intermission, Leahy invoked this spirit in seeking out the team captain, Jack Alessandrini, and demanding more of him, both in terms of leadership and in shifting to offense to spark some production. Alessandrini internalized Leahy's exhortations to personify the type of grit and determination expected of a team leader, as the coach shifted him from linebacker to guard to solidify the offensive line. Arch Ward approved the move, attributing the improved play of tackles Joe Bush and Fred Poehler in opening up holes to the presence and leadership of the captain.

Having survived the first half, Notre Dame had a decided advantage over its opponent due to the emphasis on conditioning preached by Leahy and his staff. The crazy winter practices ("tell 'em you're on the track team") and the often surreptitious summer training paid off in circumstances such as these. The Irish had more of a physical reserve remaining in their starters and in their first possession of the second half, they took advantage of it.

Perhaps the Irish had better stamina, but Leahy also

had just coached a team that had not scored a single point in a half of play, so in addition to waiting the other team out, Leahy admitted that he gathered with the coaches and "changed our offensive splits at halftime to adjust to the Texas defenses."

It worked wonders at the start of the second half. Skillfully mixing up his running assignments between Heap, Lattner and Worden, Guglielmi wore down the Longhorns on a brilliant drive, which also included a key pass reception by Art Hunter and a decent run by Googs himself. He even spread the glory on one play, pitching out to Heap, who fired a pass to Lattner who cradled it and drove down to the one yard line. On the next play, Lattner dove through the line and with Minnie Mavraides' successful conversion, came the first Irish lead of the day, 7-3.

The two powerful defenses then caused the game to devolve into a punting contest, and while the Irish won the field position battle, neither team scored. A promising ND drive, accentuated with four first downs, stalled on fourth down on the Texas 31 yard line, so Leahy called in Paul Reynolds to pooch punt it to the opposing returner Bob Raley.

Two aspects of the call appear unusual when viewed through the prism of over a half century later. Why did not Leahy either try a field goal or go for it on fourth and one? And if he did call a punt, why bring in Paul Reynolds and not John Lattner, the regular punter, who had just boomed a 51 yarder minutes earlier?

In 1952, chip field goals quite often failed, so Leahy probably did not even consider having one of his kickers try a low percentage kick. And in an earlier possession deep in Texas territory on fourth and short, the Irish did try for the first down and failed, so the coach still had that taste in his mouth.

However, the decision to use Reynolds instead of the regular Lattner at first blush borders on lunacy. On a short punt, Lattner did not need to boom a 51 yarder, but he had the experience in receiving the long snaps and in successfully punting behind his line, so it made little sense, particularly given the conservatism that Leahy embraced in these moments, to substitute a far less experienced punter.

Strangely, the punt turned the game around for the Irish, proving sometimes luck takes the odd turn. Reynolds booted to Raley, who tried to field it on his five yard line only to have the pigskin bounce off of his chest with the redoubtable Dan Shannon scooping up the bobble on the two yard line. For the second touchdown, Guglielmi handed off to Heap who bulled it right in, Mavraides converting.

Perhaps remembering the hurt put on the Irish the previous year by Fred Benners of SMU, Texas attempted to get into the game by passing, but separate drives were thwarted through interceptions by Jack Whelan and Dan Shannon respectively. The game ended with Tom Carey calling diving plays for his running backs, leaving Texas coach Eddie Price to say complimentary things about the lads that had just defeated his men.

Frank Leahy had calibrated the severe Texas heat and had planned a slugging match that only his team could win. His players looked silly in pith helmets on the sideline, appearing more like colonial governors in some remote outpost in the diminishing British Empire, yet the Old Man had correctly optimized their ability to play hard for the full sixty minutes, a point that Texas coach Ed Price conceded after

game's end. In their second game of the season the Irish defeated a better team.

The defense had improved incrementally since the previous week, preventing the Longhorns from scoring a touchdown for the first time in their last 57 games. Whereas
Dan Shannon came under criticism for his performance the
previous week, in Austin his hard hitting and ball-hawking skills came at defining moments in the game and stalled
any momentum his opponents had generated. With spectacular defenders like Lattner and Szymanski in place, and a
line continuing to gain experience, the Irish nearly shut out a
powerful team at its home stadium.

On offense, the Forgotten Four kept grinding down
the opponents, a must with gimpy receivers on the flanks.
Lattner gained the most yards for his team with 88, followed
by Worden chalking up 52 yards on 11 carries. Guglielmi
had his team's longest rush, reeling off a 29-yard run in the
fourth, while Joe Heap added the final touchdown. Impres-
sively, Googs directed his team most of the day with his fellow backs pouring it on in the fourth quarter to seal the tri-
umph. Flushed with victory, the Irish returned by charter
plane to South Bend the next day, which perhaps gave Joe
McArdle a chance to return to the store that sold him the
pith helmets and try to return them.

With Texas and its heat behind them, the Irish faced another strong opponent in the Pitt Panthers the next weekend.
Disenchanted fans and former players had accused the good
Fathers of deemphasizing sports under the Golden Dome,
fairly or not, but Pitt had openly deemphasized, with their
teams no match for any half decent opponent in the 1940s
and early '50s, but they had shifted again and by 1952 had

some very explosive backs of their own to match the Forgotten Four.

Maybe the team stayed one day too long in Austin, or the sun had bleached them, but whatever the cause, the Irish never established a rhythm all the next week long in practice. Having just defeated a formidable Texas Longhorn team far from home, most of the ND players expected a cake walk against a down-in-the-luck Pittsburgh squad coming to South Bend. Leahy saw it coming all week, urging his men to take matters seriously, to seek to improve over the week before, but nothing seemed to motivate them.

When the Pitt Panthers visited South Bend, the Irish lost their first home opener since 1942, by a narrow 22-19 margin. Similar to their experience with SMU the previous season, the team fell prey to the outstanding performance of one opposing offensive star, in this case Pitt's back Paul Reynolds who gained 167 yards on 17 carries. Unlike SMU, Pitt compiled much more of a team effort, with Joe Schmidt starring at linebacker and the backs all contributing at opportune moments with runs and receptions.

Pitt's Paul Reynolds struck with about five minutes left in the first quarter with a 78-yard touchdown run. Just before the first period ended, with Pitt back in possession of the ball, quarterback Rudy Mattioli threw a 63-yard touchdown pass to back John Jacobs, and after Paul Blanda kicked the extra point, the Irish found themselves behind 13-0. In the second quarter no one scored, but after taming Texas, Leahy found himself non-plussed at why his team had so many problems containing the Panthers.

In the third quarter, the Irish seemed rejuvenated when they took the ball from their own 22 after the kickoff.

Subsequently, the team seemed to click so much better, with a 16-yard Lattner run, topped by a 29-yard dash by Joe Heap to sustain a touchdown drive capped by a Neil Worden plunge into the end zone from 12-yards out. Guglielmi mixed up the drive well with timely passes to Heap and Worden.

Unfortunately, Pitt countered with a long drive of their own, with Mattioli scoring on the QB sneak. The defense played with spirit, having stopped Reynolds on the one foot line for no gain on the previous play, and they would not give up any points the rest of the way, but now the score stood 20-6 in favor of Pitt.

Back into the breach came Ralph Guglielmi, who again spread the wealth on offense, as Pitt's indomitable Schmidt went down with an injury. Googs completed a pass to Art Hunter which the end brought to the one foot line. As Mattioli had just done, Guglielmi sneaked it over for the TD and with Mavraides' extra point, he had brought this team back to within 7 points of the Panthers.

The Irish stalled on a promising drive in the fourth quarter, losing possession on an intercepted pass, but Pitt had its problems too, which caused them to punt to Joe Heap. All Heap did was catch the ball on his 8 yard line, run across the field and then race the rest of the way along the sideline for a 92-yard touchdown return. Pitt 20, Notre Dame 19.

At this point it all fell apart. On Mavraides' extra point kick, the referees penalized the Irish for holding. On the subsequent try, the snap from center went awry and the kick failed. Very late in the game, with ND back in possession of the ball, the Panthers sacked Guglielmi in his own end zone for the safety, and that was it.

After the loss, the expected recriminations followed, with Charlie Callahan deadpanning that "Notre Dame is practicing handshaking in order to appear gracious after losing." More concretely, Joe Doyle questioned why the Irish did not use Guglielmi more, particularly after his impressive performance against Texas. Harder to digest, how did the Irish defense play so poorly at home against a rebuilding Pitt team while shutting down Texas in Austin?

Not only had Pitt exposed the Irish weaknesses, but their boys had banged up Minnie Mavraides and end Paul Matz. Al Kohanovich moved from the defensive backfield to fill in for Matz, while basketball star Junior Stephens took over the spot vacated by Kohanovich. Replacing Mavraides presented more problems as Jack Alessandrini had to play both ways in the upcoming Purdue game to replace Minnie at guard, while either Bobby Joseph or Bob Arrix had to kick (the hopefully plenty) extra point opportunities in the game or games ahead.

Between the lines, Pitt may have won the game by repeatedly employing the "sucker shift" to draw the Irish offside. To successfully employ the sucker shift, a team's backfield formed a box formation and the quarterback ran to his right or left while his center still had not hiked the ball. If done correctly, the shift caused the defense to jump with the center still holding the ball on the ground, with a resulting penalty to the defense.

Purportedly, Purdue scouts at the Pitt game pleaded with their coach Stu Holcomb to use it the next week in their game against the Irish, but Holcomb turned down these entreaties because he equated the "play" with poor sportsmanship.

For his part, Leahy scheduled a secret Sunday practice the day after the Pitt loss to install the "sucker shift" into his offensive playbook, and then replicated the feat with key personnel the next day. Supposedly, Fr. Joyce himself could not enter the stadium while Leahy drilled the change into his men. Fool Frank Leahy once, shame on him, fool him twice...well that was not about to happen.

As much as the Irish needed to realign their offense and find their identity on the field against Purdue and some of the other premier programs remaining on their schedule, they had to also address some of the societal changes outside of Notre Dame Avenue, a difficult task for a traditionally conservative university and a very conservative (at least politically) coach. The program and the University had to confront issues of racial equality.

Wayne

ON OCTOBER 20, 1951, in a game against Oklahoma
A & M, Drake back Johnny Bright was punched in the face
by an opponent. He may not or may have broken his jaw at
that point, but he stayed in the game. A couple of plays later,
as an eligible back, he threw the ball downfield for a completion to his teammate, and then again, an opposition defender
punched him in the face, at which time he left the game for
good.

An immediate uproar followed the incident, both from
the Drake administration and from folks nationwide, as
a photographer captured the sequence of acts that led to
Bright's injury, and these sequential shots ran in a magazine,
exposing the plays in their full barbarity. The brute violence
of these assaults shocked most people, but as an ugly under-
current ran the issue of race, as Johnny Bright was African-
American and his attackers were Caucasian.

Against this backdrop, the University of Notre Dame
had begun its own first tentative steps to integrate its football team, a task that Leahy and the administration had attempted to accomplish for a while. Leahy had coached an
African-American athlete at Boston College, and he gave every indication that he abhorred segregation. With Leahy of

257

course, the skeptics who never believed a word he ever said did not suddenly give him the benefit of their doubts, but at the least, a fierce competitor like him favored integration if only as a means to gain an advantage over an opponent.

World War Two veteran Frazier Thompson had lettered in track for ND, and the Old Man gave him a tryout, but he did not make the team although he did graduate and earned a monogram (varsity letter) in track. On the 1949 team, African-American player Aaron Dyson made the varsity football team but did not play and did not earn a monogram.

In early 1950, *Ebony Magazine* ran a piece concerning African-Americans at Notre Dame, and largely lauded the University for its efforts at integration, and the positive experiences of its students of color. It did chide the University for its past practices, quite fairly, and stated that the "[c]racking of the onetime lily-white policy at Notre Dame came as a result of two pressures: 1) insistence by liberal Catholics on admission of Negroes; 2) wartime V-12 educational programs in which the Navy Department refused to kowtow to long-standing color [bias]."

Campus integration had come tepidly, with "eleven Negroes [entering] the hallowed halls...Two have graduated, seven others still attend and two more have dropped out—one to become a priest and the other because he was drafted." Most of the African-Americans on campus were Catholic and the school in part defended its past practices on the basis that with the exception of New Orleans and the parishes of southern Louisiana, most African-American communities did not harbor significant Catholic populations.

Still, Notre Dame had integrated voluntarily in juxtaposition with many state schools in the South, which awaited their own tumult as the Civil Rights era in a few years challenged their segregationist policies. Concurrent with Notre Dame's dropping the racial bar, St. Mary's College had also begun to admit African-American women to their school. The administrations attempted to make all students feel welcome and *Ebony* reported that at ND, the races interacted well together in a non-coercive environment. Some progress had occurred.

Two months later, when the Letters to the Editor flowed in, the University extended its appreciation for a balanced article while two African-Americans criticized it: one writer, an alumnus named Carl Coggins wished to straighten out the record to the effect that integration had effectively begun a bit earlier than the article intimated, while another writer challenged the conclusion that the University had not hired African-American employees until somewhat more than a decade earlier. The latter writer pointed out that Knute Rockne's trainer for the 1924 football team was an African-American named Verly Smith.

Notre Dame had a skimpy history of desegregation on the gridiron. The team did grant a scholarship to Entee Shine, primarily for his basketball prowess, but he did impress his teammates in his brief try-out with the football team as a freshman in the fall of 1950. Having feasted on opponents in the late '40s with Leon Hart at end, Shine, together with Joe Katchik and Bill Hall, fit the prototype of the future Irish tight end: tall, sturdy and hopefully athletic.

Katchik did not live up to the advance billing and Hall gave up too easily, but had Shine stayed, he might have become one of the greatest ends in the school's all-time roster. Unfortunately, he did not persist with football long at all, and transferred out of South Bend after playing some basketball, never fulfilling his vast potential. Although he left Notre Dame (and if he played football again it was for a very small school), the Los Angeles Rams drafted Shine in 1954, and after a brief time there, the team cut him. Shine did not have enough money to head back to his home in South Bend, so he worked out west for a bit until he had accumulated the funds necessary to purchase his train ticket.

Since Shine failed to earn a monogram, the task of becoming the first African-American man to do so in the Notre Dame football program fell to a thoughtful young man named Wayne King Edmonds. Wayne Edmonds graduated from high school in Canonsburg, Pennsylvania, the hometown of Perry Como and Bobby Vinton, Vinton being a high school classmate and friend. He had actually spent most of his younger years living in a mining camp and then a small nearby town. He had hardly seen a white person growing up because the mining camp town, named "No. 9," set off blacks on one side with whites living on the other and rarely did the two races come into contact with each other. Eventually, the Edmonds family decided they did not owe their soul to the company store and moved out of the camp to McDonnell, Pennsylvania.

By the beginning of high school, the family had moved once again, to Canonsburg, a small southeastern Pennsylvania town, where he grew up on the east side, an enclave of Greeks, Polish, Italians and some African-Americans. Canonsburg had a mixed heritage with race relations, with their schools integrated but its stores and movie theatres set aside by race. Oddly, on one day, Emancipation Day, the whole town got together to watch a parade celebrating the Emancipation Proclamation, and then the next day the walls rebuilt themselves. During that summer before high school, Wayne played some summer baseball as a catcher for a man named Al DeLucia who encouraged him to try out for the high school football team in the fall.

Wayne had been around town long enough to learn that Polish and Greek young men had very little chance of making the team, and African-Americans had none, but DeLucia told him, "Give it a try. I am coaching next year, so we will see if you make the team or not." Wayne Edmonds made the team. It was not always easy, because while his teammates all got along with him, Wayne faced a fair amount of racial taunting and name-calling from opposing players, particularly on teams from rural communities. After Wayne made a name for himself as a star at Notre Dame, one of his worst tormentors went around telling people what a great friend he was back in the old days with Wayne Edmonds.

Wayne's mentor Al DeLucia never stopped filling him with suggestions, making slight alterations in his game, shifting him from tackle to guard. At one point he advised Wayne to join the track team, where he proceeded to win almost every 100-yard dash he entered, in addition to anchoring a leg on the 4 x 220-yard dash. When Wayne came back one summer to school, having worked at a mill and gained 15-20 pounds of muscle, this most elegant and erudite of men looked like a football player and scouts took notice.

And all the time that a young Neil Worden glanced up at the giant clocks at the Allen-Bradley factory that seemingly foretold his inevitable future, Wayne Edmonds used to sit alone on a hill overlooking town and gazed below and thought about where his own life might lead. Wherever he looked, activity abounded, with cars driving down streets and folks milling about, but a single stretch of green lay below uninterrupted, Wayne's town football field. This, this was Wayne's out.

Many schools came to grant Wayne his wishes, with Pitt's scout maintaining the inside track throughout, with a full scholarship ride and an assurance of a graduate or law school degree to follow. It seemed like this was the place, until Bob McBride initiated a courtship, inviting Edmonds to visit Notre Dame, which he did with a high school teammate named James Malone. Edmonds had received interest from Penn State, Maryland, Penn and Colgate, but believed he would end up at Pittsburgh, until he saw Notre Dame. Some fellow West Pennsylvanians, including Jim Schrader, Huck O'Neil and Dave Flood took Wayne and his friend on a tour and a visit to a burger joint downtown. The situation seemed like a suitable one for all and he came away so impressed by the campus and its academic reputation that he signed on with the program.

The school also had an advantage in seeking the services of young Wayne Edmonds, in that he always wanted to play for Notre Dame. He undoubtedly knew that during his boyhood and before, ND had never fielded a black football player, and yet like millions of other young men across the nation, he held onto the dream.

Wayne did not believe previously that he could fulfill his boyhood dream of attending Notre Dame, but there it was, a scholarship offer from Frank Leahy telling him different. The next major hurdle was Wayne's Mom, concerned that the school might try to change him, here a Catholic school wooing a young Baptist boy. But McBride kept pitching, assuring her either he or his wife would get Wayne to a Baptist service every Sunday and then back again, a promise that the coach scrupulously kept. Somewhat hesitantly, Mrs. Edmonds gave her blessings and Wayne left the next fall for Notre Dame.

Notre Dame did not make it easy on young Wayne Edmonds for the same reasons it challenged all of its students: it was already a strong academic institution, and in the years ahead, led by Fr. Hesburgh, it became one of the leading universities in the world. In his zeal to remake the University, Fr. Hesburgh did not forget human beings and on the plane ride back to South Bend from an "away" game, Wayne woke up from a nap to see Hesburgh nudge the player next to Wayne to take his seat. Fr. Hesburgh proceeded not only to ask how Wayne was doing and if he had any issues to discuss, but began a long normal conversation about a number of topics, all undoubtedly to help the young recruit feel wanted and respected.

Not all went well. Once Wayne and a friend had to go out to the West Side of South Bend to get a hair cut because the barber on campus did not serve African-Americans. Fr. McCarragher, on one of his patrols, caught them and asked them about being in a restricted area, so they related the story to him. Nothing happened to Wayne but his friend got written up, although ultimately the matter fell through the cracks. And the segregated barber shop stayed on campus, at least for a bit longer.

Wayne's experiences with traveling with the team generally were favorable, except in some of the trips to the South. Slavery was once termed the "Peculiar Institution," and Jim Crow was almost as inscrutable to Wayne, as in some segregated areas he could sleep in the hotel with his team but not eat in the same restaurant with his friends. When Leahy found out about these types of restrictions, he blew up, and in the case of Georgia Tech, since they could not guarantee fair housing and meals for Wayne, Notre Dame forced them to play a game in South Bend that had previously been scheduled in Atlanta. Georgia Tech thus lost home field advantage in order that an odious Jim Crow status quo might live on.

Accompanying these types of issues, the administration at Notre Dame sincerely wanted to tend to its own area and ensure its own desegregation efforts proved successful, so in addition to Wayne, the team recruited another African-American scholar-athlete out of Pennsylvania, a back named Dick Washington. Unlike Wayne, who befriended everyone, Dick hung around a half dozen teammates who thought they could not be kicked off the team, not the hell-raisers that surrounded Neil Worden (most of whom were destined for success after football), but guys who just didn't get it. These associations hurt Dick's chances to make it at the school.

Some contacts through well-placed alumni did work in Dick Washington's favor, particularly on one occasion when a date had been set up between him and sultry blues singer Eartha Kitt. Leading up to the big evening, the back went back and forth about going on the date with the beautiful star or taking the safe route and staying home with the guys in the dorm, causing Wayne Edmonds to volunteer, "If you won't go, I'll stand in for you." Washington eventually chickened out, not even giving Edmonds the opportunity to replace him, a wrong move if there ever was one. On both counts.

Grace Edmonds had been warned back home to keep her son from coming to South Bend, because the priests would try to change him, converting him to Catholicism or otherwise making him something he was not, and the administration assured her that ND would not change her son. The administration was not able to keep its word to her.

Fr. Hesburgh and Frank Leahy and Bob McBride did not mean to mislead, and certainly Wayne received a first-class education and the opportunity to start on one of the most prestigious teams in the country and he had escorts to and from his Baptist services each week. But Wayne Edmonds did change. He walked into a situation ripe for desegregating and he made it happen, not just for himself but for future African-American young men who wanted to come to South Bend. And as Wayne guessed, once desegregation worked on the Fighting Irish football teams, other programs would follow the lead trying to replicate the success of that wily Frank Leahy.

No, Wayne Edmonds changed, and blessedly, the world changed with him and because of him.

Johnny Lattner's
Five Mortal Sins

THEN AGAIN, some things never change, and the annual Purdue/Notre Dame game proved no exception to the cliché, as the teams continued to dislike each other and Frank Leahy acted like a fan on the sideline.

At Ross-Ade Stadium in downstate West Lafayette, Indiana, Notre Dame defeated a favored Purdue team by 26-14, largely on the strength of Purdue's eleven fumbles, eight of which the Irish recovered. The Irish themselves coughed up the ball ten times, five times by John Lattner, although they did a much better job of recovering their own miscues or otherwise limiting the depth and nature of their self-inflicted wounds.

On a rainy or snowy day, one might expect or at least fear twenty-one fumbles, but the game against Purdue took place under fairly clear and sunny conditions. What made the game particularly violent, and which ended up with players on each team surrendering the ball, had its genesis with the recruiting practices of both schools in that era, particularly in Chicagoland. Each school raided the Chicago high school programs, with generally Notre Dame getting the most highly ranked recruits, a point not lost on the Purdue boys, many of whom wanted to attend ND. So when the games in the early '50s took place, it was almost in terms of a Holy War, where ancient rivalries having their genesis in the Chicago Catholic team rivalries spilled over to the games played in South Bend and West Lafayette.

Before the game began, the team captains met at midfield and after the Irish won the toss Leahy elected to defer to Purdue. On the very first kickoff Purdue had difficulty maintaining possession of the ball as returner Rex Brock lost the ball on his own 24 yard line after Tom Seaman hit him and Jack Lee recovered the ball.

John Lattner and Joe Heap chipped away at the distance between their team and the goal until Heap ran the ball right into the gut of the defense and lost it. Fortunately, tackle Joe Bush fell on the ball just inside the end zone for the Irish touchdown, Mavraides converting on the extra point kick.

Purdue answered, after a later brief Irish possession, with their own touchdown, led by Irish nemesis Dale Samuels, who quarterbacked his team systematically down the field, culminating his drive with a strike to Bernie Flowers. Flowers overran Irish defensive back Gene Carrabine, who had to leave the game with a leg injury sustained on the play. Samuels punctuated his drive by kicking the extra point to knot the game at 7-7.

After Joe Heap fielded the Purdue kickoff and ran it to his own 32 yard line, the offense stalled, forcing John Lattner to punt to the Boilermakers. Fortunately for the Irish, a Purdue defenseman roughed Lattner, permitting the Irish to regain the ball. Tom Carey then ran a perfect drive down the field distributing the rushing chores between Worden, Lattner and Heap. The Irish and Boilermakers proceeded to draw each other offside on a few plays until Worden bulled his way into the end zone, Mavraides converting.

Frank Leahy injected Ralph Guglielmi into the game the next time the Irish got possession of the ball and Purdue back Phil Mateja intercepted him, but then fumbled trying to run it and Tom Seaman recovered the fumble. With time running out in the first half, Guglielmi heaved a 37-yard touchdown pass to Lattner. Mavraides missed the extra point after the referees penalized his team on his first attempt.

Purdue narrowed the margin between the teams in the second half to 20-14 as Bernie Flowers made his second touchdown reception of the day. The Irish sustained a last touchdown drive of their own in the fourth quarter to round out the scoring at 26-14, with a typically bruising victory over Purdue.

The Irish defense played very well against a very strong but mistake-prone Purdue offense, led by the timely ball-hawking of Jack Lee, Notre Dame's green dahlia.

Lee pounced on three fumbles and blocked a punt, which led to his father calling him to inform him that he had just been voted Lineman of the Week. Lee modestly shrugged it off, but for that week, Jack Lee had earned his recognition as the finest lineman in the collegiate ranks in the United States.

Unfortunately for the varsity, the honors bestowed upon Lee did not extend to his teammates, particularly as they all gathered to review the game with the Boilermakers and to prepare for the next opponent, the North Carolina Tar Heels. Per usual, the varsity held its team meeting on Monday in the Law School lounge, where Frank Leahy mapped out plays on the blackboard and ran over the mistakes his team had made during the previous game. No one talked about how the varsity had just beaten a previously undefeated Purdue team, only an introspective dissection of mistakes deemed worthy of discussion transpired.

Generally, the starters had the day off after attending the skull session, but John Lattner did not get off so lucky this week. Toward the end of the session, Leahy, in his quasi-Irish brogue directed his focus squarely on Lattner: "Oooh John Lattner, why would you hurt Our Lady so this past Saturday with those five grievous sins committed against her?" The five cardinal sins, of course, were his five fumbles.

It has long since become Irish lore that Leahy then instructed Lattner to carry around a football all week long, to classes, the chow hall, the showers, to church—in an attempt to cure his "fumble-itis." One of his teammates, Bobby Joseph, even wrapped white tape around the ball to create a handle for Lattner to use for easier carrying from place to place. Many of his teachers took pity upon him.

What is spoken of less frequently, but which did occur after the team meeting on Monday, is that Coach Bill Earley then took Lattner to the practice field alone. Earley took a rope, tied one end of it to one goal post, very close to the ground and then ran the rope to the other goal post and tied it down there, also very low to the ground. Thereafter, Lattner had to hold the ball and jump under the rope without dropping the ball.

Earley had Lattner dive under the rope approximately 300 times. On occasion, Lattner's nose hit the rope and by session's end, he had a nose bloodied from the contact with the taut rope. At the end of this very tough workout, which only terminated once Lattner had snapped the rope in two parts with his nose, he returned to venturing everywhere on campus with a football, his now constant companion.

The coaching staff's deep concern about fumbling did not end with Lattner breaching the rope. A week later, still dissatisfied by the back's fumbling ways, the team ran a drill where every back on the team had to grab a ball and then run a gauntlet of the freshman team players, each of whom tried to gouge and claw the ball away from each varsity back. And then the next runner ran, again and again.

Having called out John Lattner's fumbling at the team meeting, Leahy leading up to the NC game focused on other elements of the team's recent performance, stating, "After looking at the Purdue movies, it is apparent we have plenty of work to do in the two departments of blocking and tackling." So Leahy sent his boys out there scrimmaging, with Guglielmi and Carey sharing snaps behind center, with the linemen repeatedly drilled on their blocking.

On the Friday before the North Carolina game, the team largely nursed its wounds, reviving some old plays and again stressed blocking. Gene Carrabine still suffered from an injured knee and Paul Matz ailed with a rib injury. Team captain Jack Alessandrini, meanwhile, drank hot fluids to purge the flu from his system.

Purdue puzzled Leahy. Despite his Irish having defeated a strong team, both clubs had indulged in too many mistakes to gauge the true worth of either. Last year, the Irish had barely scraped away a win over North Carolina, and while Leahy probably suspected his team had improved enough to win again, he needed to see a convincing victory to estimate how much they had progressed, as the final games of the year involved games against very formidable opponents. Repeated fumbling or missed blocking and tackling assignments spelled doom against upcoming programs like Oklahoma and Southern Cal. But as Sunday arrived and the team left Mass on October 25, 1952, the Irish had to focus on first getting past the Tar Heels.

Played in South Bend, each team scored a touchdown within the first four minutes of the game, knotting the score at 7-7, and seemingly setting the pace for a shootout. Then the teams' offenses both settled down, and with only five minutes left in the first half, Notre Dame took possession on its own 21 yard line.

What happened next helped establish Ralph Guglielmi's reputation as one of the finest "late rally" quarterbacks in school history. He swiftly completed six of eight forward passes to targets Art Hunter, Fran Paterra and Joe Heap, and when necessity called for it, even ran for a first down. With precious seconds remaining, Guglielmi then rolled out to his right, leading Heap toward the end zone, and then suddenly swirled and slung the ball to the unguarded Hunter, who made a shoe-string catch for a touchdown. After Arrix added the extra point, the Irish went into the locker room at half up 14-7.

Unlike Knute Rockne, Frank Leahy did not deliver fire and brimstone speeches at halftime. But while the Fighting Irish band marched outside, the team, nursing their spotty won-loss record, needed a spark to jump start their efforts in the second half. Receiving the opening kickoff on his own 16 yard line, Joe Heap more than provided it by running the ball all the way into the end zone as a bunch of his friends circled him and kept two Carolina special teamers at bay. Irish 21, Tar Heels 7.

Reserve fullback McHugh accounted for much of his team's success that afternoon. Had Tom McHugh suited up with the great Notre Dame teams of the 1940s, his name most likely would be trumpeted along with the almost endless flow of All-American backs of that decade, but in the early 1950s, his talents did not receive their proper due. Another part of his misfortune lay in playing fullback behind Neil Worden for four years, and Bull rarely received as much as a scratch, so McHugh waited.

By way of a slight digression, Knute Rockne produced not only great players, but smart players who thereafter went on to coach football programs throughout the country.

His most famous disciple of course was Leahy, but he peopled other former players at the heads of teams all over the place: Jack Chevigny at Texas, Harry Stuhldreher at Wisconsin, Elmer Layden at Notre Dame, and Jim Crowley at Fordham and Michigan State.

In contrast, Frank Leahy, who preached a cerebral and detail-oriented game, spawned very few coaches from the ranks of his lads, even though he had far more players under him each year than Rockne did. Terry Brennan coached at Notre Dame to mixed reviews, but while some former players served as assistant coaches, primarily at Notre Dame, few others made a mark. John Mazur later coached the Patriots, but it is hard to remember others who followed the Old Man's lead. Tom McHugh did, working his way up from the high school ranks to the collegiate level at Xavier and Kenyon.

In the '52 game against Carolina, this ND unsung hero

finally received some overdue recognition by scoring the last two touchdowns for his team. On his first score, McHugh penetrated a Tar Heel goal-line stance that had stopped the first two Irish runs from scrimmage and on the second occasion, he scampered for 22 yards until he crossed the end zone plane.

Many Irish players performed brilliantly for their quickly gelling congregation. Ralph Guglielmi coordinated long drives while fellow QB Tom Carey effectively led the team with his passes. Fran Paterra had a fine day on the ground and on defense, as the *Chicago Tribune*'s Charles Barlettt noted, Sam Palumbo "disturbed the Tar Heel backs thruout (sic) the afternoon, frequently slinging them for losses ranging up to 12 yards."

Having sat out the first game back in South Bend, Bobby Arrix now capably held down the kicker's position with the team. While he had scrimmaged in the fall as a back-up fullback, Arrix had also taken a few moments out to fool around with kicking the ball, a fact not unnoticed by the Irish coaching staff, and soon he had worked himself into position as perhaps the first kicking specialist in team history. Knowing something about kicking himself, Bob Joseph held the ball for him on his scoring attempts.

The *Chicago Tribune* reserved its highest kudos for John Lattner, who in an era where specialization had crept in, he "punted, played safety and averaged 7.4 yards in eight carries. Watching Lattner, you get the idea that here is a football player's player." He caught passes, ran once for 29 yards and intercepted a ball while on defense. But while Lattner and Worden continued to excel and Tom McHugh had demonstrated his ability, the team's other starting halfback had begun to demand his own plaudits.

Joe Heap had developed by this time into a great running back as well as the varsity's finest pass receiver. Only two athletes in the history of Notre Dame football have ever gained 1,000 yards both on the ground and in receiving during their careers, one of whom is Rocket Ismail, with Joe Heap the other.

As Heap's star ascended, Paul Reynolds' fortunes descended. Despite having an excellent freshman campaign on the ground in '51, Reynolds did not possess the sheer acceleration of Heap and did not do as many things well either. But after the NC game, Joe Doyle hinted at another reason, the requirements of Reynolds' degree in the engineering department. On Tuesdays and Thursdays, Reynolds had to attend engineering labs that ran well into practice time and since Mondays and Fridays were relatively light days, Reynolds only effectively worked out hard on Wednesdays. He simply did not have the time required by his coaches to perfect the plays, while Heap, an excellent student and a perennial Academic All-American, did.

In the next game against Navy, played in Cleveland, Heap excelled again, this time as a punt returner and as a passer, completing a 41-yard pass to Lattner. Ranked defensively first in the country against the run, Navy lost its star middle guard Steve Eisenhauer early with a broken rib. Leahy reacted by pounding the Middies with the persistent punches of the Notre Dame trio of Heap, Worden and Lattner. Bob Arrix put the Irish on the board for the first time with a field goal, followed later by a Worden touchdown run before halftime for a 9-0 lead.

In the second half, Huck O'Neil sacked the Navy quarterback in the end zone for a safety and Neil Worden scored his second running touchdown. The extra point attempts after each TD failed, but O'Neil's safety erased these errors as he and his teammates advanced to a 17-6 win against the Naval Academy. Ralph Guglielmi had a good day passing, primarily to target Don Penza.

Still, Notre Dame should have manhandled the Middies, and as Frank Leahy prepared his lads for the upcoming epic battle against Oklahoma, he may have wondered whether he had properly prepared them or if they were going to listen to siren songs as the Sooners' speedy back Billy Vessels ran over them all afternoon.

Oklahoma '52

OMINOUSLY, THE STAFF at the *Scholastic* had warned before the season that "In fact, the forthcoming campaign could be the worst of modern times." To date the Irish had won a game they had no business winning (Texas), lost a game and tied a game they should have won (Pitt and Penn) and then strung together a nice three-game winning streak; now they faced the most difficult part of their schedule: Oklahoma, Michigan State, Iowa and Southern Cal. The *Chicago Tribune* opined that they might lose three of these matches.

Oklahoma, in particular, looked like a certain loss on the schedule. Their coach, Bud Wilkinson, had laid the foundation for making the Sooners the preeminent football program in the United States, and he coached an extremely talented backfield led by quarterback Eddie Crowder, fullback Buck McPhail and halfbacks Buddy Leake and Billy Vessels.

Vessels, on the verge of winning Oklahoma's first Heisman, ran faster than most every back in the country. In watching game films of him, John Lattner commented that it appeared that the coaches had sped up the tape, but he learned to his consternation that Vessels ran as swiftly as the films demonstrated. Few gave the inconsistent Irish much of a chance of defeating the Sooners, an undefeated squad that had just blown out Iowa State by a 41-0 tally.

277

It was actually a bit worse than the average fan knew. The Split-T that Notre Dame utilized as their main offensive weapon had been taught to Leahy and his staff by one of Wilkinson's assistant coaches, Gomer Jones, and Oklahoma had long mastered what the young Irish offense still sometimes struggled with. While ND had defeated Texas and lost to Pitt, Oklahoma had beaten both common opponents, scoring 49 points against each. Indeed, the Sooners averaged over 40 points a game thus far. Mickey Mantle, one of Oklahoma's favorite sons, predicted that the "Sooners were going to stomp the Irish all season long..."

Frank Leahy received one piece of encouraging news in the middle of the week, when his candidate, Dwight David Eisenhower, won election to his first term as president, with the promise of many visits and golfing games with the president-elect for the head coach. Besides that bit of good news, Leahy had much to worry about, with defensive back Gene Carrabine, hurt in the Navy game, declared unfit to play for the remainder of the season. To fill the gap, Leahy shifted Jack Whelan to Carrabine's position and then brought in Paul Reynolds to start in the defensive backfield, with Whelan and the redoubtable John Lattner.

Fortunately for Leahy, Reynolds was poised for the defensive game of his career.

All week leading up to the game, the campus buzzed in a state of near pandemonium, a feeling matched by the opposing fans, twenty-six trainloads, 10,000 of whom had bought tickets to the game. At the eye of the storm, Leahy devised a very simple formula for victory, based on gaining three yards each play from scrimmage and denying the opposition the ball for as long as possible. Keep the explosive

Oklahoma offense off the field and continue to grind away at their defense until the superior Irish conditioning began to overwhelm them.

Stressing the ground game and pinpoint accuracy on the split-T, Leahy opted to start Tom Carey at quarterback. Having first possession in the game, the Irish went right to work but stalled after three plays. Lattner boomed his punt to Oklahoma's Jack Ging (in later life an actor perhaps best known for his roles in television's "The A Team") who returned the ball to his own 47 yard line. On the first play from scrimmage quarterback Crowder handed the ball off to his fullback Buck McPhail who dived into the line.

Wire services had run photos of the Oklahoma backfield all year, the tricky quarterback Eddie Crowder, with quick Buddy Leake and all-world Billy Vessels at the halfback positions. But the toughest of all was Buck McPhail, a worthy rival to Bull Worden. And yet on that first play, McPhail ran into an Irish wall with the result being that he not only fumbled but he shot the football into the air. An alert Dan Shannon at linebacker rebounded the ball and ran it another thirteen yards to give his team excellent field position at their opponent's 35 yard line.

Like an Homeric epic, the fates had shifted with the whim of the gods, a pattern that repeated itself all afternoon. Three runs failed to get the first down, so on fourth and short Leahy rolled the dice a bit and kept the players on the field for one last shot at the first. It worked, with Carey handing off to Lattner who ran the ball all the way down to the 12 yard line.

Carey then let his starting backs share the running chore, with third down back Joe Heap driving the ball down to the four yard line; not enough though, and Leahy faced another fourth and short, and he again kept the offense running. Lattner took the hand-off and ran it to the one yard line, his legs churning for that extra yard and the score, until a host of Oklahoma defenders joined the fray and finally muscled him down. Still, it looked like a first down until the crowd shifted their focus to a flag on the field, a penalty of five yards against the Irish for backfield in motion. This time Frank Leahy opted to bring in his kicker, Bob Arrix, who narrowly missed the field goal to the left. A stunned Arrix, followed by his holder Bobby Joseph, staggered off the field dejectedly.

Taking over, Oklahoma sputtered in attempting to establish its running game, with Vessels being stacked up like lumber on one rush by Huck O'Neil, Dick Szymanski and Jack Lee while Buddy Leake looked like he had the entire field to himself on another play until John Lattner stood him up and drilled him on a fine open-field tackle. The last play forced a punt, but while Lattner, Worden and Heap combined for the three yards on each play, the average dictated by Leahy, they too had to punt, on 4th and 1.

On the next defensive series, Szymanski came up big again, and fierce tackles by Whelan and Reynolds from their defensive back positions again stalled the opposition. On Reynolds' tackle, the unassuming Irish back nearly took the opposition runner's head off. Unfortunately, the ensuing Oklahoma punt, together with a holding penalty, left the Irish on their own 1 yard line.

Neither Ralph Guglielmi, Neil Worden nor John Lattner could dig the team out, so Lattner punted from his own end zone and a hideous bounce back planted the ball for Oklahoma on the ND 27 yard line. From there, quarterback Crowder faked a hand off and the Irish linebacking corps bit on the run. Out sprung Billy Vessels in the flats to the left and Crowder tossed him a perfect pass on the ten yard line which the speedy Oklahoma back easily ran into the end zone. With the successful Leake extra point kick, the Irish fell behind 7-0.

Again on their next possession, ND had some decent runs, no game breakers, and had to punt, this time Lattner booting it from his own ten all the way to the Oklahoma 45. On their first play, Crowder handed off to Vessels who immediately became acquainted with Dan Shannon and a vicious plant into the Indiana earth for a three-yard loss. With that play, the first quarter ended with the Irish behind, but two facts working in their favor: with the exception of one play, the defense played remarkably well and the offense ran 29 plays from scrimmage to the Sooners' 13 attempts, trends working in the favor of the underdog.

One of the issues facing Oklahoma as they started the second quarter is that the Irish had a pretty good defense and they started stacking seven men on the line to blunt the run, with the knowledge that the Sooners did not possess much of a passing game. The result, the Sooners increasingly became stymied in trying to sustain long drives and became reliant on the big plays.

The Irish defense stopped their opponent early in the second quarter, but again, once the Irish got the ball back, they kept the ball for a spell then gave it right back again. Encouragingly though, in the first drive, Lattner gained nine yards plowing behind Minnie Mavraides and also spun loose for another decent gainer, this one for thirteen yards before the drive failed.

Thereafter, both ND and Oklahoma staged futile possessions, necessitating Lattner punting the ball from deep in his territory. The ball sailed to the return man, Jack Ging, who inexplicably called a fair catch with no special team defenders around him. The Sooners missed out on that opportunity when quarterback Crowder fumbled, with Huck O'Neil recovering the ball and racing all the way to the end zone. The run was called back due to a penalty, but the Irish retained possession.

With Ralph Guglielmi now calling the plays, everything seemed to click. Heap caught a 15-yard pass to bring the ball to nearly midfield and then the line, led by Tom Seaman and Minnie Mavraides, began opening holes up for everybody. At center, Jim Schrader plowed ahead at will, with Neil Worden, Fran Paterra and Googs himself taking advantage of the holes opening ahead of them. The drive culminated when Joe Heap cradled a ball thrown to him in the flats, shook off three potential tacklers and scored the team's first touchdown, with Bob Arrix tying it with the extra point.

The future just kept getting brighter when in their next possession Oklahoma surrendered the ball on their own 33 after linebacker Dave Flood jarred the ball loose from the back and Paul Reynolds scooped it. A Guglielmi pass to Heap just missed the wide open back, and then on the next play disaster struck. Notre Dame relinquished the ball on a fumble recovered by Oklahoma's Don Brown. Two plays later, Crowder handed off to Billy Vessels—at first it appeared as if Notre Dame had stuffed him at the point of attack-but then someone turned ND lineman Bob Ready around, perhaps by a low block. Vessels then slid to his right, got past Dave Flood and Paul Reynolds and ran the ball 66 yards for a touchdown. Like that, Oklahoma led again, 14-7.

With time running low in the second quarter, Oklahoma kicked off, but instead of booting it, the kicker squibbed it and Dick Szymanski brought it up to his own 45 yard line. On a subsequent play, the Irish made no headway, but after the play had apparently ended, Minnie Mavraides slammed Oklahoma's best defender, J.D. Roberts. Roberts threw a punch at Mavraides and got ejected from the game by the referees.

Behind Guglielmi, the team stormed down the field again, making good use of the clock with short, high-percentage passes. Googs found Heap with a pass late in the drive, which his friend took all the way down to the 5 yard line. At that point, Leahy almost certainly would have urged a return to the running game, probably with hand-offs to Neil Worden, except the referees brought the ball back to the 20 on a penalty. On the next play Guglielmi threw to Lattner in the end zone, but Vessels intercepted and soon after, the half ended.

At halftime, Frank Leahy projected calm. As a student of the game and not a fan, he perceived that his game plan so far had worked reasonably well against a very strong opponent. Oklahoma had lost its best lineman, J.D. Roberts, while conversely, particularly on offense, linemen Varrichione, Seaman, Alessandrini, Schrader and Mavraides had begun to dominate. To his lads, he stressed continued ball control and deprivation of possession to Oklahoma, and waited for luck to break his way.

Notre Dame's first possession of the third quarter made it appear as if luck were not needed as Tom Carey directed the Irish 72 yards on 16 plays with wonderful fakery in the split-T. He also ran the option quite well even when the opposition seemingly had drawn a bead on him; on one play he kept stringing the defense laterally across the field until he heaved it to Joe Heap at the last instant for a good gain. End Art Hunter caught a key pass and Worden, Heap and Lattner kept running the ball down the gut with drill-press precision. Until John Lattner got hit, mugged really, on a running play, and fumbled at the Oklahoma 11 yard line, the Sooners' Kay Keller recovering.

Lattner felt awful, but his teammates just dug in harder, slugging it out in the trenches that increasingly they owned. This time the gods favored lineman Sam Palumbo, who helped break up two runs for short gains. Frustrated, Crowder dropped back to pass and threw it right into the hands of Irish defensive halfback John Lattner who redeemed his recent *faux pas*, running the ball from the 35 down to the eight yard line. Lattner in fact did more than simply step in front of a pass and grab it, Crowder called a pass play identical to his earlier touchdown heave to Vessels and Lattner read the play all the way.

From there, a Sooner penalty inched the ball to the 2 yard line, where Worden and Lattner failed to score. On the next try though, Worden displayed some of his gymnastic prowess by jumping over everyone until he shattered the plane of the end zone. With Arrix's extra point, the score stood 14-14.

But not for long. On the Sooners' next possession, on the third play, Billy Vessels followed his blockers who bowled down a number of would-be tacklers for a 44-yard touchdown run and a 21-14 lead after the conversion.

Up until now, the game had been characterized largely by ND running the vast majority of the plays while their opponents scored when Billy Vessels got free. The next Irish drive did not alter this trend as Tom Carey continued to run the T effectively. On one of the more surprising plays, Carey pitched to Heap who heaved the ball downfield to John Lattner for nearly a 40-yard gainer.

As the third quarter faded into the fourth, the Irish dropped all pretense of surprise, with Carey handing the ball to Neil Worden seven straight times. Even without J.D. Roberts, Oklahoma had some fierce tacklers like Larry Griggs, and on play after play Worden got pounded and then jumped right back up for the call. He plowed ahead inexorably to his goal and then surpassed it, as the Bull finally broke through for the tying touchdown.

Typically, a quarterback called his own plays, but Worden understood that Carey was not the one calling on him time after time—the plays emanated from the Old Man, Leahy. Worden took each assignment without complaint or concern about personal pain, he only hoped that on each play he hurt the other guy a bit more. These plays stand over a half century later as the signature moments in the great fullback's career at Notre Dame, as Neil Worden shook down the thunder from the sky.

The thunder only boomed louder on Minnie Mavraides' kickoff, fielded by Oklahoma's Larry Griggs, who crossed his 20 yard line at the same time as Dan Shannon planted him with one of the greatest hits ever registered in Notre

Dame football, one which Joe Doyle suggested "must have resounded all the way to the Oklahoma midlands." Shannon and Griggs lay on the ground like turtles laying helplessly on their backs as Al Kohanovich recovered the ball for the Irish. Probably, Shannon sustained an undiagnosed concussion as both players were taken off the field. In the stands, Dan Shannon's mother started to say the rosary.

Tom Carey took immediate advantage of the situation, handing off to Lattner for a twelve-yard gain. He then apparently took the ball from center and raced to his right as the Oklahoma tackles blasted across the line, offsides as it turned out. Carey had merely run to his right with Schrader still holding the ball, the maneuver called the "sucker shift," which penalized the opposition five yards. Neil Worden failed to score on the next play, but then Carey called a sneak and barreled into the end zone behind Schrader. Oklahoma blocked Arrix's extra point attempt, but Notre Dame had its first lead of the day, 27-21.

Oklahoma did not go quietly into the night. It ran a 60-yard drive that sputtered, then ran another drive that ended with a fumble at the Notre Dame 20 yard line, Lattner recovering. On their third and last great drive, they resorted more to the pass, not pitching the ball outside to Vessels, which had been their most explosive play. The game ended when Vessels threw a pass to one of his receivers at the end zone stripe, but defensive back Paul Reynolds capped an extraordinary day on defense by batting the ball down as the final gun sounded.

As the Oklahoma players staggered off the field, Notre Dame's fans stormed it. They appreciated Tom Carey, who had just completed his finest day as a Fighting Irish by carrying him off the field and across the way to Cartier Field before letting him down. Among the other Irish carried off the field were Joe Heap and Ralph Guglielmi. John Lattner and Neil Worden needed all the help offered to them, as they contributed fifty of the almost seventy rushes by the team. For his part, defensive star Dan Shannon, still bleary from his hit on Larry Griggs, asked Tom McHugh, "Did we win?"

Back in the dressing room, Dan Shannon's father spoke to his son and explained what happened in the game after the collision with Griggs. Oddly enough, most of the players sat around relatively subdued, having survived the rare game that probably exceeded the worst of the team's practices for taxing one's limits. J.D. Roberts, the lineman tossed out of the game for taking a swing at Mavraides, came into the ND lair to apologize.

Three-touchdown underdogs no more, Frank Leahy followed his pre-game battle plan perfectly, eking out the win. In doing so, he had completed the rebuilding of his team from the 1950 debacle. In the next 3½ years the Irish would rarely lose again and never be held to disdain as they had before the '52 game with the Sooners.

As Jack Glowser of the Cleveland *Press* saw it, "It was a milestone on glory road, a saga of defiance against odds, a shining and exalting chapter in Notre Dame's treasured volume of athletic feats. In thirty years of watching football, this writer has never seen a more inspiring performance." In other words, stop crying for the Irish, they are back.

Remember the Spartans

ON SUNDAY after the Oklahoma game most Notre Dame men attended church and basked in the era of good feelings brought about by their football team's victory, while on Monday the team took the day off from practice to rest and refit for its upcoming game against the number one ranked team in the country, Michigan State. While ND's most recent contest seemed savage, with J.D. Robert's ejection and all, the Spartans had just come off a victory against Indiana in which eight players in all got the hook.

Trainer Gene Paszkiet had to tend to Joe Bush with a bum shoulder and Minnie Mavraides with a bruised knee, the latter getting off lightly considering his tiff with J.D. Roberts. Gene Carrabine continued to suffer from his previous injuries and looked doubtful for service in the week ahead, while strangely, no mention was made of Dan Shannon, the most badly battered player of them all.

Any residual glow from the Sooners' game disappeared on Tuesday when Leahy had his men running gassers, fifty-yard sprints over and over and over. He also had Lattner punting, an unnecessary exercise given that he had kicked generally very well in the past contest, with the exception of a punt that took a bad bounce backward. Meanwhile, the

289

Spartans drilled in secret while the press learned that baseball star Robin Roberts expected to attend the upcoming game.

By Wednesday, Leahy had begun to follow Michigan State's lead, with two prominent signs posted which read "No Scrimmage," and "No Spectators." Leahy stated that "The players will be as anxious to win …And I feel certain from long experience they cannot be as well prepared physically." Following this cryptic path, he pondered what would happen to his club if Lattner, Worden, Sam Palumbo or Huck O'Neil were ever hurt while intimating his team might resort to the "long passing game."

The team traveled to East Lansing for their November 15, game against the Spartans, one of the most successful college football teams of the 1950s.

The Irish defense continued to play well, shutting out the Spartans in the first half. While the defensive backfield still relied too much on John Lattner's omnipresence, the defensive line had solidified behind Huck O'Neil, Sam Palumbo, Jack Lee, Bob Ready and Paul Matz. Similarly, the Irish had one of their best linebacking corps in the second half of the twentieth century with Dick Szymanski, Dan Shannon, Jack Alessandrini and Dave Flood. Unfortunately, the Notre Dame offense did not score in the first half either.

Irish eyes began to smile at the very beginning of the second half as John Lattner recovered a Spartan fumble on their 11 yard line. Although the offense did not drive it in for a touchdown, Bob Arrix kicked a 17-yard field goal for the Irish lead.

Fumbling had been a problem for the Irish in the first half (really all year) and in the second half State took full advantage of the opportunities presented to them. That and penalties began to sink them, errors that Don McAuliffe exploited by running two touchdowns in to place MSU in the lead 14-3.

The Irish did rally, almost cutting into the opponent's lead, with John Lattner legging out a 34-yard run; but it died with Ralph Guglielmi being stopped one yard shy of the goal line. After MSU intercepted late in the game, Evan Slonac scored the final time for MSU and the Irish lost 21-3.

Done in by interceptions, penalties and fumbles (seven of the latter), the Irish made their own bed in this game. Playing the best team in the country at their home stadium in East Lansing, with a 21-game unbeaten streak to protect, meant ND had to play virtually mistake-free ball to win. They missed that mark by quite a bit and returned to South Bend with a bitter loss and an ailing Dave Flood, who had sustained an injury to his clavicle.

The loss left Notre Dame #9 in the AP poll, with Iowa next on their schedule. In practice that week, Leahy threw his freshmen against the offensive line and back starters to generate a better running game. In place of the injured Flood at linebacker, the club alternated Jack Alessandrini and Neil Worden to take his place, meaning that the replacement would, like John Lattner, have to play the whole game. The Irish worked out in a pouring rain on Tuesday and planned a last hard workout on Thursday, designed to reduce the fumbling plague, then taking off by train for Davenport, Iowa after a light Friday drill. It appeared Gene Carrabine might have to sit out another game while Flood definitely had ended the season due to his broken clavicle. It is not recorded if Ray Bubick approached Coach Bill Earley and asked the coach if he now knew what a clavicle was.

Earley might have even smiled, as he stayed behind in South Bend's St. Joseph Hospital to be with his wife and new born baby girl. Frank Leahy too, stayed behind, reportedly with a dose of the flu.

Joe McArdle took over the head coaching duties, radically altering the way the Irish conducted business, starting with installing Tom McHugh as the kickoff returner. Most of the moves had already received Leahy's approval, and the head coach even sent out a letter in the middle of the week telling someone that McHugh would start at fullback. Some one forgot to tell McHugh this, as he learned about his start on the morning of the game on the bus ride to the stadium.

Although it had not rained recently, the turf at Iowa's home stadium was drenched leaving most Notre Dame men to conclude that someone flooded the field before the team got there, in an attempt to equalize the two teams as much as possible with artificially slippery conditions. With two fullbacks though, ND had an advantage as McHugh, and Worden preferred "grind it out" football.

Preferences aside, McHugh dropped the opening kickoff but fortuitously, Dick Szymanski recovered. McArdle kept McHugh in as the starting fullback, shifting Neil Worden over to halfback. On the Irish opening drive, quarterback Tom Carey effectively shredded any preconceptions the Iowa coaches had concerning the ND offense as the running quarterback threw successfully to Worden and Art Hunter. As part of McArdle's new-look offense, Tom McHugh carried the rock six times, with Worden providing the *coup de grace* with a short run for the Irish score, Arrix converting.

The game just got odder, with John Lattner installed as the punt returner. All he did was return one from his own 14 all the way for a touchdown, with Dick Szymanski providing the final painful block as Lattner continued his romp down the sidelines.

The Hawkeye offense encountered the ultimate "bend but not break defense," with the Irish terminating drives on their own 7, 9 and 2 yard lines at various stages of the game, ensuring a shut-out. Continuing their platooning of quarterbacks, Air Guglielmi accounted for passes of 43 yards to Don Penza and eight yards to Neil Worden before tossing a seven yarder to Heap for the team's third touchdown of the day.

On their last scoring drive, reserve halfback Fran Paterra passed to Art Hunter for 39 yards while Guglielmi scooted for eleven yards on a run. Neil Worden ended the scoring for the day with one of his patented touchdown plunges, with the final extra point failing. It was an odd game, the type Notre Dame could have won in the 1940s simply by inserting any player on their varsity in the game, still possessing the sheer ability to defeat anyone. Undoubtedly, Iowa's first-year coach, Forrest Evashevski, with only two wins in his inaugural season took the defeat very bitterly indeed.

Back in Indiana, Leahy continued his recovery from the flu as Coach Druze paid him a visit to review the scouting report of the final opponent, the University of Southern California. As Leahy continued to recuperate, Coach McArdle worked out his players indoors on Tuesday, concerned that Notre Dame might sustain another injury or two. Indeed, the week leading up to the final game was characterized more by the Irish wishing to put their best eleven on the field at all times, and hoping the harsh South Bend winter might prove an ally as the Trojans flew into town.

The inclement weather certainly helped, as on November 29, 1952, Notre Dame concluded its season at home with tin Trojans and Nixon coming. At the time the Rose-bowl-bound Southern Cal had a perfect record and a legitimate claim to the National Championship, and perhaps due to President Eisenhower's political debts owed to Leahy, he dispatched his vice-president Richard Nixon to take in the festivities. A football fanatic if there ever was one, Nixon, accompanied by his wife Pat, had a beaming smile on his face the entire afternoon during this main event.

The game itself did not live up to its billing as the ground had frozen, with "temperatures which never rose above freezing." Although no snow impeded the contestants, the young men had difficulty cutting and establishing any traction all afternoon. Frank Leahy, just back from his bout with the flu, dressed up in a heavy coat and a hoody in the midst of the frozen tundra. Observed an AP writer, "Leahy had shivered thru the game..."

The boring game only began to get interesting halfway through the second quarter when Lattner punted to USC's Jim Sears. Inexplicably, Sears lateralled to his teammate Al Carmichael, who had run upfield and was nowhere in evidence as an alert Minnie Mavraides jumped on the ball. Taking over on the Trojan 19 yard line, Ralph Guglielmi ran once, as did Neil Worden, but John Lattner did the yeoman's work, carrying the ball five times until he crossed the goal line. Arrix had his extra point kick blocked, leaving ND ahead by a mere 6-0.

Weather aside, Southern Cal roared back for two drives before halftime, but each one ended by interception, with Lattner copping one and Paul Reynolds netting the other.

The Irish mounted a good drive of their own to commence the third quarter, but when it stalled on the opposition 17 yard line, Bob Arrix trotted in and coolly drove home a field goal, a feat that won him a small headline in the next day's *Chicago Tribune*.

Seventeen-yard field goals were big news back then. The points had more significance because they closed the book on the scoring for the remainder of the afternoon. The Trojans kept trying and a Sears pass to Jim Hayes looked like a scorer until Paul Reynolds ran him down on the ND 25 yard line, the play having already covered 50 yards. No problem, Dan Shannon intercepted a pass shortly afterwards to smother the threat, causing Coach Earley to quip, "They should have known you can't throw a screen pass into Dan Shannon's [area]."

USC almost scored again in the fourth quarter with the ball on the Irish one yard line, but the sturdy Irish line held. When the game ended, the Southern Cal players exhibited the same dazed visages that the Oklahoma players had after losing a few weeks earlier.

They had thrown up five interceptions during the game, including wrongly mailed packages to Whelan and Alessandrini.

Offensively, Neil Worden ran for 73 yards while John Lattner added 66. Fran Paterra had the best average for all runners that day with 42 yards on only five carries, a feat more magnificent given the game conditions. The year 1953 looked particularly promising for Paterra, if the fates held.

For the year, Neil Worden topped the team in scoring with 60 points, all on touchdowns with Lattner leading in total rushing yardage (734) and rushing average (4.9). Joe Heap displayed his dual-threat versatility with a team-leading 29 passes caught for 407 yards, while gaining an additional 393 yards on the ground. Ralph Guglielmi completed 61 passes for 683 yards.

Lattner and Jack Whelan tied for interceptions with four apiece, although Johnny got much more yardage after his snatches. Joe Heap led the team in kickoff returns and tied Paul Reynolds for punt returns, although again like Lattner, he far outpaced his teammate in yardage gained. Flood led the team with fumbles recovered with five and Jack Lee blocked the only punt for the Irish and suffered yet another broken nose at the end of the season.

Winning the Maxwell Trophy as the country's preeminent player, John Lattner also earned consensus All-American recognition, with Huck O'Neil also named an All-American by at least one major service. Lattner flew into New York for an All-America event, then had to fly back to Chicago, sleeping for two hours on a bench in a train station before hopping on the train ride back to South Bend. Alone among his fellow All-Americans (all others hailing from other schools), he attended his classes that Monday.

While the year started off a bit shaky, the Notre Dame Fighting Irish ended up with a 7-2-1 record which included wins or a tie over five conference champions. In recognition of this most formidable accomplishment, the polls tabbed them the No. 3 team in the country.

The team elected Don Penza as their captain for the following season, and Hollywood comedian Joe E. Brown entertained the crowd at the team's annual fete on December 4. Ominously, Frank Leahy traveled to the Mayo Clinic and his doctors ordered a week of total bed rest, so he failed to attend his team's wrap-up banquet. His friends and family worried about his health, while his enemies talked about how worried they were about his health.

Brennan in the Dome

THE FOOTBALL SEASON having ended, Neil Worden no longer focused as much on the team and began to take the opportunity to stop and smell the roses. One day, while in the administration building he looked up toward the ceiling and noticed that on the third floor a bare railing stood between passers-by and a big sudden stop on the first floor. He decided to share this observation with Bobby Joseph and Lee Getschow and then mused whether or not a person could possibly do a headstand on the railing without falling down.

Of course Worden felt he had the requisite gymnastic background and acumen to complete the task, but he wondered if Joseph or Getschow had the same ability. The dare was on. The three dare-devils walked up to the third floor and indeed all thought that they could perform the feat, with the equal knowledge that if they failed, they certainly had no chance of trying out for the varsity in 1953. Worden tried it first, worrying for the first time a bit about the cost of such failure, but he accomplished the task without a hitch. By this time a small crowd had formed below to watch the spectacle. Unfortunately, they never got to witness a crash as Joseph and Getschow both proved that a head stand on the rail could be done.

297

In a less dangerous arena, the Fighting Irish basketball team made its first post-season appearance ever in the NCAA, winning its first two games until losing to Indiana in the quarter-finals. Although they did not star, Walt Cabral and Bobby Joseph played on the varsity team. Joseph also competed in the university's annual Bengal Bouts (so named for the charity aspect of the event with proceeds donated to the Holy Cross missions in the Bengal region of the Indian subcontinent), winning the 167-lb. class, as a *Dome* writer noted that he "displayed some of the best counter-punching in the bouts." Ed Sarna won the 177-lb. class and Ed Cook took the heavyweight crown, over a number of other boxers, including Jack Lee. In indoor track, Joe Heap ran well in the sprints and the relays, quitting the moment that Leahy bid him to practice.

The Army, Navy and Air Force ROTC continued to thrive, with the Air Force and Navy men awaiting their summer six-week training assignments at bases across the country. On particularly cold and hazy days, Patsy Bisceglia cut through the gloom after leaving the Dining Hall by belting out his rendition of *O Solo Mia* at the top of his lungs, a sound that nearly carried over to the Michigan border.

The school continued to sponsor its annual class dances, the Freshman Frolic, the Sophomore Cotillion and the Junior Prom and for the first time ever a Junior Parents-Son Weekend was held. The parents had the option to watch an ROTC drill, a football scrimmage, a varsity basketball game against Illinois or just visit with their child and perhaps traipse over to the Grotto. Father Hesburgh addressed the families at dinner, telling the throng, "I want you parents to feel you belong at Notre Dame as your sons are the main part of our University."

In a different vein, Fr. Hesburgh had the occasion to speak at another popular event of the day, the Marriage Institute. Throughout each March, seniors and married students attended a set of gatherings each week for four weeks, at which time a number of speakers espoused their views on this sacrament and other topics, such as conversion of non-Catholics. Fr. Hesburgh's topic concerned choosing the right mate, a well-received lecture then and a source of good natured kidding of him ever since

At another gathering, Hesburgh made a former Forties' football back feel welcome in early March when he announced the hiring of Terrence Patrick Brennan as an assistant football coach and "probable" freshman coach, at a Notre Dame Club of Chicago meeting. By all outward appearances, Head Coach Frank Leahy handled this development with class and grace, a task made more difficult by the probability that his superiors had almost certainly hired his ultimate successor.

Previously, the light had shone brightly on the Leahy/ Brennan relationship. Hailing from a prosperous Milwaukee family (the elder Brennan owned a very profitable law firm), Terry Brennan came to South Bend as a freshman in 1945, and by senior year, had starred for three years as a back under Leahy. Most importantly, he took a class with Fr. Hesburgh, making a most favorable impression as a gentleman and a scholar on the future ND president.

After graduation in 1949, Brennan accepted an offer to coach perennial Chicago prep superpower Mt. Carmel High School, a teeming feeder of talent to the Notre Dame varsity at that time. In his last three years, Brennan had coached Mt. Carmel High to city championships and developed such future Irish stars as Dan Shannon, Paul Matz, Tom Carey and Frank Pinn.

Despite Brennan making a good impression, there were two irreducible facts in the ND football program at this time: to paraphrase the priest in *Rudy*, there is a God and Frank Leahy too often acted like he thought he was God. In other words, Leahy never saw himself not coaching Notre Dame and there, in his presence, stood the young man who he had once coached who had just been anointed his successor.

Secondly, by this point, the administration at Notre Dame had ceased to treat the football program with a laissez-faire attitude, and indeed, influential people like Fr. Hesburgh and Fr. Joyce had begun to wonder if the presence of Frank Leahy hurt or helped the university, and to what extent one factor outweighed the other. To understand the era, Fr. Hesburgh had great dreams for Notre Dame as a foremost academic, spiritual and athletic institution and with the NCAA extending the scope of its own power, he rightfully feared that the football program might ruin it all.

Nearing his death, many years later, Frank Leahy alluded guardedly to his biographer some of the issues regarding bringing young men into the University of Notre Dame:

"Do not misunderstand me, I did not altogether care for the means whereby players were induced to attend our school. There were some things that occurred at Notre Dame that I did not wish to think about. They happened."

"I knew about them. I did not care for them. But in the

pursuit of excellence, one learns to make important compromises. They are not tasteful ones, you understand. But they do become necessary."

Leahy's peers, particularly those who had to schedule games against him each year, posed a threat to create a controversy around the program. The minute a disaffected young man left the program, or even worse, the school, the potential for someone blabbing about recruiting or coaching or some other aspect of the team might spur an investigation. The NCAA was growing more powerful each year and had the ability to embarrass and punish Notre Dame. By way of example, the "sucker shift" was banned after the '52 season, Notre Dame treated as if it were the only program to employ it.

If Frank Leahy did not wish to think about some things, University president Theodore Hesburgh and Fr. Joyce did not have the luxury of wishing a problem away. If something blew up around the football program, it might potentially engulf the program itself and a large part of the University's reputation in the ensuing firestorm.

So Terry Brennan came aboard because he came from this wonderful athletic background but also understood the administration's concerns that the football program was a scandal or two away from permanently blotting the reputation of the school. He had to win and he had to win honestly and within the rules, and given Frank Leahy's nature, Brennan might get the chance to take over in the near future.

Again, to his credit, Leahy welcomed his former lad as a colleague just as much as he had done with Johnny Lujack, sitting him in on all meetings of the coaches and listening to him. Yet Lujack never scared him, but after the announcement of Brennan's hiring at the Chicago club meeting, Leahy had the right to feel a tad paranoid.

For Leahy, it only got worse. The NCAA and Leahy were not ideal mates for each other, and the coach seethed at their restrictions on spring practices and the decision to implement one-platoon football for the next year. Essentially one-platoon ball meant that a team had to keep its starting players on the field both on offense and defense most of the game. Once a player left the field, he could not return for the rest of the quarter and his replacement then had to pick up his assignments on both sides of the ball.

One-platoon ball harked back to an earlier time when players lined up on offense and defense, and Leahy had long since become enamored of free substitutions and slotting a player to his best position on either offense or defense, but not both. Unless one's last name was Lattner. Due to the reinstitution of one-platoon ball, Leahy had to find not only his first-string players both ways but also his second string two-way players, and great stress was placed in mid-March of holding open practice sessions under the NCAA's 20 practice spring limit.

The spring practices resembled the commencement of fall sessions with a photo op day [to herald the upcoming 1953 campaign, Dick Szymanski (No. 19) posed next to Joe Bush (no. 53)] and on the first formal day, Leahy and the lads went right to business with a scrimmage. Indeed, Leahy reaffirmed his fervor for scrimmaging by holding a number of blue-green contests in the spring, trying to determine who his best two-way players were and at which positions. In manipulating through the puzzle pieces, the annual Old Timers game necessitated much more roster experimentation by the coaches than in years past.

Since the last few years had produced relatively few seniors, the ranks of the returning alumni had likewise thinned considerably since the fabled game in the spring of 1950. The game more closely resembled the current Blue-Gold spring game, with most of the "Old Timers" being football players who had every intention of suiting up with the varsity in 1953, added to a sprinkling of alums like Bob Williams and John Lujack. Lattner sat out with a bum shoulder and a freshman backfield started, with Don Schaefer at quarterback, joined by backs Dick Keller, Dick Fitzgerald and John Gaffney, indicating Leahy had to get more a look at his youngsters than his veterans.

In particular, Keller had a great day, intercepting Lujack for a 45-yard touchdown, and then on a punt, he caught the ball and lateralled to Fitzgerald who took it 89 yards for another score. Backs Dick Washington and Dick Hendricks ("a running find") also distinguished themselves, while Leahy groused, "I think they have progressed well with the double-duty problem the anti-platoon rule imposes, in view of the limited number of practices we are allowed under present regulations." By the time Neil Worden, Joe Heap, Ralph Guglielmi, Tom McHugh and Tom Carey took over the rout was on as the varsity coasted, 34-7.

School wide, the students from all of the halls got into line for the annual May 1 procession to the Grotto. In Fisher Hall, Frank Varrichione had to sit out the event due to sustaining a serious ankle injury. A couple doors down from him senior Regis Philbin, who went on to great fame as a television host and entertainer, knocked on Frank's door and asked if he could hide there in lieu of the procession, as he expected to receive an important phone call. Frank said "sure," and Regis hid behind the curtain of one of the closets on either side of the dorm room door.

Room by room the two friends heard the prefect check to see if all had gotten into line for the walk to the Grotto. Finally, the priest got to Frank's room and learned why Frank could not take part in the festivities. The priest then asked if there was anyone else in the room and Frank solemnly said, "No, Father." The priest, prepared to leave, but then suddenly pulled back the curtain to the closet door to find a quaking Regis Philbin, who immediately fell into line, quite literally, for the May Day procession.

A week later, the seniors had their Ball on Friday, May 8, an evening at Shangri-la, followed the next day by a trip to the dunes with their dates for a picnic. On Sunday, the dates attended church together at Sacred Heart Church. The relatively small senior football team then passed out of the school, content in being members of the great team of '49, albeit as freshmen punching dummies, but secure that they had helped commence a new winning tradition on campus.

G.I. Blues

IN EXCHANGE for shielding Notre Dame football players from selective service, the program had arranged for virtually all of them to enroll in the ROTC, with most of the lads signing up for the Air Force and a relative few others choosing the Navy. Although the Army had instituted a program of its own, it started too late and therefore bypassed most, if not all, of the senior class of 1954, who had chosen their branch of service early in their academic careers. Indeed, some of the only "Army men" around that age were the transfers from West Point to Notre Dame after the 1951 Cheating Scandal, and many of them converted to Air Force recruits.

During the summer of 1953, the bill became due for the varsity football players and their classmates at the ROTC, and in the instance of the air men, they received orders to various air bases across the country to begin six weeks of training. For many of them, they approached it as an obligation, like attending chapel services before the dawning of the sun three days a week or getting into bed early with lights out at 11:00 p.m.

For others, like Jack Lee, Bob Martin and Ray Bubick, it constituted their first truly concentrated exposure to their future vocation, service in the United States armed forces.

Bubick trained at the Barksdale base with no Notre Dame football players, although he did meet up with a Domer who had left West Point in the Cheating Scandal.

From Chicago, John Lattner planned to drive down to Bryan Air Force Base in Texas with teammate Tom McHugh and classmates from Chicago and Ohio. Lattner's brother had just purchased a '53 Oldsmobile which John and his friends commandeered for the ride south, so the drive down to the base already had a road trip aspect to it.

The young men kept at their best behavior, or at least did not get caught doing anything wrong, until a policeman pulled them over in Arkansas for some traffic violation, instructing them to appear at the local courthouse right away.

Acting as the *consigliere*, McHugh gave Lattner very specific instructions: tell the judge that you are John Lattner and that you have no money. The advice would have been good, had they been in Chicago or South Bend, but in the South the Judge either had never heard of the Notre Dame back or cared less. "Well, if you can't come up with the money," the judge thundered, you can go right to jail!" John Lattner found the money and the party continued to their destination.

Each air base varied its program a bit, but in essence, each ROTC man encountered a basic training experience. The young men fired guns at the range, learned some survival training techniques, ran obstacle courses and boned up on some of the information already conveyed to them in their on-campus classes, such as the Code of Conduct. They also learned a smattering of basic aeronautics, such as why a plane could fly at all.

In the more southern climes, the young men chafed at having to wear starched khakis in the horrible humidity. Yet for some of them, the trip constituted their first time up in an airplane, a treat for those of them who had not played on a travel team and flown out to Southern Cal or Texas. Jack Lee had memorized the physics of flight and the purpose of each gauge and instrument, so the instructor let him fly a B-29 bomber for fifteen minutes. Also during his training period, he met a man named Tom Pagna, then a ROTC jock out of Miami of Ohio, one day to become one of future Notre Dame coach Ara Parseghian's most trusted lieutenants.

Early on, Tom McHugh left Bryan, due to an astigmatism in his eye, leaving his friend Lattner to lead some of the Notre Dame men to weekends off base in Houston. At the end of the training period, John and his friends took a five-day break in New Orleans to party the night away, with the most exotic event occurring when the men accidentally chanced upon a gay bar, the first any of them had ever seen or even imagined existed.

For the young men of the Navy ROTC, they did not spend part of their summer billeted at a military installation, but rather hopped on a ship and went out on a cruise. Fred Mangialardi, George Hubbard and a handful of other Notre Dame men jumped into their seaman uniforms and started their passage on the USS Columbus, docked in Norfolk, Virginia, making ports of call at Guantanamo Bay, Trinidad and Panama.

John O'Hara, who had drifted off the Notre Dame team during the past season, also took a cruise but he sailed on the battleship Wisconsin, with ports of call in Edinburgh, Scotland and the Coast of France. He learned to say the "F" word a lot from many of the street-smart sailors on board and how to swab the deck each day with lye and holystone. Of most use, he learned to live with different kinds of people at close quarters, an absolute prerequisite for a happy naval experience. Like his friend Larry Ash, he aspired to fly planes for the Navy.

Most men enjoyed their training period, wearing fancy uniforms and making some practical use of the endless lectures they sat for during the last three years. For the football players, it permitted them a respite from Frank Leahy and any of his efforts to further condition them or instill a new offense or teach them a new pass defense technique. Oddly, the rigors of military training paled compared to their two-a-day fall practices. It also united the men, providing the Fighting Irish with another common experience in addition to their tough workouts at Cartier Field and their busy-work jobs checking people in for chapel or delivering mail.

Back in South Bend, Frank Leahy chafed, later telling his biographer: "I coached very hard and I worked far too hard. I found myself almost incapable of taking time off. I was treated in the off-season for nervous exhaustion and was ordered by doctors to relax in the off-season…But it was not easy. In fact, it was more agonizing not being involved. I knew that this would be my greatest team and I was eager to begin assembling it."

Fourth Quarter

Slaves of the Immaculate Heart

THE OTHERWISE STRENUOUS activities of the incoming freshman ballplayers commencing their acclimation process to Notre Dame student life received an unusual reprieve of tragic-comedy when six clerically garbed young men descended upon the campus to proselytize the message of defrocked priest Leonard Feeney on July 28, 1953.

Feeney had gone about Cambridge and Boston, Massachusetts preaching the doctrine of "extra ecclesiam nulla salus," or no salvation outside of the Catholic Church, and had managed to rile beloved Cardinal Cushing enough that Rome excommunicated the priest. In Boston, Jack Lee read all about Feeney and his minions parking themselves on the Boston Common each week and preaching their gospel of hate, baiting people really, and otherwise getting on the nerves of passersby.

Ironically, Feeney saw himself professing the belief that no salvation existed outside of the Catholic Church despite the fact that he and his followers were now, in essence, no longer considered Catholics. But Feeney was never one for irony. A native of Lynn, Massachusetts, he had joined the

Jesuits and had developed quite a following in Harvard Yard, an ultra-conservative in an area rapidly becoming one of the most left-wing enclaves in the United States.

He probably could have continued to preach that only Catholics could be saved, if he just said it to a small congregation and did not directly rebut dogma; but he mainly focused his energies on as crude a form of anti-Semitism as existed outside of Nazi Germany. He picked the wrong place to do it, not so much because Cambridge had begun to become a hotbed for liberal thought, but because Cardinal Cushing had a Jewish brother-in-law and saw very little merit in the Church persecuting Jewish people. He preached ecumenism while Feeney ran counter to this teaching, resulting in Boston and Rome forcing Feeney out of the Catholic priesthood.

Feeney went about forming an order, without the approval of the Vatican, named the Slaves of the Immaculate Heart of Mary and his followers wasted no time in becoming scene-makers. Like his sermons on the Boston Common, he and his adherents prided themselves as "in your face" provocative zealots. The six brothers who voyaged out to Notre Dame had come at a poor time, insofar as relatively few students remained on campus, and those that did probably enjoyed the peace. Still, the Slaves claimed that they deposited leaflets in the Dining Hall, something no college permits, with the consequent demand that they had to leave; perhaps delivered by Black Mac McCarragher himself.

The Slaves did not take kindly to demands from the damned, deciding to say a rosary in front of the library before proceeding to stop by to visit and worship in Sacred Heart Church. They never got inside. By now some administrators had contacted a few local sheriffs and a crowd of seventy people, mainly students, stood in front of the church barring the intruders from entering. It made a stark scene, more befitting a sixteenth-century setting, as six young men with "black suits, white shirts and black ties" poised in front of Sacred Heart confronting a wall of mostly other young men in light short-sleeve shirts glaring at them.

One of the Slaves shouted, "The first sign of your approaching damnation is that Notre Dame has Protestants on their football team!" The statement rang out like a declaration of war, because while many in the crowd may have privately agreed with the Slaves that the Catholic Church constituted the sole means to salvation, no one messed with the football team.

Yet there it was, one of the major stalking points of this dour little band was that Notre Dame had somehow corrupted itself by allowing Protestant football players on their team. As offensively as the Slaves conveyed their message, they historically erred quite badly. Protestant players like Knute Rockne (Rock only converted to Catholicism later in life) suited up for Notre Dame virtually from the foundation of the sport, and indeed, as head coach Rockne had featured Jewish stars such as Marchy Schwartz and Marty Brill. After Rockne's death, a Jewish end from Roxbury, Massachusetts, named Wayne Millner continued this tradition, eventually gaining induction in the Pro Football Hall of Fame in Canton.

South Bend and Chicago papers attacked the pests for their preaching, and not liking their reception, the group mercifully left Notre Dame after a "slight scuffle" and headed for Chicago to set matters straight because some papers had referred to Feeney as an ex-priest. They had shifted their focus from their views on salvation and anti-Semitism to an insistence that Leonard Feeney still possessed standing as a priest under the theory that "once a priest, always a priest." There, they tormented the Cardinal of Chicago, Samuel Alphonsius Stritch, who finally had them arrested.

Some anonymous Catholic paid for their train ride back to Boston, where the story pretty much ended, except in one of the upcoming Irish games that fall, one of Feeney's minions supposedly ran onto the field to make a spectacle of himself.

Feeney himself may have been surprised at how few Protestants the Irish had on their squad in 1953. Lineman Minnie Mavraides adhered to a Greek Orthodox tradition and Wayne Edmonds and Dick Washington followed their Baptist faith, but few other members came from anything but a strict Catholic background. A Presbyterian, junior quarterback Jim Bigelow fit into one of those exceptions, but the administration at Notre Dame and Leahy himself probably did not know it.

Recruited by a local bird dog scout in Pittsburgh named Eddie Cochrane, Bigelow had locked on the Irish radar as early as the Navy game in Cleveland in 1950. In the locker room after the game, Bigelow met the coaches and he and another recruit from the Pittsburgh area spent about ten minutes alone in the locker room listening to Leahy map out the positives of a Notre Dame education and membership on its football team.

No one asked Bigelow what religion he subscribed to, and absent rare circumstances he did not tell anyone at N.D. during his four years there. His teammate Leo Callaghan and he engaged in theological discussions now and then but otherwise, Bigelow did what he felt he had to do to fit in. He checked his hall mates into chapel as one of his campus jobs and went to Masses with the team and lined up to be blessed before the game. He learned how to execute a perfect Sign of the Cross and knew when to kneel, stand and sit during services, a skill that even some life-long Catholics never master.

Best of all, he learned how to respect others and received a great education on the ball field and in the classrooms at the University. Feeney and his followers never could have been Notre Dame men, Jim Bigelow very naturally was.

While Feeney eventually faded from sight, Notre Dame's young president, Fr. Theodore Hesburgh, shared in the spirit of ecumenism and not only renounced the Slaves' teachings, but built bridges to people of all creeds and colors, accelerating efforts to recruit and incorporate African-American students and student-athletes onto his campus.

The Catholic Church was changing, not as fast as many wanted it to change, but it no longer tolerated Feeneyism, and while it remained steadfast in its mission as a Catholic University, it had become equally serious in welcoming all. It admitted Protestant and Jewish students and the football team increasingly began to reflect American society.

Mad Dogs and Irishmen

DAN SHANNON'S FATHER, an accountant, had invested some of the family's money in buying farmland, and as many of the Irish drifted back to Chicagoland from their six-week service commitments, they found their paths diverted to the Shannon farm for some practice. John Lattner showed up, along with enough other players to form an offense and a defense, as the men exerted themselves into condition and prepared for the fall practices.

Or at least that was the idea. A neighbor had decided to bake pies and churn out ice cream, providing the football players with these sweets; for every pound lost in training, another pound or two went right back to each young man's gut. The neighbor must have been an Oklahoma fan.

When the full squad assembled in South Bend in late August, the temperatures had soared in Northern Indiana to almost 100 degrees. Charlie Callahan had staged photos for the press on August 31, with team captain Don Penza spraying Neil Worden and John Lattner with a fire hose and later, Lattner and Penza dumping water on Worden. Penza also led the Irish onto the field accompanied by two mascots, the leprechaun and Irish terrier Clashmore Mike III.

Across the country, the heat wave proved quite serious as

317

high school football player Charles Blythe died in the dreadful scourge that engulfed areas as far east as Peakskill, New York. Back in Chicago, Frank Leahy missed the first practice to attend the funeral of Mrs. Harry Wright, the wife of a 1941 Fighting Irish quarterback

To combat the heat, Leahy scheduled the first of his two-a-day practices (and some three-a-days) for 6:00 a.m. to 8:00 a.m. to take advantage of the still relatively cool morning temperatures, musing that "[i]f we drill until 8:00 a.m., it will mean that our players will be able to get in more rest between sessions. Thus they should be fresher." Undoubtedly some members of the team probably theorized that the early times did not emanate out of altruism, but rather constituted a new way to torture the men with a wake-up call at an ungodly hour. Anything to toughen the lads.

The concern for the players did not runneth over to only scheduling one session a day or at least concluding the day's work at sunset, as the team came out for a 3:00-5:00 p.m. run-through which included, among other events, running fast through a series of tied together ropes, an agility drill still practiced today. Trainer Gene Paszkiet weighed in everyone and Neil Worden barely tipped the scales at 186 pounds, although by the beginning of the season the Sports Information department probably planned to publicize his weight at about 30 pounds more.

The team also announced that Dan Shannon had not fully recovered from a spring left ankle injury, and no longer negotiated the deep cuts expected of a fullback. As Joe Doyle observed, Leahy had decided to shift this heavy hitter to end. The move benefited Shannon, but Leahy voiced his reservations that "it is expecting too much to make Shannon a qualified performer at end in the short time we have before the Oklahoma opener." One never knew with Leahy; either he truly believed what he said or he wanted to plant false hope in the mind of Sooners' coach Bud Wilkinson, who knew better. Or should have.

Shannon's shift may have been necessitated by the physical condition of the player, but since the NCAA had eliminated two platoon football, replacing it unwisely with the one- platoon set, Leahy had to shuffle several men around and pick the best two-way players available. Their talents had to include the endurance to play football for close to sixty minutes. Awkwardly, the brain trust moved Art Hunter from end to tackle, Dick Szymanski from center to guard, Mangialardi from end to guard and Sam Palumbo from tackle to guard and back to tackle again. It resembled trying to bang pieces of a puzzle into places the pieces did not fit.

For Hunter, he had now changed positions three times in three years, and he no longer took orders from the benevolent Coach John Druze. Now he had to perform to the satisfaction of the demanding Bob McBride. Wayne Edmonds empathetically watched Hunter come back from practice or post-practice "instruction" with Coach McBride and just lie down on the bench, completely inert, while his teammates dressed and headed to the dining hall or a their rooms for a nap.

Phony nostalgia aside, the change to single-platoon football not only meant that a terrific offensive tackle also had to play defensive line (where he may not have much talent or not as much as another teammate), but it also quite often robbed another man of his job. For instance, Jack Lee had started as a nose guard for two years, but since he did not play offensive center, he now had to ride the bench for long stretches and wait for someone ahead of him on the depth chart to get hurt.

On the second full day of practice the team participated in line scrimmages, emphasizing passing offensive and defensive drills. Running backs Dick Washington and Paul Reynolds nursed knee injuries and, as soon became evident, the latter back was destined for the physically unable to perform (PUP) list for the ensuing season. Partly to compensate for this loss, Blackie Johnston, who last played for the club in 1950 before joining the Air Force, had just returned on leave to resume his career on the gridiron, although this development proved fleeting.

A victim of the excessive heat, newly minted end Dan Shannon collapsed as did running back John Gaffney, the latter a victim of dehydration. Rather than truncate the practices, Leahy made grudging small concessions to the inclement weather by mandating a five-minute rest period in the morning and one in the afternoon, while lodging the men at night in the cool basements of dorms such as Lyons and Sorin Halls.

These small humanitarian concessions did not address the serious public health concerns out on the field, as some players rubbed their heads, faces and necks with towels on the sideline, and then wrung the towels so the accumulated sweat dripped into their mouths, so parched were they. Tensions arose in the halls too, when a small guard almost drove a much larger teammate through one of the dorm doors, an event so loud it startled John Lattner in a room down the hall.

Fortunately, after the third day of full workouts, rain

came and with it sixty-degree temperatures at night, somewhat alleviating the communal suffering. As the weather moderated, several minor injuries and ailments overtook various players Patsy Bisceglia with a bruised hip, Don Schaefer with pulled neck muscles, Joe Heap with laryngitis and Gene Kapish with the flu.

Heap's health concerns spawned from the intense work conditions he endured in his summer job back in Louisiana, where he installed fence around power transformers. Aluminum dust swirled all around and the temperature at its worst rose to approximately 140 degrees, so the Irish running back caught a bad flu and lost quite a bit of weight, all this before Leahy's grueling practices began.

This meant little to Leahy, who almost immediately had the lads out scrimmaging, oppressive heat aside, for ten minutes. On one play, quarterback Guglielmi pitched out to Lattner who scampered to a 36-yard touchdown behind the notable blocking of Jack Lee, while later, Worden scored on a 35 yarder of his own.

Most puzzling, star tackle Frank Varrichione had not made an appearance in camp, and while Leahy groused about only players who "wanted to play" would play for him, frantic calls went out from South Bend to Natick, Massachusetts to locate the powerful tackle. When a fourth stringer went AWOL, Leahy and his coaches hardly noticed, but when a massive talent like Frank Varrichione teetered, calls went out.

Back home, Varrichione had pondered the changes wrought by the NCAA by the return to one-platoon football and had convinced himself that he could not play defense well enough to start, so he intended to forego football and start up his studies on campus with the other students. Frank Leahy got in touch with him by phone finally and convinced the young tackle that he had the ability not only to stand out on the offensive line, but also to play well on defense. Leahy could be very persuasive, so young Frank Varrichione decided to give this one-platoon a shot, to the eventual mutual satisfaction of coach and player.

On September 5, once prodigal son Frank Varrichione attended his first practice, the Old Man shifted his focus to worrying about Joe Heap, who had never played defense before, but had to operate out of the defensive backfield, again due to the one-platoon system. Earlier, Leahy had more options, perhaps utilizing the skills of a superior defensive halfback who might complement Worden and Lattner as a blocking running back. But the injured reserve status of Paul Reynolds and Gene Carrabine, combining with the academic ineligibility of Fran Paterra, wiped out much of the depth in the backfield. So Joe Heap had to learn how to play in the defensive backfield as his mate Dan Shannon had to learn the wide receiver position on the fly.

Fred Poehler, a married pre-med student, also opted out of the program. At 6'4" and over 210 pounds, Poehler had already served a hitch in the Air Force as a surgical technician, and obviously saw his future in medicine, not in pounding fellow big men at practice and along the line at games. While Poehler's loss hurt, Reynolds' season-ending injury vexed the coaching staff much more, since the team had a surplus of strong and healthy linemen.

Losing Reynolds also left a void in the back-up punter position, in twenty-first century football, not a huge priority, yet since first stringer John Lattner might become a casualty at any time as an offensive or defensive back, the auditions began with all healthy running backs booting the ball. Some of the efforts brought a smile even to Leahy, as he observed, "Punting tryouts are dangerous in the way some of these fellows punt, they're apt to hurt themselves." Tom McHugh ultimately won the coveted back-up punter role.

The Old Man's generally pessimistic nature overtook him a few days later, when after only barely a week of formal practices, he had to scale back on his beloved scrimmages and other contact workouts due to an alarming spate of injuries to his remaining healthy backs and even some of the linemen—that, and the fact that Captain Don Penza had complained to Leahy that his practices were too intense and that the coaches had to extend mercy. Leahy did not generally take advice from players, but Penza possessed a unique ability to influence his coach, and he exercised this trait wisely in this instance, staving off an exodus from some key members of the team.

As captain, Penza effectively played his role to provide leadership to his teammates and to act as his mates' patron saint to intercede with Leahy and the coaches. But as a veteran, Neil Worden also intuited that his friends needed a break from the drudgery of the practices; so on one occasion with a bunch of backs standing around with him, he grinned and said, "Want to see the Old Man get upset?"

All of his fellow backs decided they would like to see Leahy lose it, so they all egged their teammate on. Thus encouraged, Neil Worden cleared everyone out, bent his knees and threw himself up in the air and landed, having just performed a perfect back flip. Leahy saw this and like a flock of geese taking off, started running over to Worden, screaming. "Coaches, coaches, don't let Neil Worden do that again, we will need him to do that in a game!" The running backs all cracked up, leaving Neil to ponder under what circumstances during the regular season Leahy might conceivably order him to perform a standing back flip. Then it was back to work.

Purely by accident, Wayne Edmonds on defense clipped Lattner on the fourth or fifth day of practice, an unfortunate event that caused the star to pull up with a lame ankle. At the same time Bull Worden developed blisters on his feet so severe that he had to wear tennis shoes, a frightening proposition as the defenders at the scrimmages wore metal cleats. John Gaffney suffered bruised thigh muscles which removed him from action, as Tom McHugh pulled up with a bad back, Dick Washington dinged up his knee and Bob Rigali banged up an ankle. Among the backs, only Joe Heap appeared healthy, undoubtedly because his laryngitis kept him out of the earlier practices.

Don Schaefer and linemen Jack Lee, Bob Taylor and Patsy Bisceglia also checked in at the infirmary, causing Leahy to lament, "This is the most depressing situation I've ever been confronted with....I don't know when we've ever had to call off practice before the season opened." Added Bill Earley, "If we had enough receivers we wouldn't have had any defenders or vice versa." Out of necessity, the coaches had to scale down the number of practices and the intensity of the workouts. With so few backs healthy, passing offense and defense drills temporarily disappeared from the agenda. Penza was prescient, Leahy had worked the lads too hard this time.

By the September 8 practice, the team did regain a semblance of health and managed to schedule a Blue-Green inter-squad game with Blue winning in overwhelming fashion 33-0, behind two touchdowns by Joe Heap, and single scores from Lattner, Cabral and Worden. The exercise proved counterproductive as Lattner pulled up lame for the final three quarters.

As unhealthy as the Irish appeared, Studebaker Motor Company formally announced their fiscal ill-health a couple days later by scaling back on production by one-third with plans to lay off 5,000-6,000 auto workers, an early sign of the eventual demise a little more than ten years later of that venerable South Bend institution. Meanwhile, another wizened institution, Frank Leahy continued to scrimmage and drill his young men to exhaustion in the following days.

On September 16, the varsity played a full sixty-minute scrimmage against the freshmen (sporting future 1956 Heisman winner, Paul Hornung) and disappointingly tallied only three touchdowns, with Penza scoring on a pass play and Joe Heap barreling in from 43 and 10 yards out. By consensus of the coaches and observers on the sideline, the varsity had "never looked worse." The *South Bend Tribune* singled out Lattner's replacement, Dick Washington, for particular criticism, asserting that the sub "didn't live up to expectations."

Disgusted, Leahy began to insert his second team into the game, led by Tom Carey at quarterback, joined by backs Dick Fitzgerald, Bob Rigali and John Gaffney and linemen Paul Matz, Sam Palumbo, Patsy Bisceglia, Dick Frasor, John McMullan, George Nicula and Gene Kapish.

McMullan had just received a nice write-up from the *South Bend Tribune*, which praised the "stubby New Jersey 'fireplug,'" a competitor whose heart made up for his relatively squat frame. A native of Hoboken, New Jersey, McMullan had also lettered at Demarest High in basketball and baseball and decades later, his son Kevin played minor league baseball.

As was his custom, Leahy fretted about the lack of production on offense the next day, heaping scorn on his sophomore backs, whom he contended "just didn't shape up like we thought they would." Lattner had now been sidelined for ten days, with the Oklahoma game looming, and on the 19th the varsity disgusted Leahy again as they managed only two touchdowns against the freshmen in a full half of another scrimmage. In the second half, the second team players lined up against the starters, defeating them 7-6.

To motivate Guglielmi, Leahy injected intermittent doses of negative reinforcement, alternately telling his quarterback, "You have to be a Spartan to beat them at their home." "They are much better this year than last year." "Don't throw the ball Ralph!" Comments like these were designed to sharpen the quarterback's already pronounced competitive instincts, to prove Leahy wrong if nothing else.

Unlike last year, however, Googs operated from a position of strength as the team's starting quarterback, due to the imposition of the single-platoon system. Even if Leahy and his assistants liked Tom Carey better as a quarterback, Guglielmi's defensive prowess far exceeded that of Carey, so Carey sat and Googs played both sides of the ball.

Lattner and Heap remained indisposed, engaging in calisthenics and jogging workouts as their teammates endured a bruising defensive battle. The running corps had been so depleted that sophomore Dick Hendricks alternated between the starters and the subs in the game. Neil Worden scored on a pass from fellow back Dick Washington but Joe Doyle felt the Bull had lost some "zip" in his running. Worden for his part scored again on a 27-yard run aided by a neat block by Don Penza.

Leahy lamented again after this latest futile scrimmage, holding everyone at fault, "Our offense is pretty sad...Two touchdowns against the freshmen certainly doesn't speak well for our coaching." Critical of his offense, the head coach did little except shift Dick Szymanski back to center, continuing to back up Schrader.

Having beat up on his players, Leahy eased up somewhat in preparation for Oklahoma. On September 22, the team engaged in dummy practices and then were outfitted with short-sleeve jerseys to combat the anticipated heat in Norman by game time. Frank Leahy might have been too young to remember the Alamo, but he did recall the heat in Texas last year and, while he slighted his team in public, in private he devised every strategy possible to beat the Sooners in their home stadium.

Oklahoma Redux

TAKING A PARAGRAPH from the Frank Leahy play book, Sooners' coach Bud Wilkinson began to badmouth his team in public, virtually at every opportunity that presented itself. On September 21, Wilkinson broadcast: "We have a few capable backs and some linemen who ought to play very well for us. I think we will improve just as fast as any team playing college football this year,...With this biggest game, I'm sorry to say we have the least chance of winning and the greatest chance of being really humiliated."

Having learned from a master, Notre Dame's Sports Information Director Charlie Callahan immediately engaged in one-upmanship in the game of "whose team is more pathetic" by citing the weak performances in practice by both the Irish freshman and varsity squads. When Callahan heard an Oklahoma fan in a barber shop a couple days later opine that the Sooners would win by four or five touchdowns, Callahan upped the ante: "You're so right, pahtner. My name's Callahan, Cholly Callahan. I'm from Bahstan originally, but now I handle sports publicity for those Notre Damers you were talking abaht,...Maybe you're shorting it when you said 30, 35 points. Coube be 40, maybe 45."

Determined to damn the Sooners with lavish praise and not provide them with any locker room bulletin board motivation, Leahy added, "We just cannot take a single chance on injury when we meet such a powerful team as the Sooners." And to think they called Neil Worden "Bull," when so many others in the Irish firmament slung so much more b.s.

Blustering aside, back in South Bend the varsity had to prepare for the big game and not a war of words. Nursing injuries, Lattner and Heap eschewed bone bruising contacts for "lighter drills" and wind sprints. Having only three weeks earlier seen members of his team keel over from heat exhaustion and dehydration, Frank Leahy observed, "It's imperative that you be in the best possible condition," in order to survive the forecasted extreme heat in Norman, Oklahoma.

Having listened to coaches and administrators bad-mouth their own teams, Oklahoma's Larry Griggs paid tribute to one of the heaviest hitters in ND history, before or since. Recalling his experience in South Bend in 1952, Griggs related: "I was trying to run back a kick but that Shannon...really whacked me....Hard to take him off the property. There's a player, that Shannon."

Around the same time that Griggs paid sincere tribute to a respected foe, thirty-eight members of the Fighting Irish football team flew into town and, after deplaning, drove off to their team hotel in Guthrie, twenty-five miles away from the Sooners' stadium.

The Sooners team that the Irish faced in their opening game had changed significantly, with their starting halfback and fullbacks gone, including 1952 Heisman Trophy winner Billy Vessels. With the Irish's Forgotten Four completely intact, some prognosticators had ND as favorites by as much as three touchdowns. These odds makers failed to account for the fact that Wilkinson had built up a program very similar to the Notre Dame model of the 1940s, where a team might lose many of its starters and some All-Americans for good measure, and regenerate with a championship caliber club virtually seamlessly the next year. So Notre Dame had no easy task ahead of it, plus it had to play in Norman, Oklahoma, this time and not in the House that Knute Rockne built.

On the day of the game, the field maxed out at a temperature of 94 degrees, similar conditions to the Texas game early in the previous season. Frank Leahy had taken extreme steps to ensure that his lads had the edge to deal with the heat during the Texas game and Bud Wilkinson probably foresaw many of these ploys, and either utilized them himself or had his administration not grant the opposition as many favors as they enjoyed in Austin in their victory over the Longhorns. Last year of course, Leahy could substitute at will but this year with the single platoon, he had to be very judicious about substituting as the move effectively took a starter out for the rest of the period once replaced.

Despite laboring on a bum ankle for much of the fall, John Lattner wanted to start and his coach Billy Earley strongly urged Leahy to accede to the star back's wishes, stating, "You've got to start him, he's our All-American!"

Leahy relented, but portents of looming disaster surfaced from almost the outset after Oklahoma kicked off and Irish return man John Lattner bobbled the ball, which squirted out of bounds on his team's four yard line. A disgusted head coach sought out Bill Earley, hollering all the while, "There's your All-American! There's your All-American!"

Guglielmi stabilized matters by negotiating some gains for his offense, but on the fourth play from scrimmage, Neil Worden fumbled on his 23 yard line, with the Sooners' left tackle pouncing on the ball. As the *Chicago Tribune*'s Charles Bartlett reported it, "Jack Ging, Sooner left half back, did most of the work in accomplishing the first Oklahoma touchdown, with Leake supplying the extra point to give the home boys a 7-0 lead..."

Fumble-itis victimized Oklahoma on one of their subsequent drives when Max Boydston coughed up the ball on his own 41 yard line with Irish defensive lineman Jim Schrader recovering. Guglielmi heaved a 29-yard pass to John Lattner, but then the opposing defense stiffened on two consecutive Neil Worden runs. Not a problem as Joe Heap took Googs' "over the shoulder toss" for a touchdown reception, Minnie Mavraides tying the score with his kick.

The see-saw contest proceeded all afternoon. On a Sooner drive in the second quarter, end Don Penza stepped up with some key tackles and a fumble recovery to stop it. ND did not capitalize on the good fortune, so after a punt, Oklahoma had the ball back at its own twenty yard line. The Sooners' quarterback, not much of a passer, somehow rose to the occasion enough to complete a 62 yarder to his end Carl Ellison, with only the tenacity of defensive back Joe Heap preventing the touchdown by relentlessly tracking Ellison down and tossing him out of bounds.

Sam Palumbo bundled Oklahoma's Jack Ging on the next play, but then Ging and Buddy Leake chipped away until they secured the touchdown with Leake kicking the extra point, putting his team ahead, 14-7.

Again, ND had no answer for its opposition and had to give up the ball on its next possession, causing the Sooners no damage and even less anxiety. Having his best day for the Irish, Don Penza dominated on defense, knocking down an attempted pass from Leake, and then blocking the punt attempt by Max Boydston which the Irish recovered on the Sooner 9 yard line. With both coaches beginning to "take advantage of the rule allowing replacement" late in the second quarter, Tom McHugh came in to take a run, but he, and then Lattner, only got the ball to the four yard line. Guglielmi tried to punch it in with a run to the left which failed. On fourth down, he ran to the right, faked a pitchout and then barreled in for the score, hurting himself on the attempt (as Penza had sustained an injury on his recent fumble recovery). Tom Carey came in to hold the ball on the extra point attempt, which Minnie Mavraides drilled in to tie the score before halftime.

Early in the third quarter, the Irish defense led by Don Penza and Ralph Guglielmi, recovering from their first-half injuries on the fly, foiled the Sooners again. Googs read a Buddy Leake pass attempt perfectly, intercepting the ball right in front of the opposing bench. Switching right over to offense, Guglielmi threw a long pass to a wide open Joe Heap, who ran it in past defender Larry Griggs for a touchdown, Mavraides again converting for his teammates' first lead of the afternoon.

After taking possession on the kickoff, Buddy Leake fumbled with Don Penza on defense again recovering. The Forgotten Four took over, with Guglielmi passing to Heap and dishing off to Lattner. With fourth down on Oklahoma's 14, Googs called his own number and snuck the ball to the 9 yard line and the first down. Demonstrating bull dog determination on the next play, on a hand off, Worden sailed into right tackle and found his way logjammed. Resourcefully, the small fullback renegotiated his way to his right and then plowed in for the score. With the Mavraides' kick, ND now led 28-14.

At this point, the *South Bend Tribune* reported that "the crowd quieted down to more of the Midwestern smugness and the cowboy whoops and hollers missing...." Like last year's epic, though, Oklahoma restored the balance of power quickly, riding the back of Merrill Green. Green staged a long return of one of Lattner's punts and then largely carried his team on its ensuing drive to its next touchdown, narrowing matters to 28-21.

Because of the vagaries of the one-platoon rule, Notre Dame took over under the direction of third-string quarterback Don Bucci, who did engineer a first down drive for the team. With four minutes remaining, Guglielmi came back into the game legally, but rather than run out the clock, he handed off to back Joe Heap who attempted a pass, which was intercepted.

The cowboy whoops and hollers must have thundered at this point. Buddy Leake went about passing, but unfortunately for him and his mates, an errant throw ended up in the hands of John Lattner at defensive back, killing the potential game-tying rally. A satisfied Coach Bill Earley walked up to Leahy and deadpanned, "there's your All-American!"

Bob Rigali came in and ran for a few yards as did Googs on the next play. Facing third and four, Worden took the handoff and bulled his way for sixteen yards and the game-ending first down.

Notre Dame had just meted out the Sooners' first loss at home in 25 games and thereafter the Sooners went on an unbeaten streak of nearly four years, until a team from South Bend led by Dick Lynch defeated them by a 7-0 score. Leahy played the one-platoon masterfully, with the only flub occurring when he sent Tom McHugh into the game at one point, only to have an official boot him out for already being in the game that quarter. The four components of the offensive backfield worked quite efficiently and Don Penza helped stave off a number of the opponent's drives, as did Lattner and Guglielmi with their ball-hawking as defensive backs on the other side of the platoon. Lattner's 38.7 yard punting average posted him as the thirteenth best punter in intercollegiate ranks as his team topped the polls as the number one team in America.

Boilermakers and Panthers

LEAHY PULLED BACK a bit on the varsity for the Monday practice, as Lemek and Guglielmi nursed cuts over their right eyes and Lattner hobbled from a recurrence of his chronic ankle injury. The coach excused his regulars and allowed the second and third stringers the luxury of beating up on each other. Little wonder, with single-platoon football implemented with a vengeance, Schrader played 53 out of 60 minutes in the Oklahoma game, followed closely by Lemek and Heap with 52 apiece, Hunter with 51 and Lattner, Worden and Mavraides each logging in 50 minutes of hard running and heavy hitting.

By Tuesday, Leahy returned to form by scheduling a line scrimmage, perhaps in retaliation for his perception that the offensive linemen did not adequately protect the backs. Lattner sat out again, while the team further prepared for their upcoming game with in-state rival Purdue by stressing punt and pass protection. One area of concern: the Boilermakers outweighed the Irish by an average of five pounds per each lineman.

As it turned out, Purdue could have outweighed them by another twenty pounds a person as the Irish linemen dominated their counterparts all afternoon, on another uncommonly hot and windy day at Ross-Ade Stadium. The strange weather foreshadowed even more peculiar scoring, starting off with Irish kicker Minnie Mavraides booming out a 40-yard field goal at a "wide angle."

On the next possession, Purdue fumbled on its own 29, with Joe Heap recovering; Heap then shifted to offense and with some help from John Lattner, ran the ball to the 11 yard line. The next call went to Neil Worden, who experienced the sensation of "a half dozen Purdue hands latch[ing] onto the Milwaukee bruiser but he charged on over." Touchdown Irish.

Purdue responded with a touchdown of their own, narrowing the Irish lead to 10-7, but on the ensuing kickoff, John Lattner returned the ball down the right side of the field for an 86-yard scoring run from which the Boilermakers never recovered.

By the fourth quarter, Leahy had emptied the stables, permitting many talented backups like Tony Pasquesi, Bob Taylor, Joe Bush, John McMullan, George Nicula, Gene Kapish, Dick Keller, John Gaffney and Nick Raich to see action. Walt Cabral even attempted an extra point kick, which failed, although it hardly affected the team spirit, as his teammates rolled to an embarrassingly easy 37-7 win.

Everyone contributed. Dick Fitzgerald led all runners with 90 yards on 10 carries, while one of his blocks sprung teammate Dick Washington for a touchdown jaunt.

After Purdue, the team "enjoyed" a bye-week, during which time the coaching staff decided to treat their injured players to a "full game scrimmage" against the freshmen. Lattner sat it out with a pulled leg muscle, as did Don Penza with a bruised shoulder and Bob Rigali and Don

Schaefer, also with pulled leg muscles. Leahy did not see this practice as he had left early the previous morning, supposedly to personally scout an upcoming opponent. In reality, he and Moose Krause flew down for a Sugar Bowl testimonial event in New Orleans, where Moose golfed and Leahy presumably fretted about the next game. In their absences, the freshmen were led by star recruit Paul Hornung in the game against the varsity.

The trip to New Orleans may have obscured a hidden purpose, a hinted-at first step to return the team to postseason bowl games, a tradition it had never embraced, having only played in one, a 27-10 victory over Stanford on January 1, 1925. Otherwise the junket made little sense, absenting the head coach and chief of the athletic department from campus for an otherwise overblown ceremony for the Sugar Bowl organizers, the type of event that Leahy in particular saved for the off-season and then only if a decent recruit awaited him. Moose Krause probably wanted Notre Dame back in the bowls, but the administration nixed any such development, at least for the foreseeable future.

Leahy returned to more mundane drills with Tuesday's practice, concentrating on offensive production with Guglielmi throwing mainly to his ends Shannon and Cabral. The next day the tables turned with the players firming up their pass defense against the freshmen, while a seemingly disorganized Pitt team announced the shift of its starting quarterback back to running back just days before their game with ND. Many gamblers had Notre Dame as three-touchdown favorites over Pitt for Saturday's match.

Unfortunately, this news fell at the same time that Irish players stampeded to the infirmary with Captain Don

Penza and Art Hunter pulling up with bruised shoulders, Ray Lemek and Jack Lee nursing bruised ribs and Lattner hobbling with a pulled leg muscle again. Back east, Brooklyn Dodger Chuck Dressen had a worse day, quitting the club due to his disgust with continually receiving only one year contracts from his boss, Walter O'Malley.

Meanwhile, the University proceeded with plans to honor Elmer Layden and the late Knute Rockne and George Gipp at the half-time ceremonies in the upcoming game.

Leahy's men, those that still ambulated, worked on offensive and defensive drills.

With the team so roughed up from their traditional physical game against the Boilermakers, the two-week hiatus served them well, as most of the injured souls recovered in time for their October 17 tiff at home against the University of Pittsburgh.

In that match-up the Irish took the opening kickoff but did little and punted to Pitt without undue delay. Led by their quarterback "Model T" Ford and fullback Bobby Epps, the Panthers rolled down the field for a touchdown. George Blanda's brother Paul kicked the extra point for the 7-0 lead.

Notre Dame responded in kind, with runs by Lattner, Worden and Heap and short passes by Guglielmi, until Bull Worden crashed into the line for a touchdown, Minnie Mavraides converting to tie it up.

On a later drive, Guglielmi passed to Paul Matz, apparently complete, until Pitt's Ford wrestled the ball away and ran the ball back 47 yards to the Irish nine where Joe Heap tackled him from behind. On the next play, the refs called the Irish offside, which then ushered a short run into the end zone by Pitt's Richie McCabe, Guglielmi and Worden in vain pursuit. Pitt led again by 14-7, Blanda again converting.

During halftime, as Frank Leahy repaired to the back (equipment) room of the Irish dressing area to plot the comeback of his lads, the *Chicago Tribune*'s Arch Ward retuned to his alma mater to honor some past Irish immortals. Handing out Hall of Fame plaques to Horseman Elmer Layden, Bonnie Rockne (widow of Knute Rockne) and Mrs. Paul Taylor (sister of the late George Gipp), Ward invoked the past as a nervous Leahy and his coaches sought to preserve the present.

In the third quarter, Notre Dame controlled itself better, having racked up too many penalties earlier in the game. In doing so, the lads conceded nothing in aggressiveness, pegging Pitt deep in its own territory, and when Pitt's Bobby Epps took a hand-off, defensive lineman Frank Varrichione rushed in and drilled him into the turf for a safety. And to think that only a month and a half ago, Varrichione brooded in his Natick home, concerned he might not play well on defense with the advent of the single platoon.

The Irish defense kept pouring it on, when during a later Pitt possession, tackle Wayne Edmonds stripped the ball from Model T Ford and end Don Penza recovered it on Pittsburgh's 25 yard line. Although contemporary accounts differ, it appears that next John Lattner lateralled to an open Joe Heap, who then ran down the field to the Pitt six or seven yard line.

Deep in the red zone, Pittsburgh's defense threw back Heap and Worden, but on third down Guglielmi sneaked in for the TD and after Mavraides' successful PAT, the Irish led for the first time of the day, 16-14. The Irish then seemed to have the game in hand, subsequently marching down the field, but when Tom Carey handed off to Dick Washington, the back fumbled the ball in the end zone and Pitt recovered it.

After Pitt stalled offensively, Washington gained a measure of redemption by returning the ensuing punt down to the opponent's 37 yard line. Washington gained five more yards on the first play from scrimmage and then advanced another seventeen yards on a Carey pass.

Leahy then called back the first team and after a couple running plays, Guglielmi cradled the ball in for another touchdown on third down, this time for nine yards. Mavraides kicked another extra point, good for the ND lead, 23-14, and that is how matters stood as the varsity acquitted themselves well in front of Layden and the families of Knute Rockne and George Gipp.

If only Frank Leahy had been so sanguine. In preparation for the next home game, against Georgia Tech, a team that had not lost a game since 1950, Leahy openly worried about Lattner's leg and moaned, "We'll be lucky to stay on the field...[against Tech]." Of course he always rattled on in this vein, but he must have seen during the game, and on film, not only the way his backs had progressed, but also the manner in which his linemen had begun to dominate. For the past two years, Notre Dame's interior linemen had treated the Oklahoma Sooners across from them like tackling sleds, and had opened up holes for Lattner, Worden and Heap to exploit.

Joe Doyle noticed and in his *South Bend Tribune* column, lionized star left tackle Frank Varrichione, who had just been named Lineman of the Week, not only for his safety but

for his manhandling of Pitt's All-American Eldred Krae-
mer. Hard-to-please tackles coach Bob McBride seconded the emotion, asserting that "Frank has been one of our
surprises...He has worked hard at a phase of college football
completely new to him and at a spot most frequently hit by
opponents—left tackle."

McBride might have credited the left tackle position as
the most critical in protecting the quarterback, and with Varrichione deflecting tacklers away from Ralph Guglielmi, the
junior signal-caller had more time to complete his passes to
his ends, and increasingly to Joe Heap.

Having Varrichione anchor the line was a huge advantage to Leahy as he prepared for stiff opponents like Tech,
but the Irish possessed another advantage heading into this
big game. Originally, the Irish were to travel to Georgia
for the game, but the Administration did not believe that
Georgia Tech adequately guaranteed basic civil rights in local accommodation or dining for African-American players Wayne Edmonds and Dick Washington, so the game
shifted up to South Bend.

Georgia Tech still had its 31-game unbeaten streak, but
now they had to defend it away from their fans, home team
advantage, Leahy and the Irish. Too bad Leahy took little
comfort in that fact, as he paced his floors at night sleep-
lessly, worrying about the visiting team and not taking
enough time to watch his own emerging stars, and how they
meant to acquit themselves as Notre Dame men.

As Frank Leahy paced, failing to find peace, his young
lads dreamed of gold.

A Rambling Wreck

ON OCTOBER 24, 1953, Frank Leahy's tenure as the head coach of the Notre Dame Fighting Irish effectively ended.

The day started innocently enough, the team as usual attended Mass and ate breakfast together as Saturday classes wrapped up before noon, the day of the big game against Georgia Tech with its thirty-one game unbeaten skein. But during his tenure as Irish coach, Leahy had spent way too much time preparing for opponents with winning streaks or All-Americans, and his nights away from home and near constant fretting had eroded his health. Preparing for the game, the Old Man had created a meticulous manual concerning the Yellow Jackets, detailing their plays and their tendencies. He also provided narrative concerning the players his lads had to face, all with the view to providing the Irish varsity with their optimum chance of winning.

Although Leahy had dodged many health issues during the post-war seasons, nothing fully foreshadowed the pure physical agony silently engulfing him as the game approached. He had guided his teams to three victories and had even had a bye week during the season to recharge a bit, as he and Moose Krause jetted to New Orleans. Even the day before the game unfolded in mellow fashion, as the Yellow Jacket players worked out in what Joe Doyle described as a "limbering up exercise, that bordered on the casualness of a neighborhood block party." After they left, Notre Dame ran some defensive drills and all seemed fairly normal.

Saturday was a "near perfect day for football," clear and 53 degrees cold, a welcome respite from the oppressive weather that characterized the Irish's first two games. Almost from the outset, the Irish line dominated their smaller and less-talented counterparts. Bob McBride and his fellow line coaches had trained their charges well: center Jim Schrader, guards Minnie Mavraides and Ray Lemek and tackles Frank Varrichione and Art Hunter displayed the fierce athleticism that propelled them all into successful NFL careers. Ends Don Penza, Paul Matz and Dan Shannon likewise knew how to level an opponent and Shannon in particular relished the call to do so.

Joe Doyle marveled over how all day they delivered a "constant pounding" on the opposing line, sweeping "aside the defense almost at will and crashing headlong into the secondary looking for any would-be tacklers....Sometimes as many as five and six linemen were in the secondary." A line that good blasts holes open at the point of attack, but this one perpetuated their gains by roving downfield.

After Neil Worden ran back the opening kickoff from four yards deep in his own end zone, quarterback Ralph Guglielmi called only running plays for his talented backfield to exploit the opportunities created in the trenches. Joe Heap scampered for 33 yards at one point, while Neil Worden culminated a drive by willing himself a touchdown from seven yards out.

The teams exchanged punts thereafter, but by the end of the first quarter the Irish had driven to Tech's 22 yard line thanks largely to a Lattner 20-yard carry and a pass to Paul Matz from Guglielmi. With all gears moving in a wonderful synchronicity, Leahy ordered the starters off the field and sent in his reserves. Close to the end zone, Tom Carey handed off to Tom McHugh who fumbled, with Tech recovering, thereby snuffing out this promising drive.

Leahy died inside. At a later point in the half, when McHugh erred again, the Old Man nearly collapsed. As Tom McHugh jogged into the sideline after this latest mistake, Frank Leahy approached him and moaned, "Oooh MackHue, it's all right, but I'd rather die than to do that to Notre Dame." With that Leahy fell forward a bit, caught by some of his coaches. Fortunately the half ended with defensive back Ralph Guglielmi killing a Tech drive with an interception.

Leahy tried to show no ill effects as he made his way into the equipment room, separated from his players in the main dressing room, thinking "for awhile that I wouldn't be able to make it off the field. ...Things started to whirl around in my head and I had trouble making it up the stairs behind the team. I got back into that little cubby hole (the equipment room) and then started to get an awfully severe pain in my left side and chest. I tried to write something down on a flash card, but...couldn't even grip the pencil."

In this sanctuary, Leahy sat and tried to compose himself while planning for the second half. And then he collapsed onto the floor. Equipment man Jack McAllister called out for team manager Dan Hammer to fetch a priest for the coach, while McAllister scrounged up Dr. Nicholas Johns (the team and Leahy's personal physician) outside the equipment room, yelling, "Hey doc, we need you!" Some of the players in the locker room heard someone, maybe Don Penza, shout, "the Coach is down!"

Hammer ran out of the dressing room into the stands and spotted Fr. Ned Joyce. After breathlessly explaining the situation, Hammer ran back with Fr. Joyce to the back room, with the somewhat older priest outrunning him. Fr. Joyce determined almost immediately that he had been called upon to administer the Last Rites to Leahy.

Back in the locker room, confusion reigned. Bob Rigali elbowed John Lattner in the ribs, reassuring him, "Don't worry about him, he's pulling a Rockne." Rigali's father, of course, had played for Rock, a coach who nearly always devised something at halftime to motivate the team after a rough half of ball. Independently, Joe Heap and Tony Pasquesi thought this made sense, Leahy's way of pleading to them to win one for the Gipper. Other players reacted as if the end of days had occurred.

Inside the equipment room, Dr. Johns went right to work, not a simple task with Leahy in shock, his heart racing at 120 beats a minute (blood pressure at 80/40), and exhibiting an outward gray pallor and cold sweat. Dr. Johns quickly stabilized the situation as Fr. Joyce undertook the Last Rites, and with the proper mixture of science and religion, Frank Leahy was rolled onto a gurney for transport to St. Joseph Hospital for emergency treatment. Quickly, a triumvirate of Bill Earley, Bob McBride and Joe McArdle formed to guide the team during the second half. McArdle informed the team that the coach had just suffered an attack, understood by some to be a heart attack. Before the team rushed onto the field for the second half, they all knelt together and said a Hail Mary for their coach.

In the third period the luck seemed to continue to go against the Irish. After Lattner intercepted a pass, the team shifted to offense and Guglielmi threw a pass to Paul Matz, apparently incomplete as it bounced onto the turf into the hands of the Yellow Jackets defensive back, Steve Mitchell. Unfortunately, the referee called the play an interception and soon thereafter Tech seized the opportunity to score their first touchdown and tie the score 7-7. Leahy was probably spinning around on his gurney at this point.

So now it became win one for The Fretter, back in St. Joseph Hospital, agonizing about his team and his own apparent tenuous hold on life. The lads came through for him on their next drive. Joe Heap set the pace by running the kickoff back to his 43 yard line, just missing daylight and the certain touchdown. Guglielmi dissected the Tech defense with a key pass to Matz as the line continued to open holes for Neil Worden and John Lattner. Googs iced the cake with a "touchdown strike" to Joe Heap and with another Mavraides' kick, the Irish led again, 14-7.

The fun kept coming, when the Irish defense smothered the Yellow Jackets on their next possession after the kickoff by Mavraides. As Joe Doyle called it, "On third down, [Tech's] Jimmy Carlen went back to punt but reserve center Jimmy Morris must have thought he was a spectator [as] Carlen was barely able to tip the pass from center." The ball rolled around the end zone where Art Hunter spotted it and fell onto it for his team's third touchdown. Mavraides kept his fourteen-straight extra point streak alive to increase the lead to 14 points for his teammates.

Late in the third period, the Irish second team came in again to spell the starters, with Tech running back a Tom

McHugh punt nearly to midfield. On the next play, Tech's Billy Teas burned past Tom McHugh in the secondary and his quarterback Mitchell hit Teas with a touchdown pass. Having a worse day than Leahy himself, poor Tom McHugh watched helplessly as the same Mitchell stayed in to kick the extra point, with ND now only leading by 21-14.

In the fourth period, the Irish stalled on the Yellow Jackets' 25-yard line; but on their next drive, Guglielmi rallied the team down to the opposing 1 yard line. In the midst of Leahy's illness and the closeness of the contest, it almost got lost that this day just happened to be John Lattner's twentieth-first birthday. A grateful student section at this point erupted into a mass singing of "Happy Birthday" for the gallant Irish back. Star tackle Art Hunter looked across the line at his opponent and cautioned, "Guess where the play is coming." With that Schrader hiked the ball to Googs who handed off to Lattner who breezed through a huge hole in the line for the touchdown.

Mavraides' extra point failed, thus ending his streak of successful conversions, but another more important streak had begun to grind to its *denouement*. The last run by Lattner marked the unofficial end of Georgia Tech's unbeaten string, as thereafter their offense had to contend with an Irish line that continued to stifle them. Soon time expired as the players trotted to their dressing rooms with most of the Irish varsity eager to learn about the condition of their coach. Other ballplayers, the more street-smart of the lot in particular, continued to express their doubts that Leahy had done anything except stage his supposed malady.

Back at St. Joseph's Hospital, Frank Leahy wanted to get back to the grind a couple hours after admission, but Dr.

Johns convinced him to stay to run some tests. Eventually, Dr. Johns got him to stay another few days after diagnosing him with pancreatitis, a condition he probably contracted from some of his children who had just fought off gastroenteritis. The Old Man suffered no heart attack, but he did have the stuffing kicked out of him and had to finally sit still for awhile as the sun set on South Bend, Indiana.

As late as that Monday, the "No Visitors" sign still hung up on the door of Leahy's hospital room, as he required "strong sedatives" to sleep the evening before. It is hard to keep a determined man down and by Wednesday, he had the Notre Dame practices beamed into his hospital room by special hook-up, an exercise he repeated the next day.

To accommodate their coach, the campus had driven in trucks with special mounted cameras to monitor the action from Cartier Field. A 1200-foot cable connected the cameras with a micro-wave station atop Notre Dame stadium which then beamed the action to a station atop the hospital. Word must have passed over to the University's administrators who probably regarded this zeal with a concern bordering on horror. Leahy thought nothing of it as he joyously watched the varsity first team offense and second team defense respectively beat up on the freshmen.

The cameras made Ralph Guglielmi, for one, most uncomfortable. With the cameras moving back and forth, he never knew what Leahy saw and did not see. At least in practices the coach might be clearly watching another area for a drill or other activity and temporarily not paying direct attention to his starting quarterback. Now Ralph did not know when Leahy was watching him and what he perceived, giving Leahy something approaching an omnipresence. In fact, Leahy saw that Googs positioned himself too far back from center Jim Schrader, a tendency that might cause fumbles, so he instructed his coaches to rectify this tendency.

After the practice, each player walked up to the camera and waved and barked out, "Hi, Coach" or "Hope you get better soon" or some other words of encouragement. It established for Leahy a personal bond with his players that largely went unreciprocated at this point in their lives. Once many of them grew up and got a job after a recommendation from their old coach, the ties often began or strengthened, but for now most of the lads simply mugged for the camera. Still, it warmed Leahy's heart.

Toward the end of the week, the hospital discharged Leahy, but only upon the condition that he refrain from coaching the next game. In his stead, the triumvirate of coaches reigned, as Bob McBride, Bill Earley and Joe McArdle assumed temporary power, with McArdle the "senior coach." John Lujack agreed to pass instructions from up in the press box area and freshman coach Terry Brennan volunteered to peer through a hole in the scoreboard and telephone the opponent's flaws.

Back at home, Leahy arranged to talk to McArdle and Captain Don Penza by phone before the game and at halftime in the upcoming game against the Naval Academy.

Soon Leahy would return to the sidelines and at first, apparently and outwardly, nothing had changed; but of course a seismic shift had occurred. For those in the administration tired of his not listening to them or sending over an assistant coach to meet with them, his image had irretrievably altered for the worse. Now, if a Holy Cross father or fathers wanted to see Leahy leave as coach at the end of the season, they had his "health" to use as an excuse to paint his exit from the program.

And it was not a poor excuse at that, for he had been laid low as an inpatient at a local hospital while the team ran fine without him. No one guaranteed that a similar attack might not strike him in the future, and that one might prove fatal. If this rationale did not seal the deal, soon another incident provided Leahy's critics with even more ammunition to use against him.

With or Without You

THE NAVY MIDSHIPMEN visited Notre Dame on the last day of October, perhaps hoping for an upset over the poor Irish, with their coach gingerly limping out of the hospital, and for the first quarter and the first five minutes of the second quarter, they knotted the score at 0-0. It actually could have been worse, after an early lateral from Lattner to Worden misfired. The Middies recovered the ball deep in Irish territory and had their offense come in and drive to the ND six yard line, where they stalled out. Leahy probably felt like jumping out of his bed and driving over to the stadium to take over and straighten matters out.

The team did not need him because once the offense began clicking, they smoked Navy for four touchdowns in the last ten minutes before halftime, led by two touchdowns by Joe Heap and single scores by Ralph Guglielmi and Tom McHugh.

Guglielmi scored his touchdown from fifty yards out after intercepting a George Welsh pass and running it all the way back along the left sideline. As he crossed the goal line, Ralph threw the ball over his shoulder and trotted to his bench feeling elated at stopping the Navy drive and turning the tables on them so effectively.

His good mood ended almost as soon as he got back to his side of the field when his coach John Lujack approached him and began to chastise him, barking, "Come over here! That's not the type of player we want at Notre Dame. When you score a touchdown you hand the ball to the referee and don't embarrass your opponent. If you can't do this, we'll find someone who will!"

Suddenly, Ralph Guglielmi felt much less invigorated about running the ball down the field and scoring. But he also knew that Lujack was right and rather than sulk, he accepted the instruction as good advice given and, while he had several occasions in the future to intercept a pass or score a touchdown for this team, Ralph Guglielmi from that point on always handed the ball to the referee and went about his business like he had been there before.

The repeated scoring did allow some other Irish players to demonstrate their own ability as McArdle substituted freely. Given some carries late in the second quarter, Tom McHugh and Dick Washington kept chipping away at the Navy defense until McHugh tucked it in and crossed the goal line from one yard out. The only discouraging issue surrounding the scoring spree lay in Minnie Mavraides having all three of his extra point attempts either miss or blocked, so Don Schaefer came in after the fourth touchdown to successfully convert the extra point attempt, making it 25-0 at the half.

During the halftime, Leahy spoke to the coaches by phone, but probably by then had little to say as the blow-out had set in.

In the third, Tom Carey assumed the quarterbacking duties and accounted for the fifth touchdown of the afternoon with a "spinning advance of 28 yards." Later, Gene Kapish blocked a Navy punt with Ed Cook taking over possession of the ball on the Navy 7 yard line. On fourth and three, Tom Carey flipped the ball to Dick Keller for the score, with Nick Raich rounding out the team's scoring with the successful extra point. Navy scored a garbage-time touchdown in the fourth against ND's fourth-string team, but by then the outcome had long been decided and a lot of very good young Irish players had the opportunity to play in front of their friends and families. Frank Leahy called to congratulate all.

The Forgotten Four had a great day with Guglielmi completing four out of seven of his passes while playing great defense, with Worden gaining 49 yards, Lattner 57 and Heap 27 on the ground (and 65 by air), before they turned the game over to their friends.

True to form for a Navy/ND game, even with a one-sided score, Ray Lemek, Art Hunter and Paul Matz ended up with injuries, although none of them expected to avoid "heavy work" leading up to their next game against the Penn Quakers. Heap sustained a wrenched knee, Penza and Lattner suffered from charley horses, while Walt Cabral still tried to recover from an old ankle sprain, but most men expected to play the next game.

If they had any expectations to the contrary, the inevitable return to active coaching of Frank Leahy from his bed back home squelched those hopes. Penn always seemed to be deemphasizing then scaring the hell out of the Irish once their game began.

Masquerading as Penn Quaker players, the freshmen gave the varsity a good workout in the middle of the week as Minnie Mavraides kicked field goal after field goal to get his touch back. Finally, Frank Leahy returned to practice on Thursday, only to learn that the game conditions in Philadelphia for the upcoming game were decidedly inclement with "frigid" weather accompanying a dumping of snow. The weather having caused everyone problems, the team scratched its plans to fly to Philly and instead hopped on a train.

That is, everyone but Fred Miller, part-time coach and full-time President of Miller Brewery. Flying with his wife from Milwaukee, he stopped off in South Bend to pick up Moose Krause's wife, and then headed off for Philly. During the flight through Pennsylvania, he received word that Philadelphia had ceased receiving flights due to the storm, so he attempted to reroute to D.C., but the airport personnel there also fended him off, so he headed back west and landed in Pittsburgh.

Back on terra firma, Miller procured a car for his party, it now being 9:00 p.m. on Friday, with the game starting the following afternoon. All night Miller navigated the party on, with cars and trucks stalled or abandoned on the highways leading east. After this harrowing trip, Miller made it to the Irish dressing room just before kickoff. A few hours later, he explained to the press, "It was worth the loss of sleep and travel risks just to watch Don Penza after the game. He's some captain, the way he keeps the team fighting. He may be one of the greatest Notre Dame ever has had."

With Miller safely in tow, Leahy could worry again about the weather. Once in the stadium, the Arctic conditions served to create a parity between the clubs, and if that did not level the field, the referees penalized the Irish before the game began for coming out of their dressing rooms too late, permitting Penn to kick the opening kickoff from

ND's 45 yard line! Guglielmi got the team out of that mess, but after ND punted, on its first possession of the game, the Quakers methodically marched down the field for a 62-yard touchdown drive.

Last year may have been Penn's Eddie Bell's day when the teams met, but today would be John Lattner's. Lattner caught the kickoff on his own seven, picked up a few of his teammates' blocks and then darted down the right sideline for a 93-yard touchdown return.

Minnie Mavraides got his groove back to kick the extra point and tie the game.

From there until halftime the game looked like a laugher, with the Irish mounting a sustained drive as Guglielmi handed off to Worden and Lattner. When Penn began to defend for the run, he tossed passes to Don Penza and then Lattner, to drive the ball deep into Penn territory. Mere plays later, Googs diagnosed a hole between left tackle and left end and ran the ball through for a touchdown, Mavraides again adding the extra point.

Notre Dame had again driven deep into enemy territory, with only a concussion sustained by Ray Lemek early in the quarter to dampen the spirits of the lads. Patsy Bisceglia substituted for him, playing the remaining 56 minutes of the game.

The Irish line pounded the Penn line, opening up routes for Worden and Lattner who brought the ball to the two yard line as the quarter ended.

Leahy then removed his first stringers and installed his second team to finish the half. Don Schaefer quickly scored a touchdown with a dive through the line. Schaefer then attempted the extra point, but figuring the kick would not work, he picked up the ball and ran it in for the extra point, ND leading 21-7. Backs McHugh, Schaefer and Dick Fitzgerald toted the ball the rest of the way, quite effectively, but did not score, as Schaefer fumbled one yard short of the opposing goal line.

The half soon ended, with Notre Dame apparently comfortably in the lead, with the first teamers well-rested for the remainder of the contest, having sat out the second quarter, Bisceglia excepted. Unfortunately, a rejuvenated Penn team emerged from its dressing room in the third quarter, taking the ball on the kickoff to its 33 yard line, thereafter marching down the field inexorably for another touchdown, cutting ND's lead again to 21-13.

Once more unto the breach came Lattner, taking the ensuing kickoff all the way down to the Penn 26 yard line. Ralph Guglielmi exploited this momentum shift by tossing a pass in the flats to Joe Heap, who "spun crazily and lurched down the sideline to score."

No pacifists, the Penn Quakers refused to surrender peacefully, scoring again to reduce the margin to 28-20 in favor of Notre Dame. Then the Irish defense decided to force the issue, with Sam Palumbo seemingly tackling everyone in sight. Penn's quarterback threw a pass deep in Irish territory which Lattner intercepted to kill one subsequent drive, while very late in the contest Joe Heap snuffed an effort by the Quakers to score by snaring another Penn pass deep in the Irish secondary to preserve the win for his team.

Arch Ward named Lattner and Guglielmi the two stars of the game, while positively gushing over two reserves: "There are two sophomore backs in the reserve lineup whose names we suggest you remember. They are Dick Fitzgerald, a fine runner from Evanston's St. George High School, and Don Schaefer, quarterback from Pittsburgh's Catholic Central. Both are headed for stardom. Schaefer not only is a good passer, but he can run like all getout." Ward also praised the Forgotten Four as a group: "If it wasn't Lattner, it was Ralph Guglielmi, Neil Worden or Joe Heap."

Leahy, for his part, felt elated but bushed. Interviewed after the game the coach admitted that, "I've never been so tired and completely exhausted in my life. During the game, the excitement kept me going. But once it was over and I got in here... I felt that I might collapse again." He and Ray Lemek both. Lemek spent the night at University Hospital, being observed due to his concussion, before they released him and he joined his team on the train ride back to South Bend.

Per usual, the team took Monday off, but on Tuesday, Lemek was back out there practicing with his line mates. Even at that, his situation was not the worst; during the season Joe Heap had an operation to remove hemorrhoids and, as soon as he could walk, the coaches threw him into practice and piled on the work despite clear doctor's orders to the contrary. If you could walk, you played.

The freshmen had by then learned the formations and defensive sets of the next opponent, North Carolina, so they tried to stop the varsity at Tuesday's practice. Wednesday was more of the same, watching some film of the Penn game, but concluding with "heavy scrimmages," meaning Leahy wanted the players to blast the sand out of each other. At this time, Leahy had begun to create some competition at left tackle between Frank Varrichione and Sam Palumbo (and with Paul Matz and Dan Shannon at end), so at least for those four linemen, the hitting had to be much heavier than that meted out to others.

The team held a final drill on Thursday, working on pass defense and allowing roommates John Lattner and Tom McHugh to practice their punting. As the team prepared to fly out to Carolina on Friday at noon, Leahy remarked, "I am confident my health will permit me to finish this season." Confidence extended to the odds makers, who rated Notre Dame a 28-point favorite versus North Carolina.

Having just endured a contest in a cold, cavernous Franklin Field, the Irish flew to a much more temperate Chapel Hill, staying overnight in Durham. At the stadium, the Tar Heel fans waved Confederate flags whenever their boys scored or otherwise ran off an inspiring play, but due to Notre Dame's dominance, the flags mostly stayed on the fans' laps. In one of the ironies of Jim Crow that Wayne Edmonds observed, the crowd waved the flag of the Confederacy and yet the first black player in the UNC stadium had just entered the game (due to a combination of faded memory, poor record-keeping at the time and possible confusion by the broadcaster himself, no one has conclusively determined if the honor belongs to Wayne Edmonds or Dick Washington).

In many other ways, the game resembled the recent one with Navy, with the Irish substituting freely and after a brief period of frustration, seemingly rolling at will. Neil Worden gained 151 yards and bagged two touchdowns, one on a 53-yard gallop in which he typically did not score until after he had shaken the last tackler at the three yard line. Tom McHugh ran for two more scores and, in an appearance at quarterback, Don Schaefer ran one in as well.

Dick Keller seemingly ran a kickoff back for a touchdown, only to have it called back for clipping; and fellow sophomores like Don George, Dick Hendricks and Gene Martell traveled with the team and saw some action. Keeping alive the University's tradition of producing fine centers, Jim Mense and Dick Frasor gained some experience and prepared for the day when Jim Schrader and Dick Szymanski moved on. The rout on, the Irish took out the starters for much of the game, which permitted Don Schaefer to gain valuable experience not only on offense but in kicking extra points, two successfully, in live game situations. Very soon, this skill would come in handy for Schaefer and his team.

The substitutes appreciated getting some playing time and had some fun, but Frank Leahy did not celebrate much and almost immediately began to worry about his upcoming opponent, the University of Iowa, then in the process of shutting down the University of Minnesota and their Heisman Trophy candidate, the great Paul Giel.

For once, Leahy's celebrated pessimism appeared warranted.

Fainting Irish

FRANK LEAHY would have worried in any event, but when the Iowa Hawkeyes shut down Minnesota's Paul Giel, one of the finest all-around athletes of the mid-twentieth century, his now very justified concern deepened. Once Leahy absorbed that Giel and his strong supporting cast fell by a 27-0 shut-out margin, Leahy's feelings intensified into a cold grip of near panic. As quarterback, Giel gained over 2,000 yards for the Gophers and passed for nearly as many, finishing second in the voting for the Heisman in 1953. An incredible athlete, he passed up a football career to pitch for the Giants in 1954, ending his major league baseball career in 1961. Under first-year coach Forrest Evashevski, the Hawkeyes had advanced very quickly, but Giel still should have walked over Iowa.

He did not, but then again Notre Dame had Ralph Guglielmi. In 1953 very few people, even Irish adherents, would have suggested that Guglielmi surpassed Giel as a quarterback, but he did. Plus he had three very formidable friends in the backfield and a superior line. Unfortunately, Ralph Guglielmi developed a strep throat that week, landing for one full day in the campus infirmary.

Leahy made a crucial tactical decision, deciding to focus more on the quarterback position at the expense of the other three backs, a move that flew in the face of the results of the Iowa-Minnesota game. It also spotlighted the ends, starters Dan Shannon and Don Penza, who chiefly blocked for their four friends in the backfield, and now they had to expand their role considerably with precious few days to practice. Plus the blocking schemes had to adjust to a more pass-oriented offense. In committing the team to this strategy, Frank Leahy won the first gambit in the struggle against his foe.

In recognition of the work necessitated by the change in philosophy, the team eschewed their usual light Monday workouts (and general total exemption for the starters) by holding a dummy scrimmage with almost all hands on deck, contact supposedly being kept down to ensure the team walked into its upcoming game with as full a complement of starters as possible. Neil Worden with a wrenched elbow and Sam Palumbo with bruised ribs sat out the session, while Leahy evaluated the upcoming opponent as the "most difficult" on the schedule. Tom McHugh, the future college coach, filled in most capably for Worden.

The players experienced a punishing week before the Iowa game, Leahy having arranged three hard scrimmages for his lads, because the Old Man either felt they had it too easy the game before or otherwise needed more challenges. With an uncommonly hot week and the presence of so many banged-up and tired players, tough scrimmages were the last thing Leahy should have prescribed. Indeed, Assistant Coach Earley mused, "The boys have been working hard all week and we'll have to watch ourselves to keep from leaving their best work on Cartier Field."

Over in Maryland, Coach Jim Tatum brayed that last year, the school president called him the worst coach in the country while this year he had changed his mind, dubbing him the "best coach," as his back, Bernie Faloney won "Back of the Week" honors from the Associated Press. Iowa's massively talented lineman Calvin Jones provided ND with some locker room bulletin board fodder, boasting that "These Irish are nothing special." Meanwhile, the truly peerless college football coach, Frank Leahy, continued to brood as Tuesday passed.

On Wednesday, Leahy took partial mercy on his team due to the "abnormally high" temperatures in Northern Indiana, maxing out at 71 degrees. Worden and Palumbo returned to action as he ran another dummy practice, emphasizing offensive assignments, a useful precaution for the upcoming stingy Iowa defense. At the same time, Iowa closed off its practice, running their plays off Notre Dame defensive alignments and, conversely, defending against the Notre Dame offensive playbook. Only on Friday did the practices slacken a bit.

The Irish had worked extremely hard at practice all week and by game time on Saturday, the Irish held no illusions concerning their opponent, whom they universally respected.

The game itself was completely sold-out, and early the Irish eyes smiled as their team had favorable field position and profited from some good runs by Lattner, but they failed to place points on the board. Deep in Iowa territory, the Hawkeyes' Dusty Rice intercepted a Guglielmi pass, a deflection of a throw to Don Penza, immediately shifting the momentum. On the ensuing drive, the Hawkeyes' fullback Binky Broeder did most of the damage, reeling off a 30-yard run, ended only after Joe Heap hunted him and threw him out of bounds. Heap's great defensive play merely delayed the inevitable as Iowa continued to march inexorably to score the touchdown and secure a 7-0 lead.

Both teams did little for the rest of the first period but then early in the next quarter Ralph Guglielmi generaled his team brilliantly down the field, aided by runs from Heap and Lattner, as he delivered the Irish to the Iowa eight yard line. On the next play, Guglielmi faded back and spotted a free Don Penza in the end zone and threw a beautiful pass to him, which unfortunately Penza dropped. After the incompletion, Leahy paced the sidelines, accosting his friend Fred Miller and venting, "Oooh Freddy Miller, why did you recruit a player like that for Our Lady's team?" Miller held his tongue and let his old friend lament, appreciating that humans make mistakes, young men not excepted. Still, Miller time it was not.

On the next play, Guglielmi threw again for the end zone but Iowa defender Jerry Hilgenberg deflected the pass and his alert teammate Bill Fenton picked it off to end the Irish threat. From there the game went back to a seesaw struggle with the teams' ground games and some unsuccessful Irish passing attempts.

Notre Dame got one more chance to knot the score before the half when Iowa punted to John Lattner, who ran the ball back 25 yards to the Irish 41 yard line. Guglielmi went right to work, heaving a pass to Heap for 22 yards, after which Lattner ran the ball down to the Iowa 32. Guglielmi then passed for the next five plays, the most productive one air-mailed to Neil Worden who bulled his way down to the Iowa 25 yard line and the first down

In one of many controversial plays of the day, Guglielmi

passed to Joe Heap who moved the ball down to the Iowa 14 yard line, even though the "ball squirted out of the receiver's arms." Neil Worden then punched out ground gains of six and two yards, but on third down the Hawkeyes brought Googs down on the 11 yard line.

As the team huddled up, Frank Varrichione alertly spied the game clock with only a handful of seconds remaining in the half, noting that the team could not get off another play before halftime without time being called. And Notre Dame had burned all of their timeouts. Former tackle Ray Bubick, watching the game from the stands as a student, remembered that while he suited up, the team had practiced a play for use late in the half after the offense had used all their timeouts: a designated player, generally the left tackle, feigned an injury, necessitating a referee to call a timeout with no repercussions to the offense. On the line of scrimmage, the designee, Frank Varrichione, grabbed his back and crumpled to the ground. Pursuant to the rules in force at the time, the officials called an "injured player" timeout, even though Varrichione had at best only sustained an injury to his pride.

The quick-thinking Varrichione left the game, and as time ran out in the half, Guglielmi drilled a pass to end Dan Shannon who scored his first touchdown of the year. Most in attendance did not believe Varrichione had sustained an injury; but unfortunately, earlier, Minnie Mavraides had, suffering a severe knee sprain that not only removed him from the game, but cooped him up in St. Joseph's Hospital for the next two full days. Of course the Irish had to convert on the extra point attempt to tie, never a gimme in collegiate football at mid-century, and a much dicier proposition for the team with starting kicker Mavraides injured.

Leahy yelled out to Bill Earley, "Who's going to kick?" Coach Earley called on the kicker for the second unit, Don Schaefer, who ran onto the field, fortunately not overhearing his head coach moaning on the sideline, "Oooooh my God, is that the best we've got?" Schaefer ran into the huddle and assured his teammates, "Block hard, I'll do the best I can." In clutch fashion, Schaefer drilled the point after successfully, after which the Notre Dame players and coaches repaired to the locker room, having finally tied the game.

Inside the dressing room, the Irish players basked in a state of exuberance, thrilled by the late heroics and convinced they would roll over Iowa in the next half. Then they went about returning to their lockers and either changing their tee shirt or resting for the remainder of the halftime break. Some had their injuries attended to or added some padding. Then the position coaches shifted in and spoke to the players. Leahy then gave the lads the pep talk and his lads ran onto the field intending to dominate the Hawkeyes.

After such an inspiring end to the first half, the two sides ideally should have run onto the field for the final thirty minutes filled with zeal and vigor, and maybe they did; but the defense of each team predominated as Lattner and the opposing punter, Binky Broeder, traded punts all period, three kicks apiece.

Fine defensive play continued into the fourth. One of the more modest superstars ever to suit up for the Irish, Neil Worden, professed that on defense he hardly made a tackle. Not true, and on one play deep in Irish territory, he bodily lifted Iowa fullback Binky Broeder in the air and then threw him down like a sack of dirt onto the sideline.

Unfortunately for ND, Iowa subsequently scored when quarterback Reichow pitched to back Bob Stearnes who tossed the ball to receiver Frank Gilliam who snared it and then landed safely in the end zone, to make it, after the kick, 14-7 in their favor.

Iowa now led with 2:06 left on the game clock. The indomitable Neil Worden received the kickoff and ran the ball back strongly, to his own 42 yard line. Ralph Guglielmi then took over, and after having his first pass attempt deflected by the Iowa defender, he found Lattner for receptions of 11 and 15 yards and then completed one to Heap; Notre Dame now stood on the Iowa 20. Guglielmi found Lattner again for a completion down to the eight yard line. Two subsequent passes to Heap failed and, with time running out, more fainting occurred, this time with the right tackle Art Hunter designated in advance to pull up injured, laying prostate on the field.

With six seconds remaining, Guglielmi rolled out, with all indications he meant to heave the ball to the receiver on his side of the field, but then he abruptly stopped, shifted to his left and drilled a pass to Shannon who scored his second touchdown of the day—indeed, only his second touchdown of the season. Don Schaefer kicked his second extra point of the game, and the Irish escaped with a tie against a tenacious Iowa squad.

On the kickoff, kicker Jack Lee squibbed and the Iowa up man only returned it a short distance before being tackled, at which time the game ended. A crestfallen Frank

Leahy dragged himself toward the exit carrying the self-inflicted cross that his mentor Knute Rockne would never have wished on him. Don Penza wept.

It was an odd game. Lattner, Heap, Worden and Schrader never left the field, and Guglielmi, Hunter, Penza and Lemek played nearly every minute. Frank Varrichione probably also would have played the entire game had he not swooned at opportune times. The reporter from the *Chicago Tribune*, Irving Vaughan, hypothesized that Iowa forced Notre Dame into a passing contest due to relatively ineffectual running, but the statistics tell a vastly different version: according to the paper, Worden gained 105 yards on 18 carries, Heap added "68 yards in 14 jobs" while Lattner "totaled 56 in 7 calls to duty."

The running stats do not bear out a conclusion that the Irish lost their running dimension and had to rely solely on the pass to advance. Indeed, if anything, these numbers bear out an opposite conclusion and, even more importantly, the team relied on Lattner too infrequently as he produced eight yards a carry. Maybe Notre Dame should have substituted more, particularly after a hard week of practice, or maybe they did right by keeping their first stringers in as long as possible; but as unsatisfying as the game seemed at the time, today the fact remains that Notre Dame held a very tough opponent, flush off its blow-out victory over Paul Giel and Minnesota, to a tie.

The Fainting Irish incident topped the headlines across the country as Maryland slipped ahead of the Irish into the number one position. Reporters initially attempted to interview Varrichione, who kept his mouth mostly shut, "I'm not saying anything." Less guarded, Lattner lauded his left tackle and his collapse, offering, "Pretty smart thinking, wasn't it?" That it was.

The thrust of the opposition to the tactic was that Notre Dame violated the spirit of the injured player time-out rule, a sin particularly egregious for a Catholic institution. This is the problem of a religious institution which sports a football team, an issue most magnified on Notre Dame, and it brings out the most hypocritical of critics.

Arch Ward, as expected, came to the defense of his alma mater, but it mattered little. By now two camps had long formed, those who loved Notre Dame and those who most decidedly did not. If one hated the Irish, there was never any satisfying that type of person. If the school did well, they violated their principles; if they did poorly, the team got ridiculed. Of course there was no satisfying an Irish alum or subway alum, unless the team won the National Championship.

Parenthetically, the rule changed the next year to prohibit dubious injuries to stop the clock, which by logical extension meant that Notre Dame (and all of the other schools that obtained timeouts in identical fashion) did not violate the rule, because there was none in place in 1953. Like the sucker shift, the rule changed due to the false perception that only Notre Dame employed the tactic.

The night of the game, Frank Varrichione and his roommate Jack Lee were on their bunks trying to fall asleep when a hard knock, by a briefcase, was heard on their dorm door at Dillon Hall. Lee opened the door as Varrichione retreated to the back room of the dorm, which contained the desks. A national reporter asked for permission to speak to Varrichione, who in the back room, emitted horrible sounds of pain. He finally did speak to the reporter and when asked if he really had sustained an injury, he joked, "You would be hurt too if your team was losing to Iowa."

As the days passed, Varrichione received critical mail at the University from folks across the country. Some sarcastic fans from Iowa sent him flowers with wishes for his speedy recovery, while another more belligerent soul also bought flowers but this person left a note saying, "Rest in peace you son of a bitch."

Lost in Leahy's and Penza's anguish, and the fainting Irish, were two remarkable drives engineered by Ralph Guglielmi who coolly called all of his plays and ensured his team scored with little time left. Googs played despite the lingering effects of strep throat, giving the team its gutsiest performance perhaps until Joe Montana drank chicken soup at halftime in the Cotton Bowl against the University of Houston. In the clutch, Dan Shannon snared the two passes that truly mattered once other opportunities evaporated. Leahy's prescience in emphasizing passing to the ends had saved the undefeated season.

Regardless, the lads needed sun and they needed redemption, as they directed their wrath against their next foe, the University of Southern California.

Thanksgiving

LEADING UP TO ITS golden anniversary match in Los Angeles against Southern California, the team labored all week under their new found celebrity as the "Fainting Irish," an appellation that displeased them considerably. Even the coaches seemed to sense this, for on Thursday, normally a heavy practice day, the team hardly worked out at all and then joined together in the Dining Hall for a traditional Thanksgiving Day feast together. After gobbling down their meal, they were then transported to Chicago's Midway Airport for their flight west, which arrived after dinnertime that evening. For entertainment on the trip out west, some slept, some read or talked, while in the rear of the plane, Patsy Bisceglia ran a blackjack game with Minnie Mavraides as the treasurer.

The next day, Friday, the team practiced lightly under Coach McArdle and then the national media learned that Frank Leahy had not taken the trip to the west coast to coach his team, staying in Northern Indiana instead to continue his recovery from the ailment that first struck him during the Georgia Tech game. His physician, Dr. Johns, reported that, "He simply has not sufficiently recovered from the illness..." The lads would play without Leahy.

Two years before, Bobby Joseph had talked the team into a studio tour and a meeting with Marilyn Monroe, but on this trip, without Joseph on the team, the squad had to resort to their own instincts to guide them. Judging by the efforts by Ralph Guglielmi and others, the Irish men did fine, with Guglielmi introducing himself to Debbie Reynolds and scoring a date with her after the game.

One of the first to hear about it was Charlie Keller, one of the team managers, whom Googs enlisted to get prime tickets for the game to Debbie Reynolds. The team managers played important roles in general, but on the USC weekend they worked much harder than usual. So off went Keller for tickets for the new found VIP.

Debbie Reynolds did get her tickets but during the game itself, John Lattner stole the show with four touchdowns as the Irish defeated the Trojans 48-14.

Everyone got into the production, including manager Dan Hammer. Traditionally during the late Leahy years, on punt returns the special teams had both Joe Heap and John Lattner (or Paul Reynolds) back to receive. By design, whoever received the punt first criss-crossed over to the other side of the field as did his backfield mate in the other direction, and then either continued to carry the ball or lateralled it. The play made little sense because it caused the return man to waste yardage running diagonally instead of marching straight ahead.

One of the coaches had either seen something in the way that USC lined up or had studied film and had decided to challenge Leahy's stratagem, because before the punt, a coach instructed Hammer to run onto the field during the timeout and tell Heap that instead of crossing the field once he fielded the ball, to run straight ahead along the sidelines. Dutifully, Hammer passed along the message, as Heap nodded his head in acknowledgment.

Problem was, for Hammer, particularly during the single-platoon era, no one, whether it be a player or a "water boy" could transmit direction from the sidelines directly to the players on the field. An astute referee caught Hammer and dragged him to the Notre Dame sidelines, sputtering to the coaches, "This person, this person, is out of the game." Hammer had just earned the dubious distinction of being perhaps the only Notre Dame football manager, before or since, to be ejected from a game.

Of course, the USC coaching staff had scouted Notre Dame and knew that they crossed their return men on kick-offs and punt returns so their own special teams players had prepared to defend Heap and Lattner thusly. Instead, the Trojan's Aramis Dandoy punted the ball to Joe Heap, who promptly ran straight up the field for a 94-yard touchdown, for his team's first score. That silenced the home crowd, the vast majority of the almost 98,000 people in attendance, although a fair amount of Freeway Alumni did venture out to support the Irish.

Given Mavraides' continued injured state, Guglielmi substituted as kicker and missed the extra point, his only missed point after touchdown all afternoon.

Just minutes later, Notre Dame took possession again and Guglielmi guided his men down the field, completing a key pass to end Don Penza, moving the ball to the USC 14 yard line. After driving another five yards on the next play, .

the Irish scored their second touchdown when Lattner took a Guglielmi pitchout and drove to his left. Guglielmi then converted the extra point as the first quarter ended.

Somewhat surprisingly, interim coach McArdle started the second quarter by inserting his second stringers. The back-ups early on stalled on a drive and punted, only to have it called back due to a penalty. When the team punted again, the Trojans' Des Koch caught the ball on his own 27 and ran it back to the Notre Dame 31 yard line. Eight plays later Koch scored on a pitchout, USC then trailing by only 13-7.

On the ensuing kickoff, Heap ran the ball out to his 33 yard line. On the next play, Lattner ran for the first down, a nice jaunt through the flats but one which paled in comparison to Worden's subsequent effort. Taking the hand-off from Guglielmi, Worden ran up the gut of the defense as was his custom, finding a 54-yard opening down to the USC two yard line. Worden punched it in on the next play.

In the midst of Heap, Lattner and Worden overrunning the Southern Cal defenders, the *Chicago Tribune*'s Wilfrid Smith focused on Guglielmi's generalship and mastery of the offense, noting that Ralph's "direction cannot be overemphasized. He looked over Trojan ground defenses and called quick thrusts, or optional laterals, that confounded his opponents."

Mere weeks earlier the Irish had endured the spectacle of their coach having an attack during halftime, but even though Leahy had not made his way out to Los Angeles, he had assembled and coached a naturally talented and determined group of young men who now stood poised to, not only defeat a rival before almost 100,000 largely hostile fans, but also deliver the most lopsided defeat of Southern Cal in Irish history.

And that is precisely what occurred. The Irish in their first possession of the second half foundered, but Lattner's punt fortuitously landed on the Southern Cal five yard line. Trojan fullback Addison Hawthorne ran through the Irish defensive line for ten yards, only to be met by Ralph Guglielmi who stripped the ball, Paul Matz recovering the fumble on the 15 yard line. Two plays later, with a key block from Ray Lemek, Lattner scored on a "deep lateral" from his quarterback over the right side of the defender's line, after which his quarterback stayed in to kick the extra point, extending the lead to 27-7. In the course of four plays, Guglielmi had caused a fumble, directed a two-play touchdown drive and converted the extra point.

Southern Cal answered with a 64-yard drive of its own, capped by either a twelve- or thirteen-yard touchdown run, depending on whom you believe, by Aramis Dandoy.

Mirroring the USC drive, the Irish then embarked on a 61 yard touchdown march of their own. By this time, Joe Heap had twisted his ankle, forcing his departure from the game, so Dick Fitzgerald filled in, contributing a crucial eight yard run to sustain the cause. Assisting vitally were "the power running of Neil Worden and the blocking of Art Hunter." Lattner applied the *coup de grace* with another touchdown run, this time a two-yard plunge over right tackle. Notre Dame 34, USC 14.

The Irish continued to pile it on when poor Aramis Dandoy "took a pitchout, ran to his left and was cornered. He turned and passed to Jim Contratto in the end zone—a lateral—and Contratto fumbled the ball." An alert Patsy Bisceglia took it in for a touchdown, despite a plea that Dandoy's heave constituted an incomplete forward pass.

Contratto contributed mightily to the Irish' last score of the day. Running from the Notre Dame 24 yard line, two defensive linemen nailed him in his own backfield, at which time he coughed up the ball again. Taking over at quarterback, Guglielmi rushed it to the fifty yard line, and Lattner did the rest on the next play with a fifty-yard run, evading four tacklers, for his fourth touchdown of the afternoon. The pride of Medford, Massachusetts, Jack Lee, kicked the extra point for a Notre Dame 48-14 lead, and that is how matters concluded.

Ever controversial, Notre Dame was criticized this time for rolling it up against Southern Cal, a charge not without merit as Lattner and Guglielmi had no business on the field during the final set of downs, the outcome of game not in doubt. McArdle got burned earlier when he inserted the second team into action with a 13-0 lead, one which the opposition narrowed to six points very quickly. But even the fourth string was not likely to relinquish a four touchdown lead at that point.

Still, McArdle did insert the entire Irish squad onto the field at one point or the other, and Wilfrid Smith lauded the contributions of several players, notably the Forgotten Four backfield of Neil Worden, Ralph Guglielmi, Joe Heap and John Lattner. Even there, the praise did not extend far enough as the 1953 Irish did not succeed because of Frank Leahy or a single group of eleven players, they triumphed as a congregation of faith. Faith in each other.

But now it was time to celebrate. Not having returned after his injury, Joe Heap dressed early and got out of the stadium first. After Heap spied Debbie Reynolds, he hoisted her on his shoulders, so that when Ralph Guglielmi came out of the Coliseum, he saw her right away and went right out to their date together. Notre Dame men got away with things like that back then, with Googs dating a young starlet he had never met before as naturally as if he had lobbed a pass in practice to Joe Heap.

At the end of the USC game, several ballplayers went to the home of actor Pat O'Brien, who had portrayed Knute Rockne in *Knute Rockne All American*. During the just concluded game, sophomore running back Dick Fitzgerald had run a play over his guard and tackle called the "number 32 play." O'Brien commented, "Dick, when you ran that number 32 play in the middle of the quarter, you should have cut off to the right, you would have gained an extra five yards!"

An incredulous Fitzgerald retorted, "How did you know the call was a number 32 play?"

"Because," O'Brien answered with his eyes dancing, "I used to coach at Notre Dame!"

In an LA hotel, Tom Carey and Dan Shannon had a room together and did not intend to spend much time in it after the game, so Lattner and Rigali asked them if they might use it to entertain about twenty of their friends who had traveled all the way from Chicago to see the game. Being good Chicagoans, Carey and Shannon let their teammates have the run of the place.

It might not have been the best decision they ever made, as the large party of young men had to eat and wanted to drink, so Lattner and Rigali kept ordering beer and food all evening, putting the potent potables and potato chips on the tab of unfortunates such as Frank Leahy. By the next day, Lattner and Rigali began to worry that someone might report them or figure out who ordered all of the groceries under someone else's name, but nobody said a thing that day or the next. It was not until the season had ended that Moose Krause walked up to them and deadpanned, "That must have been a hell of a party you had on the Coast," after which he walked away with not another word said by anyone on the subject.

Leaving unpaid room service bills and vanquished Trojans behind, the team flew back on an American Airlines chartered flight in pretty good physical shape, excepting Joe Heap's twisted knee.

Certainly, every member of the team had positively assisted the cause, most notably John Lattner with his four scores and 9.25 yards-per-carry average. Equally proud stood undersized guard Patsy Bisceglia and his touchdown. He carried not only his own sense of accomplishment but his family's pride, his neighborhood's sense of worth. Growing up in largely blue collar Worcester, one of fourteen children of Pasquale and Angelina Bisceglia, Patsy had joined the Navy after graduating from Commerce High.

His parents, Italian immigrants, founded a restaurant named the Wonder Bar and hired a chef from the North End of Boston to introduce pizza to Worcester in 1935. Still in existence today, the Wonder Bar continues to produce daily the best pies in the city, and all the Bisceglia children growing up helped build the family business in the Bell Hill neighborhood.

Unlike Boston almost an hour to the East, Worcester

was not dominated by Irish-Catholics. Sure, the Irish habituated the west side of town, but on the east-side the Italians held sway with Poles and Jews peopling the area around Kelly Square. French-Canadians maintained an enclave on Grafton Hill and their ethnic Catholic Church stood across the street from another perfectly good Catholic Church, one into which no self-respecting Frenchman ever set foot. Patsy went to grammar school primarily with the sons and daughters of Swedish and Armenian immigrants and almost the entire city resided on one of the three floors of a "triple-decker" residential building, which stretched for miles united in their uniformity.

After high school, he served four years at sea, two of those as a veteran of the Korean War under Admiral John E. Whelchel. Patsy earned All-Navy in baseball and football, and the Brooklyn Dodgers offered him a professional contract in 1951, but at about that time Frank Leahy came calling; after Bisceglia hit Bob McBride under the belt during his blocking audition, the University's scholarship offer pried Bisceglia away from both a career in the service and with the Dodgers.

By the time he arrived in South Bend in the fall of 1952, he represented a vanishing breed of Notre Dame players, tough ethnic fellows from a city neighborhood who had served their country in war. The teams of the mid to later '40s abounded in those types, but during the Korean War, most of the ballplayers served in ROTC as a means to stay out of the active service. Sure, there was still a Vetville on campus and some teammates like Fred Poehler had a service background, but the toughness and maturity of war vets had largely disappeared. Patsy was a throwback.

The movie *Rudy*, about '70s football walk-on/over-achiev-er Daniel Ruettiger, has inspired thousands of viewers since its release, and caused the Notre Dame admissions department to be flooded with essays from prospective students equat-ing their experiences with those of Rudy, to the considerable aggravation of the admissions reps who read the essays. And yet truly remarkable and inspirational stories preceded Ru-ettiger at Notre Dame, Patsy Bisceglia's tale being just one of them.

An important distinction of course separated Bisceglia and Ruettiger: Patsy was on scholarship, and yet as a very small guard battling much larger defensive and offensive linemen, he displayed the same type of heart and spirit and by 1955, Bisceglia started at left guard, protecting Paul Hor-nung. Until then, his touchdown at USC as the '53 season ebbed, proved also that he had soul.

How did Patsy Bisceglia celebrate his touchdown on the long flight home? Did he cuddle with a game ball or replay the fumble recovery in the end-zone or get slapped in the back repeatedly with big hammy mitts from his teammates and coaches? Nothing like it, Patsy Bisceglia ran a blackjack game at the rear of the plane.

Back in Worcester though, friends and family did puff up their chests a little more with pride for their native son, and that Sunday in one of the city's many Catholic parishes, St Joan of Arc, the priest proudly proclaimed from the pulpit the good news that "one of our parishioners, Pat Bisceglia, scored a touchdown for Notre Dame in yesterday's game!"

Back in South Bend, crouched behind his desk at Breen-Phillips Hall days later, Frank Leahy summonsed Dan Hammer into his office. "Daniel, can I see you for a minute," the great Leahy requested. "I heard you were not a good boy out at Southern Cal."

Hammer stammered out a defense of his actions, explaining that the coaches had told him to tell Heap to amend the punt return play and how sorry he was and all.

Leahy listened patiently to his manager's confession and then intoned, "Nice going."

Endgame

THE EXHILARATING WIN left a number of wounded Irish to check into the infirmary as the team prepared for its final game of the season, at home against the Southern Methodist Mustangs. Among the casualties were Patsy Bisceglia (bruised knee), Minnie Mavraides (sprained ankle), Jack Lee (bruised shoulder), Ray Lemek (bruised knee), Joe Heap (wrenched knee) and Don Penza (a bruised leg). Mavraides and Penza had sat out the entire second half against USC, so their possible presence in the lineup in the last game looked doubtful.

Leahy called off a planned drill session and instead perused the scouting reports that Coach Druze had prepared during and after the SMU-TCU game. SMU meanwhile had injury issues of its own, with its first- and second-team centers laid up and unable to make the upcoming trip to South Bend. The two schools had always played each other tightly, with none of their previous games ever decided by more than a touchdown.

Leahy required a full drill on Tuesday, having regained the services of Don Penza, Jack Lee and Ray Lemek. On that date the Irish received good and bad news, with Lattner winning the Maxwell and Heisman awards and Maryland ending up number one in the AP polls with Notre Dame second. Few doubted that Lattner earned his honors, few believed that the University of Maryland had.

The national poll news hurt Leahy, but he continued to plan for the SMU game as if it meant everything—in other words, just like any game that he ever coached at Notre Dame. On Wednesday, the squad ran a dummy practice, emphasizing passing and pass defense, with Guglielmi, Carey and Don Schaefer sharing the quarterback snaps. On Friday, the Mustang team flew into town and practiced lightly at the Notre Dame stadium, as did ND itself after their guests left for their hotel in Elkhart. As the game approached, the more mundane matters of preparing a team for a game gave way to more sentimental ones.

On Friday evening at the Pep Rally, Captain Don Penza brought the house down. To the uninformed, the selection of Penza as team captain seemed strange, as by 1953 it is debatable whether he was even one of the top twenty most talented men on the team. Had the recruiting process borne fruit as Leahy and his coaches envisioned it four years ago, Entee Shine, Joe Katchik or Bill Hall would have started at end and have achieved All-American recognition by this juncture, with Don Penza a nice after-thought.

But Don Penza persevered, becoming a confidant to all and perhaps the only athlete who had any chance of speaking to Frank Leahy during that tense '53 campaign in a manner that the coach would have listened. For their part, Penza's parents named their youngest child after the Great Leahy. Sure-handed Joe Heap almost certainly would never have dropped that pass in the Iowa game as Penza did, but as captain, Don Penza was one of the finest.

So when he walked up to address the student body for

the last time, at the pep rally before the SMU game, he ascended the steps of the mezzanine of the old Field House with the weightiest of hearts, having never forgiven himself for dropping those passes against Iowa. Addressing the crowd, he started, "I just want to say to my teammates and fellow students, I'm sorry..."

And got no further. At that point Don Penza broke down and the students began to cheer wildly, screaming and yelling for more than a half hour in support of their captain.

No one from SMU heard the cheers or appreciated that Penza had awakened the echoes, but they stood no chance of defeating the University of Notre Dame. No chance.

The next day, it took very little time for the Irish to strike, once the game commenced. SMU went nowhere on their opening drive, punting out of bounds to the ND 39. Guglielmi ran for a couple yards on the first play from scrimmage and then on the second, the great quarterback pitched to Lattner who ran left, drawing as many of the opposition defenders to him as possible and then at the last moment, threw his second pass of the season to Dan Shannon. Shannon had gotten behind two SMU defenders, including their great back Jerry Norton and raced to the four yard line before being tackled. After an SMU offside, Neil Worden did what he did best, bulling over end for the team's first touchdown, with a relatively healthy Minnie Mavraides kicking the extra point.

SMU answered convincingly, driving all the way down to the ND nine yard line on their next possession, but key tackles by Ray Lemek and Joe Heap, together with an incomplete pass ended the promising offensive outburst. The Irish then engineered a sustained thrust of their own, which almost resulted in a touchdown, when SMU's great Forrest Gregg planted Lattner on the SMU two yard line on third down. On fourth, an incomplete pass ended the drive and SMU took over on downs.

Not for long. With third down and five to go on their own ten yard line, SMU's quarterback McNutt faded back but Irish end Paul Matz slammed him, knocking the ball loose, which Frank Varrichione tracked down in the end zone for an Irish TD.

Just before the second half, Guglielmi manufactured another sustained set of plays, with Leahy substituting fairly liberally. Dick Fitzgerald got in some runs and Paul Matz ran several plays from offensive end. At the SMU 24 yard line, Matz raced left toward the end zone, drawing off most of the opposing defenders, while John Lattner sneaked down the right side line, where Guglielmi found him virtually undefended for the score. Notre Dame went into halftime up 20-0.

The second half went much the same as the preceding thirty minutes, with even more substituting from Leahy. All seniors got into the game, including wonderful men like Rock Morrissey, Paul Robst, Bob Martin, Art Nowack and Armie Galardo, all of whom could have thrived at many powerhouse programs and had easier practices and more creature comforts provided to them from alumni. But they chose the tough route and received the appreciation of their fans and fellow students in this, their last game.

Leahy also saw to it that Dick Keller, Nick Raich, Gene Martell, and Dick Frasor got some playing time, as the Irish cruised to a 40-14 win. During the game, the students raised one finger and repeatedly yelled to the reporters that their team and not Maryland was the finest in the country. As the *Chicago Tribune*'s David Condon reported, "There were many in the press box who conceded the error." Captain Don Penza turned over the game ball to fullback Tom McHugh.

For their part, the Irish players lifted Frank Leahy upon their shoulders and paraded around the stadium, taxiing him to his wife Floss' seat, where the coach blew her a kiss. The stadium still contained thousands of cheering fans, screaming loudly for their great coach and the fine team he assembled and nurtured for years. The players then transported the Old Man to the locker room, where a banner hung up that read, "Thru these portals pass the National Champions of 1953."

In the dressing room a jubilant Frank Leahy assured everyone, "I'll be back next season if they want me," while across the room Fr. Hesburgh answered, "Frank has been told he can stay as long as he wants."

A Time to Refrain from Embracing

BEFITTING THE CONCLUSION of an undefeated season, the campus erupted in celebration. In the midst of revelry, this star-crossed 1953 season somehow seemed fated for an unhappy ending, which in fact occurred after the SMU game when Ralph Guglielmi and Joe Heap forgot to sign out and returned past hours, getting caught red-handed. They both came out of their meeting with the campus authorities with suspensions for the remainder of the term, with the instructions to leave the University grounds within twenty-four hours. Effectively, this punishment negated all of their work to date for the first semester, even though Heap for one had just won All-Academic recognition again nationally.

A disconsolate Joe Heap took a train all the way down to New Orleans, not saying a word to his family. When he detrained, he called home and his father answered; and when Joe said, "Hi Dad," Mr. Heap did not think it was him, assuming it was one of his brothers. In fact, he worked his way down all of Joe's brothers first, before finally saying, "Joe, is that you? What are you doing here?" A crestfallen Joe Heap fessed up and perhaps seeing that his son had suffered more than any parental punishment might add, he just made one simple demand: "You're going back to Notre Dame, right, Joe?" "Yes, Dad," Joe confirmed; and that was all that they said about it.

For Ralph Guglielmi, Woody Hayes was always just a phone call away, and the Ohio State head coach and new Michigan State coach Duffy Daugherty swiftly went after both Googs and Heap. Ralph may have followed the siren song out of South Bend but for local businessman Julius Tucker, who had a long conversation with the young quarterback, stressing that rather than remaining upset, he should learn a lesson from the experience and remember he was like everyone else. Googs took those words to heart and when he heard that his friend Heap meant to return, he too decided to stay with the Fighting Irish.

It took nearly two weeks after the incident for the press to catch on, with the top administrators largely keeping a tight lid on the story. Characteristically, when asked if the two talented backs could return to campus at the conclusion of their suspension, Black Mac McCarragher briskly replied, "That's strictly up to them."

Black Mac could not spoil all of the fun, and for the ballplayers a "Champions Fete" dance had been set up for them and their dates, at which time John Lattner attended with a Chicago girl named Joan Satton. The festivities did not end with speeches and dancing, as four of the Massachusetts men, Frank Varrichione, Jack Lee, Patsy Bisceglia and Minnie Mavraides, had formed a singing group named the Hungry Four, and serenaded their teammates and girlfriends.

Not only did the young men sing at the Champions Fete, they began to entertain crowds at other venues in a fairly circumscribed area of the Midwest. Singing such hit songs of the era as *Eh Cumpari*, the combo began by charming crowds on campus, including a gig at Vetville, and even gaining an appearance before the Chicago sports writers, at which time each cantor received the princely sum of $30.00, and wore a Red Sox jersey provided for him for the occasion. At a South Bend event the quartet sang a bit off-key, causing Varrichione, Lee and Mavraides to crack up laughing, which greatly upset Patsy Bisceglia, who held greater aspirations for the group. When his friends did not stop laughing after the show ended, an exasperated Patsy shouted out to them to be serious, after all, "that's how the Four Aces got started!" Sadly, the Hungry Four stayed hungry.

On a more somber note, football scribes avoided the Christmas rush and began their speculation concerning Frank Leahy's future almost at the precise second that his players lifted him up on their shoulders and carried him off the field at the end of the SMU game. The very next day, David Condon from the *Chicago Tribune* openly wondered whether the coach might return, particularly in light of his health issues in the fall.

Fr. Hesburgh professed no knowledge of the terms of Frank Leahy's contract or even its location. He did not have to, because Frank Leahy had coached his final game at the University. It mattered not at all how many years he had left or did not have or what a buy-out might entail or any other legalities, because after his lads defeated SMU, the cheering had stopped for him.

Although it was not fully appreciated at the time, the *coup de grace* for Leahy probably came with the publication of the December 7, 1953 issue of *Newsweek* Magazine. The magazine's sports editor, Joe O'Brien, had spent a week in South Bend after the Georgia Tech game interviewing Leahy and many of his players, coaches and University officials. Behind the scenes, Joe Doyle filled him in on the facts and what credence to give to rumors or quotes from others.

Either Leahy knew or should have known that a huge national publication did not dispatch its sports editor to any location for a week unless it meant to produce a major story, but uncharacteristically he let down his guard. Rather than assure *Newsweek*'s audience that he felt great and fully intended to coach forever, Leahy prattled, "At times lately...I think that coaching the Notre Dame football team is a job for a younger man."

That unfortunate quote set the tone for the entire article, in which two unnamed sources speculated about Leahy's possible successor as a race between Indiana head coach Bernie Crimmins and current Irish assistant coaches John Lujack and Terry Brennan. O'Brien strongly hinted that Leahy was leaving and Leahy missed his last opportunity to lobby for the salvation of his job.

On December 8, the campus observed the Feast Day of the Immaculate Conception of the Blessed Virgin Mary, although in New York, John Lattner had a banquet to attend, this one to honor him as the Heisman Award winner for 1953. John took his mother out for the festivities, her first time on a plane. Famously, John and his mother went out with the Heisman representatives to many of the New York popular clubs of the day and when the club-hopping went past midnight, one of the Heisman reps suggested slowing down a bit, and Mrs. Lattner dutifully complied. She stopped drinking mixed drinks and restricted herself to ordering beer.

The next evening the team assembled for the annual Notre Dame Club of St. Joseph Valley banquet, to honor the team. At this time it was announced that former Mt. Carmel stars Paul Matz and Dan Shannon had been elected co-captains of the team for 1954. The AD at Iowa, Paul Brechler, spoke (Coach Evashevski was a *persona non grata* as he became a very vocal critic of ND soon after the Iowa game ended), along with Moose Krause, Frank Leahy and Fr. Joyce. Fr. Joyce officially heralded the changing of the guard at Notre Dame by limiting his remarks to keeping intercollegiate football clean, a *de facto* slap at his own coach who had established and earned a reputation of doing whatever it took to win.

Fathers Joyce and Hesburgh wanted to win also, but they also wanted Notre Dame to serve as an ethical beacon to Catholics everywhere and as a top intellectual institution. Winning at all costs conflicted with the ascendant vision of the University held by the two people who mattered most. It is not known at this juncture if Leahy knew he had been axed, but if he had not yet received the word, he probably began to see at least some pronounced outlines of his fate in the speech Fr. Joyce rendered.

Unfortunately, the coaching situation helped obscure the accomplishments of some of the truest men Notre Dame has produced, a phenomenon that history has only perpetuated. Besides earning the Heisman Trophy and another Maxwell Award, John Lattner garnered another consensus All-American recognition, with Art Hunter and Don Penza also receiving All-American selections by various groups.

Neil Worden led all rushers with an astounding 859 yards gained on only 145 carries for a 5.9 yards-per-carry average. To the present, Neil Worden is twelfth all-time at

Notre Dame for career rushing, with all the other players ahead of him on the list having played four years at back, Worden only eligible to have rushed for three years.

John Lattner rushed for 651 yards on 134 carries while catching 14 passes. He also snared enough interceptions in his three years of varsity service as a defensive halfback that again, at the beginning of the 2009 season, he stands third all-time for career interceptions at Notre Dame. Ralph Guglielmi picked off five passes as a defensive back to lead the team that year, but his major contributions came in leading the offense to an undefeated season. Joe Heap gained 314 yards on the ground while leading the team in receptions with 22, and as usual, netting Academic All-American honors. At fullback, Tom McHugh narrowly out-gained Heap to place third in rushing for the year.

The line had developed into one of the finest in Notre Dame history. Hunter and Penza left the program as All-Americans and at the end of the 1954 season, their mates Frank Varrichione and Dan Shannon were similarly honored. Patsy Bisceglia earned All-American recognition at the conclusion of 1955, including first team in the AP and third team in the UPI line-ups. Jim Schrader, Ray Lemek and Ed Cook all enjoyed long NFL careers well into the 1960s, while Tony Pasquesi and Minnie Mavraides also played in the NFL. Six Irish linemen enjoyed NFL careers of at least nine years in duration, with All-Pro honors rightfully accorded to these men.

In the midst of the holiday festivities, as the students crammed their last bit of studying in before the commencement of Christmas Break, Frank Leahy sat in Purgatory not knowing his fate for the coming year. Some routines went on like normal, with Coach Druze playing handball against some of the players, but few if any of them saw Leahy around. This was not unexpected, as word had gone out that he had to avoid commitments for an extended period of time after the season ended, a practice he had first adhered to the previous year.

Not everyone was having a bad time, as John Lattner, Art Hunter and Neil Worden received invitations to play for the East All-Stars in the East-West Shrine Game in San Francisco on January 2, 1954. Worden watched his coach try unsuccessfully to set up running plays with people from different colleges (some who used the T-formation, some who did not, with little time to coordinate the backfields) instead of simple pass plays and foresaw a big defeat for his team. The players all visited a child at the local hospital with Lattner coming in a bit late due to a previous speaking engagement at St. Mary's High School in Augusta, Georgia, where he played a round of golf at the famous course.

When he flew back to the Shrine Game practices, he promptly separated his shoulder during a scrimmage. Rather than have it popped back in by what appeared a painful procedure on the sideline with the coaches, he rotated his arm around until it went back into the socket. Still injured, he put on the best effort possible during the game itself at Kezar Stadium, but he and his mates lost to the West squad by 31-7, as Neil Worden predicted.

Back in South Bend, the intrigue surrounding the future of the football program continued. One evening Joe Doyle, while dining in a restaurant, walked past the bar only to see one of the University's chief administrators speaking quite earnestly with Frank Leahy's physician, Dr. Nicholas Johns.

It was not that innocent; Johns had prearranged to leave the door slightly ajar for Doyle. The administrator tried repeatedly to convince Dr. Johns to state publicly that Leahy had to resign due to his health, a proposition that Johns did not feel like accommodating. The clouds continued to gather.

Grantland Rice pounded more nails in the coffin for Leahy on January 23, 1954, when in his syndicated column he lauded a recent Rules Committee determination against the calling of injury timeouts when no one had sustained an injury. Answering a colleague who supposedly questioned why he criticized Notre Dame when other programs did much worse, Rice thundered, "The only answer was— Notre Dame is Notre Dame. Many of the others are unimportant. Notre Dame is never unimportant. Through Knute Rockne, Jess Harper, Gus Dorais, George Gipp and especially the Four Horsemen, Notre Dame carries more in the way of tradition than most of the others—fair play, spirit-all that matters."

In the face of this condemnation, Leahy only enjoyed a brief respite when many of his lads received good news from the country's professional football teams. Befitting an undefeated club, the Irish seniors fared very well in the National Football League's annual draft, held on January 28, 1954. The teams picked three Irish in the first round, Art Hunter by Green Bay with the third pick, John Lattner by the Steelers with the seventh pick, and Neil Worden by the Philadelphia Eagles with the ninth selection.

The Chicago Bears chose Fran Paterra in the fourth round, while their cross-town rivals the Cardinals drafted Tom McHugh in the sixth. The Eagles provided Neil Worden with company by picking up Minnie Mavraides in the fourth round. Similarly, Pittsburgh, in addition to Lattner chose Irish end Don Penza in the eighteenth and tackle Joe Bush in the twenty-eighth round. The Redskins tabbed Jim Schrader with their second-round pick, while the '49ers drafted Sam Palumbo as a "futures" pick, essentially locking up his rights until the next year.

Leahy had set up John Lattner with Julius Tucker (the same gentleman who counseled Ralph Guglielmi to swallow his pride and return to ND after serving his suspension) to look after his interests. The Bears under George Halas had put feelers out, but the proposed salary of $8,500.00 was too low for Lattner, so the calls from his home town stopped. Someone in the Lattner camp also intimated that Vancouver in the Canadian Football League had the "inside track" on his services, a massive concern to the NFL since the previous Heisman winner, Billy Vessels, had signed the previous year with a Canadian team.

On draft day itself, Lattner got a call from a representative of the Pittsburgh Steelers who informed him that they had drafted him in the first round. The coach of the Steelers, Joe Bach (a former Notre Dame football player himself) came out to South Bend and met with John and Julius Tucker, and offered him a $3,500.00 signing bonus and a three year contract at $10,000.00 a year, with no year guaranteed. After his brief flirtation with the Canadian League ended, John signed on the dotted line and became a Steeler. Julius Tucker never required a penny for his services, while Bach shortly thereafter retired as coach.

Neil Worden heard about his selection when he got a knock on his dorm room door one day, with someone from Philadelphia asking to speak to him. Not only did cell phones not exist, no one had a phone in their room, so Worden had to jog down the hall to the communal phone, and then speak to a secretary from the Philadelphia Eagles. She asked him some questions and then sent him a contract. Once he received it, he compared their offer to those extended to his teammates, thought it seemed fair, and signed it and mailed it back to the Eagles. Just like that, Neil Worden had his first job after graduation lined up.

The Los Angeles Rams made two quirky picks, choosing end Joe Katchik in the tenth round and Entee Shine, the basketball player who lasted two weeks on the freshman team, with its twenty-seventh round selection.

A serious selection, Tom McHugh learned of his destiny one day back home in Toledo when, as he waited for a bus, he looked at a local newspaper box which contained a headline that he and another local player, George Jacoby, had been named in the NFL draft. As one of the top picks of the Cardinals, he attended a press conference and signed up with the team for $6,500.00 a year.

But for McHugh the story did not end there. After he signed, Wally Ziemba, no longer a Notre Dame coach and now a coach of the Canadian Football League's Ottawa Roughriders, visited his former player in his dorm. Zealously, Ziemba laid out his case for McHugh working north of the border and then sweetened the pot with an offer of a $1,000.00 bonus and another $7,500.00 to follow, outstripping the Cardinals' offer. McHugh decided to cast his lot with the CFL, a development that rained hell upon him from the Cardinals' ownership, but Tom McHugh stuck with his decision and prepared to play the next year with Coach Ziemba and the Roughriders.

And that was the NFL draft. For a little more than half the seniors on the varsity squad, the results signaled the effective termination of their football careers, unless they chose to play in Canada or join a semi-pro league.

Publicly, at least, Frank Leahy continued to twist slowly in the wind, betwixt pursuing a championship in 1954 and a final exit from the school he so loved. In part, the fans did not detect much of a difference because the winter practices that they did not supposedly know about largely did not occur as first Christmas break and then January exams took precedence over the players' attention.

One evening in January, Dr. Johns received a phone call from the old Stevens Hotel in Chicago, where Frs. Joyce and Hesburgh sat with Leahy and columnist Arch Ward. As Dr. Johns understood it, he was being asked to back up Leahy if the Old Man resigned and attributed the exit from Notre Dame to concerns for his health. Dr. Johns agreed to in the event the press queried him.

On January 31, 1954, Leahy formally walked the plank, telling an AP reporter that he needed to quit due to ill-health, maintaining that, "It's a tremendous weight off my mind to get out of the game, as much as I love it." He also asserted that doctors had told him that another attack like he had at the Georgia Tech game might prove fatal, as he made vague references to future opportunities he might pursue in business. The confirmation came off the heels of an official announcement from Fr. Hesburgh accepting the resignation.

Speculation concerning his successor focused on Bernie Crimmins, an excellent candidate as he had coached at Notre Dame for several years and had recruited many star players for the varsity. He had served as head coach at the

University of Indiana for the past two years, so he also had credentials at running a major football program. Fred Miller for one, doused such ruminations, pointing the Associated Press more in the direction of John Lujack or Terry Brennan, coyly suggesting that the University had already chosen their man.

Miller knew what he was talking about. The very next day, February 1, 1954, the University removed any doubt by naming Terry Brennan the next head coach at Notre Dame. A former All-American running back for Leahy and the Irish in 1948, Terry had led a charmed existence, born into a family headed by a very prosperous Milwaukee attorney. After leaving Notre Dame, Terry himself had obtained a law degree and had successfully coached Chicago high school powerhouse Mt. Carmel for three years before being hired to coach the Notre Dame freshmen in '53. Now, at age 25, he ascended to the head coaching job at his alma mater with many of the stars of the previous season returning.

Brennan said all of the right things at the announcement, promising, "I am both thrilled and humbled at the opportunity of taking part in a great coaching tradition. I appreciate the confidence that has been shown me and hope for the support of all Notre Dame men throughout the country..." With considerable grace and dignity, Frank Leahy wished his former player well and offered to help him in any way, as the death knell began to toll for such coaches as Bob McBride and Joe McArdle. An era had truly ended.

But while Leahy suffered, many of his lads enjoyed the opportunities afforded them as young athletes who people wanted to see. For example, a promoter from the South Side of Chicago, a fellow by the name of Kirby, proposed to John Lattner that some money might be made now that his amateur career was over. No one played football during the winter back then and Lattner was not going to box, so Kirby lined him and some of his friends up in green uniforms and barnstormed them through the Midwest as the Johnny Lattner All-Stars, an unlikely basketball squad consisting of Lattner, Neil Worden, Tom McHugh, Don Penza, Bob Rigali and Bobby Joseph.

Only Lattner and Joseph possessed even a minimal amount of college varsity experience on the court, but still the contingent found itself playing about twenty games that winter against players from the Chicago Bears and Cleveland Browns as well as other semi-pro, schoolboy or company teams.

Oftentimes, the fellows left campus at mid-afternoon to drive to their game, which they invariably lost, and then returned to campus about twelve hours later, well past the bed-checks and lights-out periods. At Alumni Hall, where Lattner and McHugh roomed together their senior year, a kindly priest did not enforce the rules as vigorously as he might and on a good night, each player earned about $50.00 to $75.00, a healthy paycheck in relative terms. Not bad pay, considering that tuition for one year for non-scholarship athletes was about $750.00. Although Lattner was the draw and perhaps the most skilled cager, he never earned a penny more than his mates.

The lone exception for everyone was the exhibition against the Cleveland Browns, led by Hall of Famers Otto Graham, Marion Motley and Lou "The Toe" Groza. Groza starred as both a lineman and kicker, and his brother Alex was one of the finest basketball players in the country.

Unfortunately, a gripping ice storm hit the Cleveland area so few fans turned out and while the Browns' players got their full gate, the Notre Damers only got about $10.00 apiece. Between the first and second halves of the game, Lou Groza entertained the audience by teeing up basketballs and trying to kick them into the net, a feat he never quite attained, although his friends did win the contest itself in a rout.

On another occasion, in Mansfield, Ohio, Neil Worden, dribbling the ball down the court at the time, spied a beautiful blond woman in the stands. Keeping his priorities straight, Worden left the ball to dribble itself and ran into the seats to sit on the lap of the blond woman. Other teammates exhibited more zeal for the Lattner All-Stars, most particularly Bob Rigali. Learning his old high school and college teammate meant to attend the Maxwell Award ceremony, to receive his second straight recognition as the greatest college football player in the country, Rigali told him to "cancel it." Lattner did not cancel the Maxwell Award fete and his friends did play in his stead, and the Lattner All-Stars probably lost again.

Leading up to the Senior Ball, on Friday May 7, 1954, Bobby Brown and his Dixieland Quartet played at the student center while a Charleston dance contest kept the revelers busy. The next day came the annual Old-Timers Game at the stadium. A number of departing seniors had partied pretty hard the night before the game, and having not practiced or otherwise kept themselves in top condition since the SMU game, they presented very little in the way of opposition to next fall's varsity. In Terry Brennan's first game as a coach, he guided his men to a 49-26 pasting of the Old Timers, before over 22,000 spectators, over twice as many who attended the previous year's Old-Timers Game.

The Old Timers led by 26-22 until they became un-glued, as Ralph Guglielmi passed effectively to Joe Heap and freshman quarterback Paul Hornung engineered three touchdown drives of his own. Dean Studer, Jim Morse and Don Schaefer ran the ball most of the rest of the way, as Heap rested a balky hip.

The evening of the Old Timers game, the Senior Ball took place at the Naval Drill Hall with the usually dreary building decked out like an Austrian village complete with a fountain in the square. Ray Bubick's cousins in the Bur-genland region of East Austria would have felt at home. Dates received "engraved jewel boxes" while tripping the light fantastic to the crooning of Ralph Marterie and the Four Friends. This time, John Lattner reunited with his first girlfriend Peg McAllister and the next time the two danced together in a formal setting, it was at the reception of their wedding.

The senior lads, freed from Leahy's spring practices, be-gan to think seriously about their future, and at this time, many of them became very interested in the young women they dated. Neil Worden fixed up Jim Schrader with his fu-ture wife at this time and Worden himself let his mind drift from McAllister's locker room over to St. Mary's College across the highway. Before his suspension, Joe Heap had dated a nursing student there named Marie Berg, and af-ter he returned to New Orleans, Neil began dating Marie. While Heap served his penance in New Orleans and fell in love with a girl back home (whom he married before his se-nior year), Neil fell in love with Marie Berg, the woman he later married. The old gang was breaking up.

Graduation itself was a bit anticlimactic, more of a show for the parents than anything else. Traditionally, some students appropriated the bust of Notre Dame's founder, Fr. Sorin, from Sorin Hall and placed it in a boat and cast it out into one of the campus lakes, and this year proved no exception. What stood in John Lattner's mind most clearly was that roommate Tom McHugh appropriated a pair of his shoes on his way out the door and took over a half century to buy him a pair in return.

Some of the students, like manager Dan Hammer, went to law school or some other graduate school, while others went into the military, while most others began their lives of gainful employment. For some of the team players, their football careers ended with the Old-Timers game while others suited up for the National Football League or the Canadian Football League.

On August 13, 1954, John Lattner and teammates Neil Worden, Minnie Mavraides, Jim Schrader and Art Hunter participated in the College All-Star game against defending NFL champions the Detroit Lions, before a crowd of over 93,000 at Chicago's Soldier Field. The Lions pretty much ran the board, winning 31-6, and at the conclusion, Neil and Minnie caught a flight out to Philadelphia and Lattner flew out to Pittsburgh to join his new team in an exhibition game against the Chicago Bears.

New Steelers Head Coach Walt Kiesling put Lattner right in the game the next evening, using him on punt returns and the like. Waiting for one catch, Lattner put up his hand at the final moment to signify a fair catch, with notorious ruffian Ed "the Claw" Sprinkle warning him, "If you don't put that hand up right away in this league you'll get killed." On the next play, Lattner heeded the warning, shooting up his hand almost as soon as the ball left the punter's toe. No longer a Notre Dame man or a college all-star, John Lattner had entered the ranks of the professional athletes. The young boy who had left his family in West Chicago and had choked up the first time he viewed *Knute Rockne, All American* in Washington Hall had grown up. He was a Steeler, on his way to Pro Bowl recognition in his upcoming rookie season.

Overtime

FRANK LEAHY repeatedly referred to his 1953 Fighting
Irish football team as his greatest ever, greater than his 1943,
1946, 1947 and 1949 National Championship clubs and all
others before. The 1953 team was also the finest team in
the country that year and a quirk of the time has dishonored
their accomplishment, and it is past time to straighten out
this historical oddity.

The UPI and AP services voted Maryland the number
one team for 1953, with Notre Dame coming in second in
both polls, a vote taken before the bowl games that year. In
the Orange Bowl that year, the University of Oklahoma defeated Maryland, shutting them out. At the end of the season, bowls included, the only major undefeated team in the
United States was the University of Notre Dame, and virtually all of the polls named them National Champions.

Of course earlier in the year, Notre Dame had de-
feated the Sooners in Norman, but Pittsburgh tied the
Sooners later that year. Notre Dame defeated not only the
Sooners but the team which tied them, the University of
Pittsburgh. Maryland lost to Oklahoma in a neutral site.

In the 1953 season, Notre Dame played a far more rigorous national schedule than Maryland. Going into the '53
season, Notre Dame scheduled six opponents who made one

or both of the UPI and/or AP Top Twenty at the conclusion of the 1952 season: Oklahoma, Pittsburgh, Purdue, Georgia Tech, Navy and USC.

After the 1953 season had concluded, the Irish had played three teams who ended up in the top ten AP/UPI polls for the campaign: Oklahoma, Georgia Tech and Iowa.

By contrast, the University of Maryland scheduled only two teams who had made the 1952 top twenty polls, the Universities of Alabama and Mississippi. In the regular 1953 season, while Notre Dame played three opponents who ended that year in the top ten, Maryland only played one team which ended up in the top 20, Alabama, ranked outside of the top ten.

At the end of the 1952 season, Maryland's windbag coach, Jim Tatum boasted that only Billy Vessels and John Lattner from <u>both</u> the Oklahoma and Notre Dame squads could play at Maryland, with their wonderful depth of players. Tatum, as he was about so many things, missed the mark by more than just hyperbole.

In the NFL, only two of Maryland's 1953 players had distinguished careers, Stan Jones who had a Hall of Fame career with the Bears (seven Pro Bowl selections in thirteen years) and Bob Pellegrini who made no Pro Bowls, playing nine years, mainly with the Eagles. Their star back Bernie Faloney played in Canada and everyone else either did not make an NFL team or had a very short tenure if they did make a cut.

The four starting backs from Notre Dame all were drafted in the first round of the NFL draft, the only occasion in history a backfield of four all were drafted so high. Ralph Guglielmi played well into the 1960s, mainly for the

Washington Redskins. Neil Worden played in 1954 and then served in the military until he reentered civilian life and played a final year with the Eagles (coincidentally Minnie Mavraides played for Philadelphia those same two seasons). John Lattner made the Pro Bowl in his rookie year and then received a career-ending injury in the military. Joe Heap had a short career also, but could have starred in the NFL if the business world did not promise much more for him and his family.

Besides the backs, Notre Dame placed several linemen in the NFL, with six of them enjoying careers of at least nine years as a pro. Frank Varrichione played eleven years, roughly divided in service between the Rams and the Steelers, earning 5 Pro Bowl honors.

Jim Schrader played ten years mainly with Washington, earning three Pro Bowl honors, while Ray Lemek suited up for the Pro Bowl on one occasion during his nine year stint with the Redskins and Steelers, and Art Hunter made the Pro Bowl once in his eleven years as a pro. Ed Cook had a ten-year career with the Cardinals and Atlanta Falcons.

Starring at both center and linebacker with the Baltimore Colts for thirteen seasons, Dick Szymanski also earned three Pro Bowl appearances.

ND won the Helms Athletic Foundation honors, Billingsley, Board, Devold, Dunkel, Litkenhous, National Championship Foundation, Poling, Sagarin and Williamson Services. UPI scribe Oscar Fraley admitted that after Oklahoma defeated Maryland in the Orange Bowl, "The Fightin' Irish of Notre Dame belatedly won the national collegiate football championship while sitting in the living room." Colonel Dave Egan of the Boston *Record* seconded the emotion, "I regret that the football writers of America have made such complete nincompoops of themselves in hailing Maryland as the nation's No. 1 team and dropping Notre Oame (sic) into the No. 2 position."

They were right. Notre Dame won the national championship in 1953 *by consensus* and it should be recognized as such today. After all, they earned it.

***

With the exception of Joe Heap riding onto the St. Mary's campus on a steed, no one ever put the backfield of Guglielmi, Lattner, Worden and Heap on horses like the fabled Four Horsemen of Notre Dame. Grantland Rice never wrote a memorable poem about the Forgotten Four nor did they ever grace a United States Postal Service stamp.

But that which is forgotten can later be remembered, and the Forgotten Four were simply the greatest backfield in Notre Dame history.

Joe Doyle, who first covered the Irish almost sixty years ago, always has thought so, as he has written on many occasions, including in this book's foreword. As Doyle has pointed out, none other than one of the Four Horsemen himself, Quarterback Harry Stuhldreher, believed that the Forgotten Four were the finest he had seen.

Stuhldreher gave his reasons for favoring Googs, Lattner, Worden and Heap, and there are so many valid reasons for so honoring the Forgotten Four. They played together as a unit for three years and synchronized their movements, so critical for an offense that relied on the option. But they also possessed so many tools: Googs blocked, Lattner and Heap occasionally passed the ball and Worden either could bull through anything or at least leap over it.

Independent of their talent on the gridiron, they possessed superior athletic skills: Googs and Lattner were recruited by the leading basketball programs in the country,
Worden could have made the Olympics as a gymnast and
Heap was one of the fastest people in America during his
years in South Bend.

Plus, with the exception of Worden who played linebacker, they excelled as a defensive backfield in addition to
their prowess on offense. Lattner and Googs intercepted a
lot of balls and no opposing runner was safe so long as Heap
tracked him down. And had colleges favored four-men- defensive backfields in the early 1950s, Worden probably would
have been tabbed as a particularly bruising safety.

Notre Dame has produced great backs since the Forgotten Four, but rarely have the players in the later editions
played as a unit with other greats for an appreciable amount
of time, and there are a number or reasons why this is so.
That being said, the Forgotten Four are the greatest combination of backs.

Their like will never be seen again. In college as well
as the professional ranks, four-men backfields have disappeared and with the continued de-emphasis of the fullback
position, even three-men sets are endangered. But Googs,
Lattner, Worden and Heap did perfect the four-back set,
each riding his college accomplishments into a first-round
selection in the NFL draft.

***

The graduation of Neil Worden and John Lattner broke
up the great Notre Dame backfield, leaving new coach
Terry Brennan the task of replacing them and hopefully leading the team to new glories under his regime. Don Schaefer

and Paul Hornung filled in at fullback while Jim Morse and Paul Reynolds took over Lattner's old right halfback slot.

Many of the fine players who lost their starting roles with the institution of the single-platoon system the year before, regained them with the graduation of other players such as Jim Schrader and Art Hunter. Others rose up in the depth chart, so it appeared as if morale might improve for those young men.

Although the single-platoon system ultimately proved a misguided retro movement in college football, finally scrapped for good in 1964, it did mask one stubborn fact for the Notre Dame Fighting Irish football program, that being a very poor recruiting haul for the players entering into their sophomore year in the fall of 1954. Paul Hornung was a superstar, but after him, only a handful of players in that class might have played for the Irish during their stellar years under Leahy in the '40s and then again from 1952-1953. No matter who one blamed, this weak class in large part destroyed Terry Brennan.

It mattered little in 1954 though, with Ralph Guglielmi leading a veteran unit fully capable of defeating every team they faced, and it nearly worked out that way. By the early part of fall of '54, too many hard feelings built up to ensure an undefeated season, starting with the relationship between Coach Terry Brennan and stars Ralph Guglielmi and Joe Heap.

At a certain point, Brennan ceased addressing Googs directly, choosing to bark out to a coach, "Tell the quarterback to do (fill in the blanks)." Heap felt that he was getting less playing time as the coach wanted to bring the new boys along, and lost all respect for his coach when after a team meeting, Brennan challenged some of the team to fight him. A player could hate Leahy and resent being worked like a mule, but the respect remained. When Brennan lost his star quarterback and back, only the hard feelings remained.

Matters reached a boil when Brennan permitted Leahy to make a pep talk at halftime in the Texas game, an encounter that Notre Dame dominated far more than the 21-0 final score indicated. Inviting Leahy to speak before his lads was an extraordinarily gracious gesture on Terry Brennan's part, and it had the desired effect of firing up the troops, but it caused some harm as well.

Before young men who had been motivated to achieve greatness, Leahy looked most impressive, particularly since he appeared much healthier since the lads had last seen him. Unfortunately, Terry Brennan, a man in his mid-20s, paled in juxtaposition and Brennan must have sensed it immediately, because after that his graciousness toward Leahy never resurfaced.

***

The team yielded nine picks in the NFL draft, with three first rounders: Ralph Guglielmi by the Redskins (who also drafted Bob Ready), Frank Varrichione by the Steelers and Joe Heap by the Giants. The Colts drafted Dick Szymanski in the second round and the Cardinals picked Tony Pasquesi in the fourth. The Browns drafted Paul Reynolds and Sam Palumbo in the fourth round while the Bears tabbed Dan Shannon as a sixth round choice.

With Guglielmi gone, Terry Brennan could start to work Paul Hornung into the mix at quarterback for the '55 season.

***

It took several hours for the priest to drive to the Lake Oswego Hotel. He had received a call that someone needed last rites, so he gathered all of his necessary items to perform the service and immediately trekked up to his destination. Father Ted Hesburgh was driving up to give Frank Leahy his Last Rites.

Of course it was not the first time Leahy had been administered this sacrament of the Church, Fr. Ned Joyce had famously undertaken this task at halftime during the Georgia Tech game of 1953, but with Leahy, twenty years later riddled by the effects of leukemia, this would be his last time to make peace before passing on. Leahy had initially called Notre Dame, searching for Fr. Hesburgh, and as soon as the University staff located the priest, he found out where Leahy was situated and took right off for the destination.

That evening, Fr. Hesburgh was greeted by an extremely ill Leahy and his wife Floss. Hesburgh heard confession and then administered the Last Rites. As described by Leahy's biographer,

> They spoke of many things, even social conditions, arch-liberal cohabiting with ultra-conservative. It had been an extremely warm meeting, a tying-up of long forgotten loose ends. It was a thoroughly unexpected gesture on the part of two undemonstrative men.
>
> They walked together to the parking lot, Leahy wobbling on his arthritic legs and Father Hesburgh moving with firmness and authority. They commented on how unusual it was to find such staggering heat in the midst of a normally rain drenched Oregon summer. Then they said farewell. It was Frank Leahy's last living touch with Notre Dame.

***

That is one snapshot, this is another. One of the most difficult courses at the Air Force Academy is electrical engineering. Two brothers, sons of former Irish coach Bob McBride, needed a bit of help and were referred to Ray Bubick for tutorial help. The McBride boys were the sons of Bob McBride, the tackle coach who decades earlier kept Bubick awake at nights, and when he did sleep, induced nightmares.

Bubick had long since made peace with his past, attending an Old-Timers Game and in general, viewing his experience at Notre Dame with a much more balanced perspective than he had while there. Not only did he help out the McBride boys, he later dined with Bob and Mary McBride when they came to Colorado to visit their sons. McBride was no longer the demanding coach and Bubick no longer was the scared kid, they were friends forever, tough former linemen at the University of Notre Dame.

***

Bubick was not the only Notre Dame man in the Classes of 1954-1957 to serve in the military. Bob Martin, reserve quarterback to Mazur, Guglielmi and Carey, flew combat missions over Vietnam and lived to describe the experience, whereas Larry Ash augured in very early in his career and became either the first or one of the first members of the Class of 1954 to die.

Most people pulled two-year hitches, and many of these former ballplayers suited up again for the fierce competition that military bases staged against each other on the gridiron. John Lattner hurt his knee so badly during his service hitch that he never played professional football again after he left the Air Force.

He did receive a memorable call from Minnie Mavraides in the late 1950s to play against Senator Bobby Kennedy in one of his notorious touch football games outside of Washington. They all ate at Bobby's place, amongst Bobby and Ethel and their brood and then went out to play serious football. Lattner's and Mavraides' team ran up the score in no time, but no matter how many touchdowns they scored, Bobby would not let his team quit.

Growing tired, Lattner asked Mavraides what they should do, having long grown tired of this endless game. Mavraides responded that Kennedy never quit, no matter how behind he and his teammates found themselves, so he suggested that they let Kennedy win. So Lattner, Mavraides and their friends threw the game and once the Kennedy club pulled ahead, the game ended.

For years, Bobby Kennedy related how he and his friends had not given up in the face of adversity, eventually defeating a football team led by a former Heisman winner. John Lattner had something more, he had a great story to tell.

***

Guglielmi, Heap, Lattner and Worden all enjoyed success after football in their chosen careers, and they still get together frequently. Their team reunites too, most recently in the fall of 2008 at the San Diego State game, where they were announced to the crowd at halftime, sporting hats that read "1953 Undefeated National champions 9-0-1" on the side.

***

Joe Katchik concluded his football career after the 1960 season as a defensive end with the New York Titans, now known as the Jets.

***

Some players on the 1953 team have disappeared, some have passed on. The ones that have died are just residing elsewhere, for as most of the teammates grew up believing, once a soul has passed, he or she becomes part of a Communion of Saints and then prays for those still on earth.

So the celestial Irish are still working on behalf of their earthbound teammates, with Don Penza undoubtedly leading the way. And when one of the Lads does enter Heaven, the fellow with the bow tie and furrowed brow nervously speaking to St. Peter is none other than Frank Leahy, the coach of the 1953 undefeated national champions.

"Get in, Lad, and hurry about it. I just spoke to God and he has allowed us to practice during Holy Week."

ABOUT THE AUTHORS

Don Hubbard is a 1981 graduate of Georgetown University and a 1984 graduate of the Notre Dame Law School. He has practiced law as a trial attorney in Massachusetts for the past 25 years and lives and practices in Boston where he resides with his wife Lori, son Billy and daughter Caroline. He has written two previous books: The Heavenly Twins of Boston Baseball *and* The Red Sox Before the Babe.

Mark Hubbard, ND '72, MBA, Wharton School, is an independent business consultant, specializing in media, entertainment and sports. He is the author of Business Wise Guide: 80 Powerful Insights You Can't Learn in Business School.

Corby Books
....Check Us Out....

Corby is a new, innovative publisher with a diverse and interesting line of books. For the dedicated Notre Dame clan, we offer CELEBRATING NOTRE DAME, a lavish coffee-table photographic view of the campus, by Matt Cashore, with text by Kerry Temple. A close look at life on campus is the subject of KNOWN BY NAME: Inside the Halls of Notre Dame, by Fr. James King, Rector of Sorin Hall. And THE HEART OF NOTRE DAME: Spiritual Reflections for Students, Parents, Alumni and Friends by Nicholas Ayo, CSC. A biography of one of the great scholars in Notre Dame history is WHEN FAITH AND REASON MEET: The Legacy of John Zahm, CSC by David B. Burrell, CSC.

For the family, we have CREATING HAPPY MEMORIES: 101 Ways to Start and Strengthen Family Traditions, by Pam Ogren, and ST. NICHOLAS IN AMERICA: Christmas as Holy Day and Holiday, by Fr. Nicholas Ayo. Business executives will benefit from BUSINESS WISE GUIDE:80 Powerful Insights You Can't Learn in Business School, by Mark O. Hubbard and STOKE THE FIRE WITHIN: A Guide to Igniting Your Life by motivational speaker Charlie Adams. Don't miss FRUGAL COOL: How to Get Rich Without Making Very Much Money, by Prof. John Gaski. And a wonderful read is THE IRISH WAY OF LIFE by John Shaughnessy. Don't miss CREATIVE AGING by Joan Zald.

Other new titles include the bestselling I HAD LUNCH WITH GOD: Biblical Inspirations for Tough Times by Dr. Kathy Sullivan, NONPROFIT GOVERNANCE: The Who What and How of Nonprofit Boardship by Thomas Harvey and John Tropman, MAY I HAVE YOUR ATTENTION PLEASE: Wit and Wisdom from the Notre Dame Pressbox, by Mike Collins and Sgt. Tim McCarthy, FORGOTTEN FOUR: Notre Dame's Greatest Backfield and the 1953 Undefeated Season, by Donald Hubbard and Mark Hubbard, THE GEESMAN GAME by Wes Doi and Chris Geesman.

For full details, log on to corbypublishing.com